WHEN I THINK BACK

WHEN I THINK BACK

The War Letters of Fitje Pitts

1943–1945

EDITED BY TILGHMAN PITTS

Cover Design: Alexa DePaulis
Cover Photograph: Jane Pitts

Dedicated to my mother
Fitje Lavinia Pitts
June 6, 1917–October 31, 2008

–And–

To all the Red Cross "Girls" who served in World War Two

The Red Cross, with its clubs for recreation, its coffee and doughnuts in the forward areas, its readiness to meet the needs of the well and to help minister to the wounded has often seemed the friendly hand of this nation, reaching across the sea to sustain its fighting men.

GENERAL DWIGHT D. EISENHOWER

TABLE OF CONTENTS

Editor's Note

Editing letters written seventy-five years ago is a tricky business. Fitje Pitts was a gifted observer and storyteller. Nonetheless, she often ignored accepted rules of grammar, rarely capitalized words and used "m" and "r" interchangeably. At times her cursive was close to indecipherable. I made minor edits to Fitje's letters to correct spelling mistakes and grammatical errors, and to clarify confusing passages. That said I kept edits to a minimum in order to preserve the voice and style in her writing.

Tilghman Pitts

Fightin' Fitje Pitts

If there was a moment when I fully grasped the significance of World War II in my mother's life, and the impact she'd had on the many people she served as a young Red Cross volunteer, it was during a trip to France in 2000.

My brothers, Toby and Steve, and I arranged to take her to Beaumont sur Oise, France so she could visit a town she'd last seen fifty-five years earlier. Before we departed Toby contacted the Chamber of Commerce, which assured us that someone, perhaps a historian, would guide us through the town. We arrived, unprepared for the magnitude of the reception our mother received.

We flew to Paris and spent a few days enjoying the City of Lights before piling into our rented car

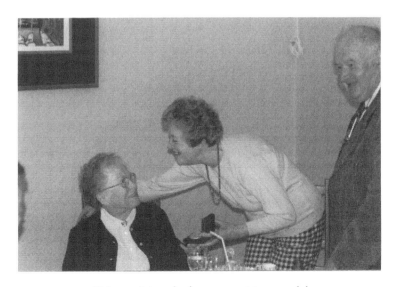

Fitje receiving the honorary citizen medal
from the Mayor of Beaumont sur Oise, 2000

and driving to Beaumont sur Oise. Arriving shortly before noon on a beautiful June day, we were greeted by over fifty people, some old enough to remember our mother. They gathered at a corner of the long-abandoned airfield, which from October 1944 to April 1945 had been home to the 386th Bomb Group. A plaque commemorated the 386th; American and French flags flew on either side. Bands played and speeches were made as the grateful citizens of Beaumont sur Oise treated her like an honored member of their family. In many ways she was.

Later at the luncheon in her honor French and American pennants festooned the ceiling of the banquet hall. Unaccustomed to being the center of attention, our mother sat at the end of a long table. The mayor made her an honorary citizen of the town. She seemed pensive, her memories perhaps transported back to a different time, when she was twenty-seven and single, a witness to great events.

After lunch we drove back to Paris. "Did you have a good time?" Steve asked. "Oh yes," she replied. "Wasn't it wonderful? All those kind people stopped what they were doing just so they could have lunch with me." She paused: "They must lead such boring lives."

I don't know if the people honoring our mother led boring lives, but this much is certain; the French will never forget what the Americans did for them during the darkest days of the war. That's why so many citizens of a small town forty kilometers north of Paris turned out to honor an eighty-three year old woman with whom they had shared the last bitter winter of World War II.

Fitje Lavinia Pitts was born in her parents' summerhouse at Hammond Hill in Saunderstown, Rhode Island on June 6, 1917. They named her after Fitje Lavina Canfield, her paternal grandmother. Her nickname was Binni, perhaps because a sibling's interpretation of Lavinia was easier to say than Fitje, a Dutch name, which is pronounced, "Fight Cha."

Like so many of her generation, war disrupted her life. As a woman she could have been an arm-chair spectator to the war, but that wasn't who she was. Outraged by what the Japanese, "those sneaky little bastards," had done at Pearl Harbor on December 7, 1941, Fitje decided to serve in some capacity. While she never looked for a fight, she never shied from one either; it was part of her DNA.

Her great-grandfather Colonel Herman Canfield of the 72nd Ohio Volunteers died in the Civil War early on the first day of the Battle of Shiloh on April 6, 1862. The after battle reports of Sherman and Grant cited him for heroism for having held off a Confederate attack, giving Sherman the opportunity to regroup and repel the Rebel advance.

Her father, Dr. Herman Canfield Pitts, served in World War I twice. Impatient that the United States had not yet declared war on Germany, and afraid he'd miss what might well be the biggest event of his generation, he joined the Harvard Surgical Unit, sailed to Europe on December 16, 1916 and served with the British Expeditionary Force in Flanders. After the United States declared war on Germany on April 2, 1917 he resigned his commission and returned to the States where he enlisted in the American Army and returned to Europe.

While Fitje was not imposing in a physical sense, she possessed a large personality. According to her childhood friend Ibby Taft Freeman, she was fiercely protective of her family and friends. She was petite and while not athletic, had an athlete's build. She used to brag that she was the fastest runner at Lincoln School in Providence where she grew up; she was six years old at the time. Despite her stature when angry she wielded a welterweight's punch and a longshoreman's tongue. She did not suffer fools and possessed an acerbic wit with which she deflated the healthiest of egos with alacrity.

Fitje graduated from Smith College in 1939, and soon after attended the Katharine Gibbs School where she learned the secretarial skills young woman were expected to acquire. Later she moved to New York where she worked in the IBM Pavilion at the 1939 World's Fair. When the war started she was working for the Rhode Island Department of Social Services. She was bored; the war provided her with an escape, the excitement and adventure she needed.

She first tried to enlist in the Women's Army Corps. Rejected because of a heart murmur, she joined the American Red Cross. After six months of training in Washington, D.C. and New York City, she boarded the Queen Mary in New York Harbor on June 23, 1944 and sailed to war. The Queen Mary normally accommodated four thousand, but refitted as a troopship there were nearly fifteen thousand passengers and crew on board when my mother sailed. She was one of only two hundred eighteen women. One of her cabin mates was Kathleen Kennedy, sister of the future President. Soon after they arrived in London Kathleen invited her to a session of Parliament as the guest of Lady Astor. Fitje declined saying she was too busy.

As children, my brothers and I were proud of our mother. She was the only mother among all of our friends who had "been in the war." We knew she'd sailed to war on the Queen Mary, and was attached to bomb groups in England, France and Belgium. Occasionally she would let us rummage through a trunk filled with memories from her time with the Red Cross: her uniform, clippings, and a dagger carried by the Hitler Youth, its hilt emblazoned with a swastika. An American soldier she met on a driving trip from Belgium to Czechoslovakia after V. E. Day in May 1945 gave her the dagger as a souvenir.

Fitje was ninety-one when she died on Halloween morning in 2008. On two occasions before she died, my brothers and I accompanied her to Europe to revisit bomber bases to which she was attached during the war. The first visit, in 1997, was to England to visit Great Dunmow in East Anglia where she was attached to the 386th Bomb Group, the second, to Beaumont sur Oise. We thought we knew a great deal about her wartime experiences. We were wrong, there was much she never talked about. It wasn't until nine years after she died that we learned how much.

In September 2017, we discovered one hundred and forty-seven letters she wrote to her family between January 1943 and November 1945. We also found the diary she kept aboard the Queen Mary. Several months later we found fifteen letters she sent to her cousin Tim Pitts. It was the first that any of us knew of the existence of the letters as they were not stored with her other war memorabilia. As she numbered the letters in the order in which she sent them, we know a few are missing. Those that survive represent a historical treasure trove. Not only do they open a window on a part of Fitje's life we knew in the most cursory way, they are a unique look at war as told through the pen of a young woman and Red Cross volunteer. The letters are funny and they are sad. They are about friends and lovers. They are about danger, but never about fear.

With the discovery of her letters, I thought about the many times we asked her to write an account of her experiences during the war. She never did, we thought. Without saying anything to us she began a narrative in the mid '90s. We don't know if she intended to surprise us, or if she assumed we'd find it after she died. For reasons of her own, she stopped writing halfway through her experience.

We found the narrative several months after I'd finished transcribing and editing her letters. It is, essentially, a road map of her activities from her training with the Red Cross in Washington, D.C. to her posting with the 386th Bomb Group in Great Dunmow, England. While she did not write about her time in France and Belgium, V.E. Day, or what she witnessed in Europe after the war ended, I use her narrative as a starting point; in a sense it represents the perfect forward, written by her, capsulizing the first half of her experience. Her letters from France and Belgium are vibrant and instructive. They serve as their own road map.

At the same time we found her narrative we discovered a short story, possibly written by Fitje, titled "Warren and Hinkie." Warren "Red" Farwell and J.C. "Hinkie" Hinkle were tail gunners on B-17 Bombers who my mother met during her brief posting to the 91st Bomb Group. As it is the closest she comes to talking about men in combat, I have reproduced the story as a stand-alone chapter.

It is a shame that we did not see these before taking her to England and France. The knowledge gained by reading her letters and the narratives would have allowed us to ask more questions, to learn more about who she was and the people with whom she served. Although we did not, the letters paint a vivid portrait of Fightin' Fitje Pitts before she was our mother.

We now know Fitje was attached to three combat groups, including the 95th and 91st, both Eighth Air Force units, which flew B-17 Heavy Bombers. She was with the 95th for four and a half months before being transferred to IX Bomber Command, a non-operational base. She was there for six months before transferring to the 91st. After a short posting with the 91st she joined the 386th Bomb Group, which was part of the Ninth Air Force and flew B-26 Liberator Bombers. She stayed with the group until the end of the war. When the 386th returned to the U.S. three months after V.E. Day she transferred to the 27th Air Transport Group in Villacoublay, France and stayed with them until she left Europe.

Fitje never wrote about casualties or missions. To do so would have violated the strict censorship rules imposed by the military during the war. In that regard they are not a "traditional" war story—great battles, hand-to-hand combat, or the horrors, as described in accounts like *With the Old Breed: At Peleliu and Okinawa*, by E. B. Sledge. These letters represent a young woman's firsthand account of day-to-day life on bomber bases during World War Two. They are about pets, the men she meets, frustrations, travels and friends. Some letters read like scripts for a MASH sitcom episode. Her sister must have commented on the lack of serious news in her letters, as Fitje wrote her a chiding letter saying that there were limits to what the censors allowed her to say.

There are letters, especially the ones written after the 386th moved to France, where she hints at the terrible reality of war. Fitje had a sharp eye for detail and a journalist's skill for painting pictures with the words she wrote. Reading her letters one meets Big Barn Smell, Rip Cord Russell, Urban Rudner, and her pet dog, which the men named V.D. She describes the locals she hires in England, France and Belgium.

As the director of Red Cross Aero Clubs she met people from all walks of life, the kinds of individuals she would never have met if not for the war. Her mother must have written questioning if she was "moving in the right circles." Fitje responded: "They are all our friends and we are here to be their friends. You could never understand how it is and I wish you were here yourself because everyone is at their worst, and also at their best. Our presence here and our relationship to them and theirs to us couldn't be, at home. In order to live at peace with everyone we must be strictly impartial and "friend-ship," like it is in your own hometown, doesn't even enter into it." It was perhaps the perfect job description. Most of the men were very young, barely out of their teens. While she was there to run the Aero Club, she was also a surrogate mother and sister. Her letters often talk about the men who "hung around" the club. To them, my mother and the other Red Cross "girls" were an important link to home in a world gone mad.

It is tempting to flip through pages, reading only the letters that for whatever reason are more interesting than others. I believe it is a mistake to do so. While the letters chronicle the progress of the war, they are, more than anything else, a coming of age story. She was a recent college graduate who sailed to Europe very much a girl on her first trip abroad. They take us through her stages of development, from wide-eyed sightseer in London to the frustrating realization that her task was one for which no amount of training could have prepared her. By the time she flies to France with the 386th, she no longer naïve. She is an independent woman prepared for whatever she encounters, a seasoned professional.

Fitje packed a lot into her twenty-nine months in Europe. Her first flight was in a B-17 Bomber, she was in London when V-2 Rockets fell, and along the way, accumulated at least three lovers. Before sailing to England the only times she had been out of the United States were during Prohibition when her father took the family from their summer cottage in Maine across the border into Canada to buy liquor. Before returning to the United States she traveled to England, Scotland, Ireland, France, Belgium, The Netherlands, Luxembourg, Czechoslovakia, Germany and Switzerland. She rested on the Riviera, flew into war-ravaged Berlin, and smelled the "peculiar sweet smell of death."

She appreciated the magnitude of her experiences in Europe and realized that nothing about the life she would return to in America could compare. In a letter to her sister Jane, dated February 6, 1945, Fitje wrote what I believe is her most poignant passage:

> *I would love to write you a letter about life as it really is over here, but I guess it will have to wait until I get home. When I think back over the last two years and realize how it has been and what I have done and how I have changed I die at the thought of coming home. I mean it scares me. In spite of it all, I am sure I am better for the experience. I hope I am right.*

But eventually she left. The Red Cross reduced their numbers in Europe after the war ended. Initially, she wrote of her desire to stay, or of transferring to the Pacific or C.B.I. But, after the Japanese surrendered on August 14, 1945, it was time to return to the United States. Fitje was one of few American Red Cross volunteers to serve over twenty-five months in Europe during the war.

On November 17, 1945 Fitje boarded the George Washington in Le Havre and sailed home. The ship docked in Boston, Massachusetts on November 25th. She collected her luggage and boarded a train to Providence, arriving shortly before three in the afternoon. Thanksgiving that year was on

November 22nd, the Thursday before she got home, but her family agreed to wait until she arrived to celebrate. It was a moment she looked forward to.

No one met her at the train so Fitje took a cab to her parent's house at 65 East Orchard Avenue. She walked in the front door to find that the family had just finished dinner. They had not waited. She put her bags down and burst into tears. Fitje was home, her adventure over.

WHEN I THINK BACK

CHAPTER I

Fitje's Narrative

Fifty years have passed since I came home from Europe after the war, and when I read over my letters to my parents I realize how much I have forgotten and lots I remember, but couldn't write about because of censoring.

I can't remember now how I heard about the overseas program, but after Pearl Harbor, December 7, 1941, as we mobilized, many programs were quickly organized for women, the WAC, WAVES, etc. The Red Cross overseas program appealed to me because it was a chance to get nearer the action without being a member of the military, the WACs and the WAVES. The WAVES never left this country.

The day the Japs bombed Pearl Harbor I was at the Matteson's house on Hammond Hill for the weekend. We were having Sunday lunch when it came over the radio and Mrs. Matteson dropped her coffee cup. Her son Sim was in Pearl Harbor with P.T. boats. He was O.K. and survived the war.

I was working as a social worker for the Rhode Island Department of Social Welfare, but switched to the Red Cross Home Service while I was awaiting the result of my application. I must have gone to Washington for interviews, and if so, I most certainly spent the night in Baltimore and saw my future husband who was in the throes of getting divorced.

After acceptance, I went to Washington for uniforms, physical, etc. I think I stayed at the Burlington Hotel and my letters say my double room was $6.00 a night and I worried about paying my roommate's $3.00 when she left to go somewhere, Australia I think. We had a $2.50 food allowance and the airmail stamp on my letters to Rhode Island cost $.06. One thing that stands out in my mind was a trip to the FBI firing range where we learned to fire different types of guns, including a Thompson sub-machine gun. Luckily I never had to put this knowledge to use. For a while several of us went to Alexandria, Virginia and lived at the Cromwell Arms on Duke Street. We worked from 2:00 to 11:00 at a USO club and sometimes went with the motor corps to take coffee and donuts to men at maneuvers in the vicinity. You have to understand that in this all out war the whole country seemed mobilized. We no longer heard from groups like the America Firsters. It seems that attacking our own country brings us all together and I remember well this instant feeling of oneness in the country. I don't believe that a war in the Persian Gulf, or in anyplace that doesn't touch our country personally can generate the same feeling.

At the beginning of May, some of us went to New York where we stayed at the Midston House on Madison and 38th Street. It was a hotel strictly for women and I don't believe they exist anymore. There I took a map reading course, which necessitated finding one's way from point A to point B in Central Park, etc. I must have learned something but don't remember what. One week we went nightly, forty-five minutes by subway, to Ft. Hamilton, which was a staging area at that time, and there were soldiers constantly coming and going and we heard lots of fascinating stories. I saw my first boxing match there, and I hope it's my last!

Jane was living in New York then and we arranged a code so she'd know when I left the country.

The last thing I did in New York was to act as hostess at the service men's lounge at Grand Central Station. This was a lounge on the balcony over the entrance where servicemen in transit could sit and have coffee, etc. They would go to sleep on benches with signs pinned to them, that said things like, "Wake me up at ten o'clock." Lots of foreign servicemen came in, and I remember one French aviator who drank a cup of coffee and asked the price. When I said it was free he said, "My God, America is a wonderful place," as he rushed off to catch his train. I wish I could know what happened to some of these young people. Of course they seem younger and younger as I get older and older!

Fitje and her sister Jane in Brooklyn, June 1943

Sometime after June 1, 1943 I went home to Providence for a few days leave and no sooner got there than the RC called me to come back to Washington. I went and busy days followed while we signed this and that and had shots, etc. I note somewhere that I had $47.60 sent semi-monthly to Dad to put in the bank for me. In those days we had a victory tax deducted from our salaries, which stopped, I believe, when we left the country. That doesn't sound like much in the way of savings, but when I got home, I invested it with Dad's help and in future years was able to buy two cars.

Eventually we went back to New York with our luggage and were billeted in the St. George Hotel in Brooklyn, waiting to embark. We were issued bedrolls, gas masks, fingerprinted, etc. We even had the fun of going through the Army Gas Chamber, with and without masks.

At 7 o'clock PM on June 23rd busses took us to a pier in the Hudson and there was the very beautiful and majestic Queen Mary, right next to the Normandie. We struggled aboard the Queen Mary with our equipment—knapsacks, helmets, pistol belts, canteens, first aid kits, heavy coats and raincoats, as well as suitcases. Don't remember where my footlocker went on or how and when it caught up to me.

There were fifty-three in the Red Cross group and something like 218 women in all, counting Red Cross, nurses and a troupe of USO girls going over for six months to visit camps in England and North Africa. I understand they got no pay but don't know if this is true. Four of us were in a stateroom and told to stay there until the chaplain could arrange a place to meet. The portholes were, of course, painted over for the blackout so we couldn't see from our stateroom, but from somewhere I remember seeing the Statue of Liberty after we sailed at high tide, around 11:00 AM on the 24th, and a great many voices singing *God Bless America*! It was very emotional.

We ate twice a day, at 9:00 and 7:00. There were six shifts to each meal, and it was a job to get everyone fed. All night long we could hear the Sgts. saying, "Hurry up men or you'll miss your meal." I have noted that for breakfast we had grapefruit, bacon, eggs, toast and coffee so we must have been pretty well fed and I don't remember being hungry. We had boat drills of course and the captain spoke over the Tannoy* system explaining air attack drills and boat drills. He impressed on us the importance of obeying all instructions for the safety of the ship, which, he said, was more important than all the lives on it. Until that time I had always thought I was important, but from then on I realized how little difference a life like mine really makes.

There were 15,000 troops on board and sleeping places for only half, so each day they changed places. The half with no beds slept in the hallways, anywhere they could. Below decks was hot, stuffy and crowded. It never quieted down anywhere and it must have been very hard on the troops.

After the ship sailed, we were given more freedom. The game deck was reserved for officers and women, although it was a job to get there through the hordes of soldiers milling around. I hated to think what would happen if we had an emergency. Of course we had to have our life vests with us at all times. From the game deck we could watch the many gun turrets and in return the soldiers seemed to spend their time looking through binoculars at the girls!

It was a safe feeling to see the huge Navy balloon overhead. I think it was with us for two days, then a day with no escort, and then we could see planes from England circling in the distance. The Queen Mary was very valuable to the war effort.

Baths were in salt water of course and I only took one. In the evenings we played bridge with an assortment of officers and Red Cross Field Directors. The lounge was crowded with a variety of nationalities and much singing of songs—Scotch, English, Australian, (*Waltzing Matilda*) and of course American. It was very difficult to sleep because of the heat and continual noise and announcements over the Tannoy system. I don't ever remember feeling tired though, I guess the excitement kept us going. I didn't see how the men could stand it cooped up below decks. Everyone was excited and part of the milling around was due to nervous tension I suppose. Rumors were rampant, probably none of them true. For example, some G.I. was murdered and buried at sea during the night, we changed course because of subs and were near Bermuda, etc. Actually it got colder, and the Tannoy system blared forth telling the men sleeping on deck to bring warm clothes. At one point two

* British public address system

5

Kathleen Kennedy in London, c. 1944

Liberators flew over, both very low. There was much speculation about where they came from. Some said Halifax.

Kathleen Kennedy and Catherine Spaatz (daughter of General Spaatz) were in our group and Kathleen and I became friends. While we were on the game deck, Kathleen and I and another Red Cross girl got talking to a lieutenant in the ship's crew (the navigator) who asked us to the wardroom for tea. Of course we went and had a delightful time and were asked back for cocktails the next night. Kathleen arranged for the ship's crew, English of course, to bring her stuff from home. Don't know if it ever worked out.

On Sunday we went to a Protestant service in the lounge. The singing was lovely; *Ave Maria, My country Tis Of Thee, God Save The King*, etc. There were such interesting people to talk to. Sigmund, a Pole now in the RAF, had quite a history. He came from Warsaw where he joined the underground in 1939. Having been warned that he was under suspicion, he fled to Russia where he was interned and sent to Siberia. He escaped with sixteen companions and got to China. Later they discovered that there was a new agreement and he would have been freed, so he gave himself up to Russian officials and was told that he was a Russian citizen since his part of Poland now belonged to that country. He was forced to join the Red Army Air Force, but deserted and got to England, and joined the RAF. He had been training in Canada and was now on his way back to England. I assumed his story was true, but who knows.

Crossing the ocean in wartime, on the Queen Mary, was certainly one of the most thrilling and exciting events of my life. I don't remember ever being nervous or frightened and I think perhaps this is more apt to be if you have responsibilities at home, like a wife and children.

We landed off Grennock in the Firth of Fourth very early in the morning. It was light of twilight all night long and we spent the evening on the rail watching Ireland go by and Scotland's rocky coast approach. I remember thinking Ireland should be green and it was. We anchored quite far out and were taken ashore by launch. The women were the first to disembark amid lots of cheering from the troops who must have had an awful trip and were naturally very glad to be near land again.

We got on a troop train immediately and set off for London fairly quickly. When we passed through towns or isolated homes women or old men or children would lean from their windows and wave and give us the "V" sign. (Churchill's sign) Local women's groups gave us tea and sandwiches at stations along the way.

It was a long trip, and we got to London around midnight, as I recall. I don't remember how we were assigned quarters or where we stayed, but it was in a private house near Green park. I do remember that I slept until 12:00 noon the next day—very unusual for me! Needless to say, I had never been in a blacked-out city before and it really was black at night. The bomb damage was horrendous! Kathleen Kennedy was in the room next door and I remember her trying to get in touch with her fiancée or whatever he was at the time. She was going to the House of Commons with Lady Astor and asked me to go along. I didn't go, and that's one of my great regrets. I had an appointment—something about my assignment—I forget just what.

After about a week during which I did a lot of sightseeing around bomb-damaged London, I was assigned to the 95th Bomb Group in the 8th Air Force as assistant director. Jean Plageman was to be the director. This was in late June 1943. The 95th was a B-17 group of heavy bombers in East Anglia, between Eye and Diss, at Horham. A bomb group had four combat squadrons and about seventeen units attached—i.e. ordinance, finance, medical, etc.

Here I might mention my great admiration for the British people. Their generally cool nature under aerial bombardment was amazing and catching as Americans behaved calmly too. I never saw any panic at all. I remember that one night I went to a restaurant with a captain in a tank company who I met on the ship. We started back to my room in the blackout and met up with a man delivering milk, so we drove around with him for a couple of hours. Quite an experience in blacked out London. It was very hard to find one's way around!

America had great faith in the B-17 (Flying Fortress) for daylight, high-level, precision bombing, with the use of the Norden Bomb Sight, which could only be used in daylight. The B-17 was a rugged plane with lots of defensive firepower. The British had given up daylight bombing as too costly in men and planes. They had been fighting since 1939. In the end, the British did the nighttime bombing and the Americans the daytime, so Germany could be pounded non-stop.

There are two books in my bookcase about the 8th Air Force—*Courage, Honor & Victory* by Ian Hawkins and *Target Germany.* They can tell you about the missions, etc. I can remember the Forts taking off and getting into formation to gain altitude over the base. I seem to remember that it took a long time, but, of course, they had to be at high altitude when they crossed the coast of France, into enemy territory. When they returned, you could count any missing by the gaps in the formation and, it was a great relief when there were none. They would circle the base for a long time to lose altitude to land and I seem to remember that the planes with wounded aboard would shoot a red flare so that they could land more quickly and ambulances could meet them. We always took big vats of coffee to the briefing rooms when we saw that the planes were about to land.

The British people who worked for us were great. I guess we had about eight in the club, which had once housed the British NAAF (equivalent to the ARC) when the RAF was stationed there. They did the cleaning and made the snacks for the snack bar. We had sandwiches, tarts and things like that, depending on the supplies we could get—really quite good. The snack bar, and in fact the whole club was always crowded in the evenings once we got it going, but we had to start from scratch, hiring, buying, scrounging, etc. We got some supplies from the ARC warehouses in London and some we bought on the English market. We had Ping Pong tables, a snooker table and a library, as well as a snack bar. A wonderful English woman used to sit in the library some nights and do mending for the soldiers.

Her name was Mrs. Widdrington, a canon's wife, and I visited them once for two or three days. It was wonderful!

Nowadays, to encounter a native of a foreign country is nothing out of the ordinary, but in 1943 there were many who hadn't traveled but a few miles from their native villages, so Yanks were a great curiosity to the British and vice versa. After a while they became very friendly toward one another and the prejudice and suspicion disappeared.

The Americans, on the whole, are very sentimental and bestow lots of affection on children and animals, whereas the English men seemed to distance themselves from children especially. They did love animals. There were many rather nondescript dogs and cats on the bases I was on, well fed and well treated and passed from hand to hand as crews went home or were missing in action. We had a cat named "Lieutenant Clark," and the GI trash men took great pleasure in catching a mouse with their heavy gloves and putting it in our window early in the morning. Lieutenant Clark got excited when he heard the truck and the squeaking and crunching that went on was pleasant for him but not for us.

There was a TB hospital for children near the base and on visiting day a group of G.I.s would always go, bringing gum and chocolate, etc. The children weren't at all interested in their parents, but loved the G.I.s. "Here come the Yanks," they'd yell! I was very proud of my countrymen and still am. At Christmastime we had a party for the children around the base and it was very popular with the children and with the men who saved their candy rations for the kids.

We charged a small bit for the snacks; I can't remember how the money was handled. We had an English accountant who lived on the base and had a minimum of morals if any. It was my first introduction to this sort of thing! Her home, where her mother lived alone as her father was somewhere with the British army, was nearby. One night we had an air raid and a German plane was shot down. The pilot bailed out and a little later there was a knock at this woman's door. When she asked, "Who is it?" a German voice answered. She was afraid to open the door and eventually the man went off. He was never found so someone must have helped him. Some said there was blood on the porch the next morning, but I'm not sure that this is true. We had a Tannoy System speaker in our room and periodically we'd hear "Red Alert" over the speaker. We always went back to sleep and woke up again when the "All Clear" sounded. Funny how used to it you got.

I remember one night after a mission a crew came in late to the mess. They had been shot down in the Channel and rescued by the _____ (I forgot the name). They were so excited!

The 95th Bomb group was activated in June of '42 at Barksdale Field in Louisiana. They departed for the ETO in March '43, began operations in May '43, and their permanent station was Horham in East Anglia. They flew 321 combat missions and dropped 19,769 tons of bombs from May 13, 1943 to April 20, 1945, and then seven "Chowhound" missions to feed the starving Dutch in May of '45, and four "Revival" missions to return POWs and displaced persons. The group lost 599 killed in action, and had total casualties of 1,734 POWs, wounded, etc. The 95th was the only group in the 8th AF to receive three Presidential Distinguished Unit Citations. It was the first USAF group to bomb Berlin, in March '44. Jean stayed through the war and went home with them the summer of '45, but I left in November '43 to go to IX Bomber Command.

Bomber Command was, of course, much smaller, not being a combat group and there was lots of rank around. I had been promoted to Director and my assistant was Martha Brush, from Zanesville, Ohio. We started from scratch, hiring, scrounging from utilities and the quartermaster and visiting the Labor Board and the Ministry of Food for ration cards and help (about fifteen). We lived in a Nissen hut right opposite the club. It had two bedrooms and a bath and eventually we got a manager, Mrs. Warman, for the kitchen. She lived in the other bedroom.

A Deerfield friend of Hermie's was on this base, Roger Williams, the public relations officer, whose father Ben Ames Williams had just written a book that became a best seller, *Leave Her To Heaven*. He sent the manuscript to Roger, and I got to read it!

We had a wonderful staff. On Christmas every one of them showed up for work! Poor Mrs. Warman! I learned that her husband and her two sons had all been killed, I think, in the RAF.

One day two English officers came in to ask for our garbage to feed a baby pig they had just bought. A few days later they said they were going to sell the pig and eat the garbage it looked so good. Still later they complained that the garbage was no longer the same good quality! Still later they invited us to come help eat the pig. I was glad I didn't know it personally.

Mice bothered us, and this is how the G.I.s said they dealt with them. They balanced a ruler with a piece of cheese on the end over a pail of water. The mouse walks out to get it and falls into the pail and drowns. "However," they said, "the mice are getting smart and now another mouse sits on the other end!"

There were WACs on this base, one of them, May March, was at Smith when I was there. She was secretary to Col. Lewis, the commanding officer. I read in my letters that Roger Williams wrote a story about an experience we shared. He showed it to me and I laughed and laughed. It was confidential and censored but he promised to send it to me after the war. I never got it and I can't remember anything about it. Since Roger is dead, I guess I'll never know. The only thing I remember is going to a dance in some town with him. We went with others from the base in an Army truck with a driver. Almost as soon as we got there, the air raid sirens blew, and the building was closed. We went to a little town park and sat on a bench. Roger had a bottle, and he drank a lot and I very little. He got so drunk! When the all clear sounded the dance was over and I was afraid I would never find the truck in the black out. Roger was too drunk to be any help. I did, and we got back to the base. I ducked in the hut quickly and locked up so he couldn't get in. He knocked for a while and then we heard a sliding noise. Some G.I.s were there with Martha. Roger had passed out just outside the door. They carried him to the officer's quarters and left him on the path outside the door of his hut, where I presume someone rescued him. They bought his glasses to me and I meanly enjoyed returning them the next day!

I only remember two air raids here. When one occurred it was dinnertime and we were in the officer's mess. We went outside and I was looking up feeling sorry for the German pilot with the searchlight on him. Suddenly I was tackled around the knees and I struggled to stay on my feet thinking I was being criminally attacked. Then I heard the whistle of the bomb and it landed somewhere fairly nearby, but no particular damage was done.

The other time was at night. We were in bed when the red alert sounded. We heard the rat-a-tat of the fighter shooting at the German plane and then the loud bang as it crashed on the base. We jumped out of bed, grabbed each other's coat in error and went to the air raid shelter. This was the only time I ever went to one and did we get a lot of teasing—two girls in pajamas with about thirty men! The pilot was killed, but the two crewmen parachuted and the Tannoy system started crackling, "Watch out for two parachuters on base," then one of them and then done, so both were captured. I hoped it wasn't true, but I heard the G.I.s took souvenirs from the dead pilot such as teeth, articles of uniform, etc.

Here I might mention that British expressions were sometimes hard to understand. One form of greeting was something that sounded like "Watch your cock," which, roughly translated seemed to mean "How's it going?" This naturally startled the men. One evening I arranged to go somewhere with an Australian liaison officer on the base and he said, "I'll be at your quarters early to knock you up." This was naturally a little startling to a twenty-six-year-old virgin. When an Englishman gave directions, he always said things like, "Go to the bottom of the road" (I never learned where that was) and "You can't miss it." (I invariably did.) I learned to love the English accent and their ways of expressing themselves.

This base, of course, was a command not an operational base. The headquarters offices were up the hill in a lovely old mansion with beautiful gardens around the huge reflecting pool. The gardener was still there taking care of it and we were able to pick peonies when we wanted to. As I recall, the generals and the colonels lived in this building and the rest of us lived in Nissen huts. There were several USAF combat units nearby, but the missions were planned from headquarters, and on occasion Col. Thatcher would ask us up to the operations room to sit while the next day's mission was planned. We'd go after the club closed at 11:00 and sit there most of the night with our knitting, just listening to it all. I always wondered why he wanted us up there.

I think it was about this time that the Buzz Bombs began to fall on London. It so happened that Martha and I were in London on leave, staying in the apartment of a friend of Martha's on Baker Street, near Hyde Park. There was only one bed, so we took turns sleeping on the floor. That particular night I had the bed and was sound asleep when the first one came over. The guns in Hyde Park startled me so that I jumped out of bed right on Martha's stomach. After that first night the guns didn't shoot at them. The next day some English people were saying that small German children piloted them. I'm glad that wasn't true. Once later, when I was in London with our truck and driver, Urban Rudner, getting supplies, a Buzz Bomb came right along beside us slowly. The engine stopped, and it crashed into a group of houses. We didn't wait to see what happened.

Since IX Bomber Command was not an operational base, we were relieved of the job of taking coffee down to the airfield when the planes came back from missions. We had our share of casualties though in the form of jeep, weapons carriers, etc. accidents. In one, the boy a WAC named Pinkie was crazy about was killed, and when she recovered from her injuries, I went on leave with her to Scotland. Someone flew us to Liverpool. We arrived in the middle of the night and what an eerie place it was—got a train to Edinburgh and somehow ended up at a little inn on the shores of Loch Lomond. It was a nice trip, but I don't remember much about it or how we got back to the base. There are always American soldiers around in jeeps or some other vehicle who would go out of their way for American women and we may have hitchhiked.

This is one of the conversations I overheard between two G.I.s one day:

"When I get home from this war, I'm going on the most glorified drunk."
"Me too. I'm going to bed with a bottle on each side."
"Not me. I'm just going to have a bottle on one side."
(Laughter)
"Well, you can still have a bottle on each side."
"That constitutes a bottleneck."
"Who wants to neck a bottle?"

There wasn't much intellect around!

I think I was at IX Bomber Command Headquarters until May of '44. I had asked headquarters quite a while ago to transfer to a group scheduled for France after the invasion. I was disappointed to be transferred to the 91st Bomb Group just outside of Cambridge but was assured that this was only temporary because they needed a temporary director. This was a huge permanent base that had been an English base before the war. It was the first base to be taken over by the Americans. We were living in luxury and I was homesick for my rough life at Bomber Command. (The movie *Memphis Belle* was filmed there.)

The club had two stories, and it seemed strange to go upstairs to my office. My assistant Jean, who was very nice, was a diver who was in the Aquacade at the World's Fair and in Vaudeville in New York before the war. Her first husband, a pilot, was killed almost as soon as he got to England and she had an eight-year-old son, living with her parents. She was married at that time to a Special Service officer who was also in England, but didn't seem to be too happy with him. Jean organized a great show—very funny and successful. She was an excellent assistant. So from the smallest aero club in England I went to the biggest, but only for a very short time—about a month. Being back on an operational station was sort of depressing. The gunners seemed younger and I guess they were as the war went on and on. Hinkie and Red, gunners, were the two I was fondest of. Red said once, "When we head for home, Fitje, I can see your smiling face and I just hope I get there." I don't know whether or not they survived. One of them was from Bell Buckle, Tennessee, if there is such a place!

In early June 1944 my wish came true, and I was transferred to a combat group. The 386th Bomb Group, in the 8th Air Force, a B-26 group. As you may or may not know, the B-26s were made right here in Baltimore at Martins. They were called the "Flying Prostitutes" because they had no visible means of support—also the "Widow Maker" a rather ominous title. Roger Freeman, was on the base, which was nice and not nice, as I had to worry about him. He was Ibby Freeman's husband, a friend from home. I had never had anyone from home to worry about before. Thank God, Roger came safely home. Since we were friends from way back and saw a lot of each other everyone kept kidding him and saying, "I thought you were married Roger." Anyway, he went home soon and I was relieved.

The 386th sent a B-26 up to Cambridge to pick me up and since it was rather sudden, I packed while the plane was circling the field. We quickly got back to the same routine of meeting all the missions with coffee and donuts.

My assistant was Mary Haynesworth, and she was a character, <u>very</u> promiscuous, very, and very nice. We lived in a Nissen hut right across the road from the club. Our accountant was Pat Dean, who was born in South Africa. Her parents were medical missionaries in Singapore when she was a child, and she grew up there and went to boarding school in Borneo. She told me that when she finished school at seventeen or eighteen and went back to Singapore, a boy she knew kissed her and she thought she was having a baby. Can you imagine being that naïve? Pat and her mother left Singapore as the Japs were nearing (her father had died) and crossed the Pacific to California, and then the United States to New York. In New York they joined a convoy going to England. Somewhere in the mid-Atlantic the ship was torpedoed and sailors in a Canadian Corvette pulled Pat and her mother out of the water. Pat was literally pulled out by her long dark hair. They had always slept in their clothes on the ship so when they landed in London this was all they had. Pat's mother, a nurse, got a job in London and Pat ended up as an accountant on our base. I don't remember now, but she must have gotten her training in London. She was very young and very pretty and had a difficult time coping with

Pat Dean, 1944

all those horny young airmen, which she did mainly by ignoring them.

Mary and I had a cat, of course. The cat immediately had kittens—four, I think. All night long she would wake us climbing up the metal side of the hut to go out the window. Shortly she'd return through the window and down the metal side saying Brrup-Brrup to let the kittens know she was coming. We didn't get much sleep for a while.

One of the officers on the base was Bob Meservy, better known as the actor Robert Preston. I've forgotten what his job was on the base. He was very likeable. A lot of Hollywood actors and actresses were involved in war work and came to the base frequently with USO shows, etc. Everyone loved them! The following come to mind, but there were many more: Marlene Dietrich, Jimmy Stewart (in the service I think), Clark Gable, Bob Hope, Vivian Leigh, etc.

CHAPTER 2

Basic Training

February 27, 1943–June 23, 1943

The Red Cross was the only civilian service organization permitted to work with overseas military personal during World War II. Red Cross personal served the G.I.s in a variety of capacities, often providing a valuable respite from the realities of war.

Those who served abroad did so as nurses and "Donut Dollies." They staffed service clubs such as the well-known Rainbow Corner near Piccadilly Circus in London, and in Red Cross Club Mobiles, often close to the front. Others, like Fitje, were attached to bomber bases where they worked in Aero Clubs. Their task was difficult and at times dangerous. Eighty-six Red Cross personal died during the war, thirty-four men and fifty-two women.

After being rejected by the Women's Army Corps because of a heart murmur Fitje volunteered for the Red Cross. Standards for acceptance were stringent. It required applicants to be college graduates, in excellent health and at least twenty-five years old. One might wonder why my mother's heart murmur did not result in her rejection. It might well have been that her father, a surgeon, had influence with Dr. Frank T. Fulton who gave Fitje her physical.

The Red Cross sent Fitje to Washington, D.C. for training at American University in January 1943. She wrote on February 28, 1943 that with the first stage of training complete, her education turned to the practical skills she'd need. She received instruction in motor mechanics, map reading, how to make coffee and donuts, and how to run a movie projector. Further, she received training in entertainment and club administration.

After finishing her practical training, Fitje gained field experience. Shuttling between Washington, Richmond and New York, she worked at a Pepsi Cola club in Washington, the USO booth in Grand Central Station, the Red Cross at Ft. Hamilton in New York, and at the club in the Midston House, a women's hotel on 38th Street and Madison Avenue in New York City.

Her letters during this period are a mix of news and gossip. She tells her family about her training and the people she meets while talking about meals with friends, trips to Baltimore to visit cousins and a weekend in Princeton. As the months pass she is increasingly impatient, ready to get her orders and move on to the job she has trained for.

The orders came in late June. On the 27th Fitje boarded the Queen Mary and sailed to Europe. While basic training had been extensive, Fitje was soon to discover how little prepared she was for the magnitude of the task ahead.

February 27, 1943
The Burlington Hotel
Washington, D.C.

Dear Mother & Dad,

It is almost one o'clock and we still are not dressed, having had breakfast sent up to us on trays. You should see our rooms, the worst mess. We are trying to repack and organize our things and wash our dirty clothes. I am sure that when we leave, we will take all of each other's things. It is particularly difficult because we all wear the same size uniform.

It certainly was nice to see you, Dad. I am still wearing the gardenia you gave me and it still looks very fresh. We polished off the tangerines for breakfast this morning.

Last night I had dinner at Franny and Herb's with Scotty who is visiting them for the weekend. I am going there for lunch, too, and we are going to have roast beef! You see I am certainly well fed. I even had four big slices of bacon for breakfast.

We have been advised to prepare ourselves for a good long wait before anything else happens. Of course rumors fly around, but the general consensus seems to be that we will be here for several weeks. Now that the first stage of our training is over our hours are very short (9:30-4:00) with an hour and a half for lunch and all we do all day is play games, etc. Next week I am going to take a four-day course in motor mechanics and map reading. Later on if we are still around we will probably go to New York for a while and learn how to make coffee, and doughnuts, and how to run movie projectors, etc.

Now that we have been divided into different groups I am beginning to know more people and have a better idea as to who I might possibly be with. There are lots of very nice and interesting people—one particularly nice girl from Pasadena who spent last year in Chile working with Albert Harkness at the Cultural Institute in Santiago.

I am hoping to see Rose and Charley but I don't suppose they know where they are going next. I am also hoping Jane will come down, maybe next weekend since I am not so afraid of leaving immediately anymore. Franny has been looking for a job but has not found one yet. She seems to feel very well. That's too bad about Mr. Gardner. Will you send me Hermie and Ann's address?* I don't seem to have it and want to answer Ann's letter. Will you also ask Johnny to write me a description of that good card trick he showed me if he has time, as I can't remember? I am going to specialize in fortune

---

* Fitje's brother Herman and his wife Ann

telling, I think, for my contribution to the entertainments and am looking for a book on it so I can learn how. I will send you postcards more often. The time seems to be flying by and I didn't realize I had been lax in writing.

Thank Lucy for her letter.

Love to all, including Jones and Bridget.[*]

Binni

✍

March 14, 1943
Washington, D.C.

Dear Mother & Dad,

Have just spent a very active and pleasant weekend with Jane and John, Franny and Herb, Scotty and Tim.[†]

The group started to gather yesterday afternoon around 5:00, first Tim, then Jane, then John, then Franny and Herb and last of all Scotty around 9:00. The meeting place was the cocktail lounge here at the Burlington. We went to a nifty little French restaurant for dinner (some of us had steak—I had liver and bacon) and then came back to Jane and John's room and sat around the rest of the evening. Every place in Washington is so crowded Saturday night that there is no use trying to go anywhere.

This morning Jane, John and I had breakfast at the Statler. It was so late that we had to order a la carte and the bill for orange juice, coffee, scrambled eggs and bacon for three was $5.10! (90 cents for three cups of coffee, $1.10 for three glasses of orange juice in regular orange juice glasses) Then we came back to the hotel and Jane took pictures of John and me in our uniforms, which she is going to send you. We spent the rest of the day at the Well's and Jane and John left about 5:00.

Johnny looks very well. I think he has gotten quite a bit thinner and looks very tan. Jane looks well too. She says the Clements are all back now and Pat's husband has been home on a 10-day furlough.

I am sorry Bridget has been so sick! You must have been having a hard time without her. There seems to be a lot of sickness around here. Everyone where Carol lives is getting the measles. I, myself, never felt better in my life and am certainly getting all the rest I need. I am developing an enormous appetite, which is too bad since I have to keep my meals down to $2.50 a day. No longer does a small breakfast of toast, coffee and orange juice satisfy me, I have to have bacon and eggs and the whole works. The shots don't affect me in the slightest. I have three more tomorrow, two more the next Monday and then they're finished.

We are still completely in the dark as to what is going on. No Club Mobile people have left for weeks now, and there is quite a crowd of us around. Some of them are getting very bored, but I have enjoyed

---

[*] Jones and Bridget worked for her parents.

[†] Jane was Fitje's sister. John McLaughry, who Fitje often calls "Big John," is Jane's husband. John was in the Marines. Tim is her cousin Tim Pitts who lived in Baltimore.

myself so far and am not yet sick of living out of my suitcase and being ready to leave at a moment's notice. I will not know whether I am going to N.Y. or not for more training until the moment actually comes, but I am hoping that I will. Jane seems to be writing to see what the Clements do before she decides. I think the farm idea sounds wonderful except that she says she is going to grow bangs again if she does it.

Thank you for sending the shoes, Mother. I find I am going to have more room than I thought, the knapsack holds so much.

I will have to hurry to get this in the mail in time. I can't believe that Johnny is really getting ready to go to college. It was so nice to talk to you all the other night. I won't call you this week unless something important comes up, but will call you again soon.

Love,
Binni

❧

March 24, 1943
Washington, D.C.

Dear Mother & Dad,

I'm afraid it's been quite a long time since I wrote you a letter, but the time is slipping by so fast and I have no idea when the last one was.

Have just gotten back from having dinner with Janet and Doug and doing my weekly ironing, which I have to take around to Janet's or Franny's to get it done. It seems silly now to think I don't part with my things long enough to take them to a laundry, but I know that if I do, I will be sure to have to go without them, and it takes a week to ten days to get anything done around here. At last we are beginning to feel the shortage, slightly, in the form of not being able to have buttered toast for breakfast. Not much of a hardship.

This week I have really worked hard. Three other girls and myself volunteered our services in the offices, and were immediately put the work making graphs of the ages and draft classifications of the men overseas. It is quite interesting and it's nice to feel useful for change. Some of the people are getting very discouraged and think nothing is ever going to happen. We get the inside dope, though, and I feel sure that something will happen soon.

After work Tuesday, Thursday, and Saturday, I go right to the Pepsi-Cola Service Club where I stay until 9:30 serving hamburgers and Pepsi-Cola, and doing a million other things. It is a lot of fun. The club is very nice, enormous, and packed every night. The big feature is the record-making machine where people can dictate letters in the form of records to send.

Alexia was transferred to New York last Monday, with quite a large group for further study, and practice, in the service clubs around there. Since she went I have been occupying this enormous room by myself. I knew it was too good to last though and now I have been told that I must either move into a suit with three other girls, get a roommate, or pay $3.00 a night myself as the room is $6 and the Red Cross will only pay $3.00. I am going to call one girl tonight who I think may move in with me. I hate to give up this room and move in with three other girls but I suppose it would be good for me. I have to keep reminding myself that I must be flexible but I also love being exclusive while I can because I know it won't last for long.

I got a letter from Johnny today saying he and Jane are coming again this weekend so I have made a reservation for them here. It will be nice to see them again. We have been limited as to weekends, so I guess I won't be able to get to Baltimore again for a while. Last weekend it was lovely. It snowed all day Sunday, and we saw two red Cardinals out in the gardens in the snow. The two babies were there, and they really are sad together. Clinton (Kink's baby) is so cute and Knobby (Alice's baby) whines and cries all the time. Cousin Dorothy and Norman take complete care of Alice's baby and Alice never lifts her finger.[*]

It is so nice to get letters from you all. I wish I could have been home last weekend when the rest of you were all there. Maybe someday we'll have the whole family altogether, under one roof. I have not seen a robin here yet dad. I think there must be a shortage of them in Washington, as I looked all day today. I can imagine your disgusted having to eat chicken. I'm sure it would never be a hardship to me though. Too bad about Johnny[†] and college, but I'm sure it won't do him any burden to delay for eight months.

Tell Ann I am going to write her one of these days. Is Hermie a 1st Lieutenant yet? Does Lu see much of Ibby?[‡] I am worried about Jones and the meat rationing. What are you going to feed him? Send me Bridget's address so I can send her a postcard. Give my Love to Mrs. Aldrich and Aunt Minnie.

Love to all.
Binni

March 27, 1943
Washington, DC

Dear Mother & Dad,

It is pouring rain again. Saturday always seems to be raining down here.

Yesterday I went to the FBI where I shot a Thompson Sub Machinegun-.45-caliber. Please be sure and tell Johnny I did it just for him.

I am looking forward to Jane and John being here, although I have to work tonight until about 9:30. I guess they will do something with Herb and Franny.

Love.
Binni

---

[*] "Kinks" was Tim Pitts' younger brother Clinton and Alice was their sister. Alice was married to Norman Gardner. Cousin Dorothy was their mother.

[†] John was Fitje's younger brother. He was sixteen and apparently deferred by Yale University. He was admitted eight months later and after graduation continued his studies at Harvard Medical School.

[‡] Lu refers to Fitje's sister Lucy. Ibby is Ibby Taft Freeman who was Lucy's closest friend.

March 30, 1943
Alexandria, Virginia

Dear Mother & Dad,

Well here we are in Alexandria living in an old, small, very nice, little inn and working in the USO club.

Friday I heard through the grapevine that I was going, but we were not told officially until Monday morning and then had to pack and leave about two hours later. What a mad rush. Six of us came here. Everyone in our class has been sent somewhere now, some to Richmond, some to New York, etc. I am just as glad to be here as it really is awfully nice and very near Washington—one half hour by bus.

We work in the club from 2:00 in the afternoon until 11:00 at night with an hour or two off for dinner. They do not seem to care whether we are here or not so we are very independent. Supposedly we work six days a week with Thursdays off. Yesterday we fooled around the USO all afternoon addressing envelops and making new menus and last night we went with the motor corps, to a Searchlight Battery, with coffee and donuts. There were about fifteen men there having maneuvers and it was very interesting. They showed us all about how light worked and we watched them spot planes for a couple of hours.

We are sent here for two weeks unless transportation is available within that time. After that I will go back to Washington. I think it would be best if you sent my mail to: American Red Cross, Print Craft Building, 930 H Street, Northwest, Washington, as I can get it every day or two, and it is so in definite how long I will be here.

Jane and John seems well last weekend. We didn't do much as I had to work until 10:00. Sunday we had cocktails with Franny and Herb, and then Jane and John went sightseeing. Franny, Herb, and I had lunch (fried chicken) at a very nice place, sat around all afternoon, and then went to Charlie and Carla Freeman's for dinner. Carla's mother and some other people were there and it was very nice.

Thank you for the shoes, Mother. I have been trying to have them dyed, and heels put on some other shoes. I took them to three places, the only three in Alexandria, this morning and none of them would promise any work in less than three weeks! I guess I will have to learn to do them myself, as I certainly can't part with anything for that long.

I hear there is a chance of you going to New York next weekend. Wish I could be there too. Jane is afraid that she will catch measles from Ibby. If so she will get them about then. I thought the pictures were very good. Jane gave me a set.

I have no guess as to when we will be off. I only know that people have been leaving lately. The last of the older group left Monday, and I should be in the next group. When that will be I don't know, maybe months. I don't feel a bit as if I were ever going to leave. I don't know who will be in my group. Our particular set has been all broken up and sent to different places. We are hoping to be reunited at the port of embarkation, as probably forty or fifty will leave at once. We are not assigned to actual groups until we reach our destination.

I will send you the telephone number of the USO tomorrow and you can call me there between 7:00 and 11:00 if you want to reach me. We are not supposed to use the telephone here at the inn and unless it is an emergency as the only one is the manager's private number.

Love.
Binni

∽

April 11, 1943
Alexandria, VA

Dear Mother & Dad,

There is great excitement around here today, as seven of us are getting ready to leave for New York tomorrow night. We are not quite sure what for, but imagine it's nothing exciting—just for more training. We are going to spend tonight in Washington and report at headquarters at nine on Monday, with our luggage. I will call and let you know where I am in New York and will be looking forward to seeing you there.

I really hate to leave here; it has been such fun. I don't know whether I ever told you much about the USO, it's awfully nice. Quite large, with a dance floor, reading room, a big lounge, a dark room for developing pictures, a soda fountain, offices etc. There are lots of soldiers, and Coast Guard, and Marines here every evening. Monday we have movies, Wednesday and Saturday dances, and other nights there are different things in the way of entertainment. We are kept busy making decorations for the dances, and doing all sorts of things. For example, one boy just bought his blouse in here for me to iron. It's all you can do to write a letter because you're interrupted so much. At this very moment I am carrying on an argument with the boy who comes from St. Louis who doesn't see why anyone lives in the east.

There are also some amazing people around here, one private who, before he was drafted was a brain surgeon in Albany, New York. He's a German and not a citizen so he cannot get a commission. Another buck private got his PhD at Harvard and is a very good friend of Mr. Dehood's, who taught me Pareto at Smith.

There are three other privates, all artists, who worked in advertising and commercial art before the war. They're awful nice. Friday night they invited Trudy, the girl from China, and myself up to the studio of a friend of theirs for dinner. We went and Trudy cooked them a Chinese dinner. It was the most amazing place way up on the top of the building owned by a Mr. and Mrs. Gillam and their two children. The Gillam's live in a trailer park in back of the gasoline station and spent most of the time in the studio.

Thursday we took the train to Richmond stopping off in Frederick on the way up to see the historical spots. I went to see Ann in Richmond. She and Stevie look fine. Don was away so I didn't meet him.

Really I just hate to leave this part of the country I love it so.

We think we will probably take the train to New York Monday evening. I will call you up Tuesday and tell you where I am—probably at the Midston House.[*]

I am sending back the ration books, as I don't see how I can use them in New York.

Much love
Binni

May 5, 1943
New York, N.Y.

Dear Mother & Dad,

I am enclosing this thing from the Red Cross in Providence about my 1943 income to be put with my other papers if you will, thanks.

At last the weather is nice and I am sitting in the sun on the roof. The only trouble, it is quite cold and I'm sure there is no chance of getting any sunburn.

Yesterday was my day off. I met Jane, Pat, and E. May at the Museum of modern art late in the afternoon and we went to see the movie, *Camille*, which was playing there. Then we all met Clem, and had dinner, and I almost died laughing at Clem's story of her experience on that Salt Island that Jane had already told us about. After dinner Jane and I went to Carnegie Hall to hear The Passion of St. John, in which Brian was singing. We got there very late and didn't like it very much as neither of us like choir singing particularly. Brian's orders have been changed and he is not going to go home after all. He expects to be about twelve hours flying time from England and very much back in active service apparently. He says Jim has another son. I am so glad that trail see had a son too.

Working in the Grand Central is a lot of fun. Most of the boys who come into the USO lounge have about an hour or two between trains to kill. They go to sleep on the benches with signs pin to them: "Wake me up at 10:00", etc.

Lots of foreign soldiers are coming in, of all sorts. Monday night a French aviator came in who looked absolutely no older than John. He spoke very little English and had just arrived here. He swallowed a cup of coffee quickly, as he only had ten minutes to catch a train and when we told him it was free he looked so surprised said, "My God America is a wonderful place." I wish I could know somehow what happens to some of these people who I talk to for about ten minutes.

Don't worry about me coming home alone mother because there are three of us here and we all come home together.

This afternoon I'm going to see *Lady in the Dark* with Gertrude Lawrence (in it) with Pat's sister, Clem, and one of the Red Cross girls. I also took your advice, Dad, and went to see the gun exhibit in the Chrysler Building. Too bad Johnny can't see it; he certainly would like it.

I'm afraid our chances of getting to England get slimmer and slimmer as time goes on. In fact we are

[*] Located at 22 East 38th Street and Madison Avenue in Manhattan.

beginning to think that we are being saved for some absolutely new place where they are just beginning this. Well there's no point in guessing, but so many people have left lately that there must be a reason for us still being here.

It was so nice being home over Easter and seeing everybody. I will plan to come home over my birthday now and see what happens. My horoscope, which someone recently gave me, says that I am not going to travel until July 2nd through 6th.

Love.
Binni

May 14, 1943
New York

Dear Mother,

I thought you would like a little first hand information on what Princeton is like these days. I spent Tuesday night with Mrs. Henry Young the aunt of Mary Taylor Cook who is in the Red Cross, in a wonderful big home on Rosedale Road just outside of Princeton.* I was amazed at how much I knew about the streets and the people from hearing you talk about them. The only trouble was it poured all the time we were there, but it was lovely. The leaves were all out.

I met one friend of yours, Mrs. Brigham, who used to be Elizabeth Duffield, and her mother. Her sister Weller took us to see an apartment that Mary was looking at for her father, and Mrs. LaVake who runs a jewelry store remembered you very well and said you were a "lovely girl". Sister Weller said there are lots of applicants for your house, which I saw.

I did not go to see the Armstrong's because we only had one morning and were dependent on Mrs. Young for transportation because of the rain. Mrs. Young knew them and the Scott's and everyone else I had ever heard you speak of. Mary's grandmother lives at the Princeton Inn and we went there for lunch. I am seriously considering renting your house from you after the war it is so nice there.

Am still working at Grand Central and have, in fact, requested the assignment for another week. I have heard some of the most amazing stories there and I'm sure I've met someone from every different branch of the Armed Forces; allied as well as our own. Last night some sailors told us that a big ship (one of those we hope to go on) came in a couple of days ago with a load of German prisoners, eight of which escaped through a porthole but made the mistake of swimming under Pier 92 which is the Navy pier and were of course captured by the Navy. Most of the sailors are barely over twenty and one nineteen, had stars for two major battles Midway and Coral Sea and had been right near the Vincennes and picked up some of the survivors when it went down.

---

* Fitje's mother Lucy McDonald Pitts (1885–1970) was born and raised on Mercer Street in Princeton, New Jersey. Her father was a Presbyterian minister and in the later 1890's, mayor of Princeton. The house on Rosedale probably refers to 89 Rosedale Road.

His ship was hit in five places but not sunk. What the sailors hate most are the "90-Day Ensigns" and the "Lymies" (English sailors, however you spell it) and what they talk about most is getting home again.

Today I am having lunch with Jane, E. May and Mary Digman and must go as it is getting late. Andrew is stationed at Ft. Belvoir in Virginia and is coming up this weekend, which seems rather silly, as I have to work Saturday and Sunday nights.

Love to all,
Binni

May 23rd Sunday
New York, N.Y.

Dear Mother & Dad,

I am glad you are having one nice day in Mystic. Saturday was so awful here but today is lovely. Last night after work I went out with Andrew and didn't get in until very late so it is now about 11 o'clock and I have just finished breakfast in my room, a luxury I only indulge in on Sundays!

Tonight, unfortunately, is our last night to work in the lounge. It was such fun I hate to leave. Next week I am going to be in the office at the Headquarters in the Midston House. No more sunbathing during the daytime! Again rumors are going around and again everyone is packing, but this time I refuse to be fooled. I suppose maybe the change in events has had something to do with our delay but anyone's guess is as good as mine.

Andrew has been down at Ft. Belvoir in Virginia for a couple of weeks training in something special and was on his way back to Kentucky last night when he stopped here. He doesn't seem to think he will get overseas for a long time to come.

About those Special Service Kits, Dad, we have them in the lounge to give out to groups of soldiers or sailors who are about to go on long train trips. They are small canvas bags with about fifteen different kinds of puzzles, a checkerboard, and a pack of cards in each. We give away about twenty-five every two weeks. They are also given out at the ports of embarkation. The soldiers seem to like them pretty well, but it seems to me there are better causes than that. N.Y. is simply wonderful to men in uniform. They can get theatre tickets free, eat free, sleep free, there are about ten dances for them every night and dozens of canteens, etc. If things aren't free they get special service rates.

We have had some amazing people in the lounge lately. Last night eight English sailors came in handcuffed together with about fifteen guards, and one of the prisoners told me a long and wonderful story about murdering someone. He said the others were his assistants. I never did find out what they really did.

I will have to wait until tomorrow and find out what my hours are before I know where I can come home or not. If not next I probably can the weekend after that.

Mary Taylor Cook's connection with Princeton is that she was born and brought up there as her father was in business in Trenton. Now her mother and father are separated and her mother has moved to N.Y. to be near Mary until she leaves, but her father's sister, Mrs. Henry Young and family live there on Rosedale Road in a great big house with pillars and lots of land around it, that must have been there in your day, Mother. We stayed with them when we went. Their oldest son, in the Air Corps, was killed in Africa. Mary's mother is awful nice and is always doing things for all of us. She works at the lounge, too, a couple of nights a week.

Hope you had a nice weekend.

Love,
Binni

May 24, 1943
New York, N.Y.

Dear Mother & Dad,

Hope you had a nice weekend in Mystic and like it enough to go again.

This week my assignment is hostess in the lounge at the Midston House, a very nice lounge given us by Mrs. Happen who serves tea to us there every afternoon. There isn't much to do there which is the principal reason why I have a chance to write letters. My hours are all mixed up 9:00 to 2:00 today, 2:00 to 7:00 tomorrow, etc. I have to work both Saturday and Sunday and also next Monday so I'm afraid I won't be able to get home this weekend. Maybe the weekend of my birthday though, depending on what my assignment is.

I haven't seen Jane all lately but I'm having dinner with her tonight and expect I will see her more now that my hours are different.

There are now about seventy club mobile people up here and any number of others. The Red Cross is offering all sorts of apologies for the delay and everyone is getting very restless including myself. As usual we really think it won't be long now and will probably be more exciting than it would have been if we going earlier. I had a wonderful dream about leaving, in which the convoy was about ten rowboats tied together.

How is Bridget? Is she okay now? Give her my love.

Love.
Binni

June 4, 1943
New York, N.Y.

Dear Mother & Dad,

What weather we are having. Yesterday the temperature was 104° in the sun. I suppose you are having the same thing in Providence. It doesn't seem possible that a short time ago we were complaining of the cold.

Our assignment this week is wonderful, except for the commuting, forty-five minutes by hot crowded subway. The Service Club we are in is in the restricted area of Fort Hamilton, which is a staging area and therefore very exciting as solders are always coming and going. I have seen lots of souvenirs brought back from Africa. Because it is a restricted area they cannot have dances in the club but they have some entertainment every night—movies or a variety show. We help with the movies and the Public Address System and generally try to make ourselves useful. The personnel are very amusing. Two Army hostesses who dislike each other intensely run the club and that makes the atmosphere rather strange. The two soldiers assigned there were formerly a N.Y. songwriter and a singer. We are treated wonderfully because we are the first Red Cross girls to be there and everyone goes out of his way to show us things. There is a wonderful Colonel who has been especially nice. Last night for example just as we were leaving a soldier came in to say he wanted to see us so we hopped in a car and were driven to the arena where there were some boxing matches going on that he thought we would enjoy. I didn't, I think they're awful but we had to sit through them anyway. Today we are going out early to be his guest at lunch and go to a parade in the afternoon.

The other girl with me is very nice. Her brother was shot down over France and reported killed a few months ago and she is very excited at present as she saw a picture in the paper that she is practically sure is him in a group of German prisoners. The Red Cross is now checking on it. Yesterday she and I went out to Long Beach for the day and got beautiful sunburns. It was lovely there, but too cold to go swimming.

Tomorrow is my day off and I am having dinner with Jane and Pat. Next week I am going to take an Army map reading course and a course in water safety both of which should be interesting. After that I will try to get home.

I am glad you liked the bowl. I thought it was lovely. Thank you for your letters. I am glad the garden is doing so well and wish I could see it. I have no hope of ever leaving, Dad, so will probably see you on the 18th if I don't get home before that.

Love,
Binni

June 18, 1943
Bethesda, Maryland

Dear Mother & Dad,

Well, Washington again and is it hot! I am glad I don't have to spend the summer here.

We are staying way out toward Bethesda in a small guesthouse. It is very nice and particularly nice to be out of the city after being in N.Y. for such a long time. I had dinner with Franny and Herb both

Wednesday nights and Thursday night and am going to see them again Saturday for the last time. They both seem very well. Franny is going to be on the hill after Wednesday for the summer and is planning to call you when she gets there.

We have been kept quite busy down here but it is all very exciting. As there is a large group it takes much longer to get everything done. It is a very nice group, too. The powers that be are certainly not letting us in on any secrets and we are completely in the dark and very baffled by the various things that are happening so don't be surprised at anything.

I expect to be back in N.Y. shortly and will try to get in touch with Jane but do not know whether I will have time to or not.

Until you hear differently my address, effective now is:

C/O American Red Cross
National Headquarter
930 H St., NW
Washington, D.C.

Until you are notified differently, which should be fairly soon, be sure and write to the above so I will hear as soon as possible.

This letter is so stupid because there is so much I would like to write but can't. I am so glad I got home last weekend and saw you all and so sorry I didn't get to see Ann. I hope she is better now and I am going to write her soon but so far our letter writing has been limited.

Much Love to you all,
Binni

P.S. <u>Please</u> don't forget that what you know about my activities right now is <u>very</u> confidential.

June 23, 1943

Dear Mother & Dad,

I have thought of you so often during the last few days and hoped that you weren't worrying about me and that you could know of the exciting and interesting things that are happening.

At the moment I am sitting on my upper bunk in a stateroom for four where we have been told to stay to keep out of the way. There is great confusion of many people coming on board, etc., and I wish we could watch it all. This letter will be mailed after we leave.

I wish you could have seen us getting aboard so loaded with stuff we could hardly move and so excited! I can't believe the day has arrived at last. I was so sorry that I didn't see Jane but as you can see we didn't have much time and were not permitted to contact anyone. Did she get any time off to see Johnny? I got your letter mother and am so glad Ann is better.

When I was in Washington I signed my allotment and you should get $46.60 semi-monthly to put in the bank for me Dad. Eventually it will be $50 when they stop deducting the victory tax. Don't forget that the first $200 and something belongs to you in payment for the stock you got.

My writing is terrible as I am using my helmet for a desk. I am sure you will hear from me again soon. In the meantime much love to all of you.

Binni

CHAPTER 3

Queen Mary Diary

June 19, 1943–July 1, 1943

The Queen Mary set sail from Southampton on a voyage to New York on August 30, 1939. It was the ship's last peacetime voyage until the war ended. After passengers disembarked in New York, the Queen Mary sailed to Sydney, Australia where she was refit as a troop carrier; the largest and fastest troop ship in service during the war. Once refitted, The Queen Mary could carry over 15,000 crew and troops, seven times her pre-war capacity. Nicknamed the "Grey Ghost", the Queen Mary was so instrumental to the allied war effort that Hitler put a bounty on her, offering $25,000 and an Iron Cross to any U-Boat captain able to sink her.

Fitje most likely received her orders in Washington, on June 18,1943. She returned to New York on the 19th and stayed at the St. Georges Hotel in Brooklyn. Over the next four days she was fingerprinted, her official photograph was taken, and she received her final clearance. Red Cross personnel were issued winter uniforms and other equipment. They learned to roll bedrolls and put on gas masks. Once comfortable with the gas masks, they went through a series of live gas drills. Everyone was required to go through a gas chamber three times—once with masks on, again removing them before exiting and finally, putting them on after entering.

On June 23rd Fitje and fifty-three other Red Cross "girls" boarded the Queen Mary at Pier 93 on the Hudson River in Manhattan. They carried suitcases and knapsacks, pistol belts with canteens and first aid kits, helmets and heavy coats. The following day after lifeboat and air attack drills the ship sailed.

Fitje began a diary on the same day. Written as a letter to her parents, she never mailed it, as wartime censorship prohibited it. The diary is a moving account of a wartime crossing.

The ship was crowded, which limited space below decks. The men had to sleep in shifts. Fitje wrote that the noise of troops on deck and announcements that continued unabated make it difficult for her to sleep. Because of the logistics of feeding 15,000 passengers—there were six shifts to each meal—they ate twice a day, at 9:00 AM and 7:00 PM. She writes that none of the inconveniences mattered as the experience of sailing to war on a troop ship made the voyage too exciting for the discomforts to trouble her.

Fitje shared a cabin with ten other Red Cross volunteers including Kathleen Kennedy, daughter of the former ambassador, Joseph Kennedy, and Catherine Spaatz whose father, General Tooey Spaatz, directed the U. S. Strategic Air campaign in Europe. They dined at the captain's table several times, most likely because Kathleen and Catherine were part of the group.

There was risk associated with a wartime crossing, but she never wrote about her concerns. Instead, she described the people she met, the inevitable rumors of U-Boats and mines and her day-to-day activities.

Despite the danger, they arrived in Europe without mishap. The Queen Mary passed Ireland just after noon on June 29th. Later the same day the ship turned into the Firth of Clyde and dropped anchor off Grennock, Scotland. Early the following morning the Red Cross contingent disembarked first. They boarded a train for a long slow trip to London, arriving after midnight on July 1, 1943.

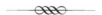

June 24, 1943

Dear Mother and Dad,

We are now sitting in our stuffy little inside stateroom for four, as we have been told to stay here until the chaplain can arrange a place to meet with us all. There are 218 women on the ship. Fifty-three of us, and two units of army nurses, as well as ten USO chorus girls, who are going over for a six-month tour of camps in England and Africa (No pay I understand—don't know if this is true.)

We have hardly seen daylight since we got on the boat last night, as all the windows are painted over and we are as yet not allowed to go on deck, as the men are sleeping on most of them. The ship just sailed, having left this morning at high tide around 11:00. The stewards and waiters tell us we are going to land in Glasgow and are going the northern route so will see icebergs. They are all so proud of the ship and no wonder.

We eat twice a day, at 9:00 and at 7:00. There are six shifts to each meal in order to get us all fed so naturally we can't expect three. A good breakfast of grapefruit, bacon, eggs, toast and coffee. After breakfast officers, RC and nurses had a meeting in the lounge. The Capt. talked to us and explained air attack drill and boat drill. Also impressed on us the importance of obeying all instructions for the safety of the ship, which he said was more important than the lives on it. At present there are around 15,000 troops aboard.

Immediately after the meeting the air raid drill was staged and after that a lifeboat drill. While these were going on the ship pulled out. We watched the Statue of Liberty come into sight and go out of sight and sang *God Bless America*. We all wonder, of course, when we will be back again.

Coming back from breakfast we went through part of the ship where the troops are. A great many colored troops are living there. I felt so sorry for them, it was so hot and stuffy and smelly. The ship must be jammed, as it never quiets down and people are crowding around all over the place.

Evening

Also what a safe feeling to watch the huge navy balloon, which will stick with us for another day.

Took a bath and washed some clothes in salt water and then ate an enormous dinner to make up for the meal we missed—soup, salmon, vegetables and plum pudding—and spent the evening in the lounge playing bridge with an assortment of officers and a Red Cross field director. The huge lounge is jammed all the time with officers and women and there are continual announcements over the PA system, mostly blackout warnings. The officers spend a good deal of time singing. As there is a variety of nationalities great variety of songs—Scotch, English, Australian (*Waltzing Matilda*) as well as American.

It is difficult to sleep because of the heat and noise, which is continual. The first night I got no sleep at all, but am hoping to do better tonight. I don't see how the men stand it—cooped up below decks—the smell of hot bodies is terrific. Everyone is excited and part of the "milling around" must be due to the nervous tension.

Watches ahead 1 hour–6/26/43 Sat.

This morning I was planning to get up early and see the sun rise but of course I never did. The weather is getting much cooler and it is quite overcast. The loud speaker is blaring forth about the men sleeping on deck bringing warmer clothes. Every day at noon the men change. The men on deck go below and those below come up. After the usual drills we went to the sun deck. Saw two Liberators fly over, both very low. Much speculation as to where they are from. Some say Halifax. We are now approximately 1000 miles from America! Spent the afternoon talking to a twenty-year old RAF boy (Scotch) returning to London after six months training in Canada. He is a navigator—before the war in civil service. Also talked to the ships navigator who told us many interesting things—he has been on the ship for four years. He says normal capacity is 3000, including crew. He says that tomorrow we will have a British plane escort us instead of American and asked us if we'd feel as safe.

The soldiers stand outside the officer's area and are very much interested in any celebrities on board. I pointed out K. Kennedy and K. Spaatz (general's daughter) to them. Some of them are so cute and we try to spend time with them.

While we were on the game deck Doris Anderson, Kathleen Kennedy and I got talking to a lieutenant in the ship's crew who asked us up to the wardroom for tea. He is the ship's navigator. We went and had a delightful time. Three army nurses also came and about seven officers. They asked we three back for cocktails. In the evening we stayed on the tennis deck until black out time, talking to several fascinating people—some officers in command of colored troops told us of all the trouble they have with them. A Liberator came and flew round and round the ship and it was a lovely clear evening after the rain. They say we will pick up more escort planes tomorrow as we are now in dangerous territory. The lounge was simply jammed later in the evening—much singing and bridge playing as usual. The men were sleeping crowded in the halls and squares as the decks are wet from the rain and it is cold out. Little sleep as usual but I guess I get a lot more than most of the men. We wake up very early hearing them going down to the first breakfast at 7:00 AM, and hearing the MPs say "Hurry men, hurry or you won't get any breakfast." Set watches an hour ahead tonight. Weather is much cooler.

Sunday 6/24/43

Catholic masses are being held for the men all over the decks. A Protestant service was held in the lounge at 9:45 and I attended it. Some of the RC girls sang in a choir and Josephine Harris sang *Ave Maria* and a duet with one of the men. I do not like the chaplain on the ship but the service was impressive, especially singing *God Save The King* and *My Country 'Tis Of Thee* at the end, which brought tears to my eyes. The weather is cold and cloudy. After the boat drill we went up on deck where we spent the rest of the day. For lunch we had tea, biscuits and chocolate, which one of the boys brought up.

Talked to very interesting RAF boys John and Sigmund. Polish, Sigmund has quite a history. He comes from Warsaw. After the German invasion in 1939 he joined the underground movement. Having been warned that he had been apprehended, he fled to Russia where he was interned and sent to Siberia. He escaped three times. The first two times he was caught and given in all a twenty-one year sentence. The third time he and six companions escaped to China. Later they discovered that there was a new agreement and he would have been freed so he gave himself up to Russian officials. He wished to go back to Poland and join whatever army they had but was a Russian citizen as that part of Poland now belonged to Russia. Consequently he had to join the Red Army air force. When his unit was evacuated from some place in the north he left, went to England and there joined the RAF. He has been training in Canada. He and the Irishman have wonderful senses of humor and we can never tell whether they are telling the truth or teasing us.

We discovered that by jumping up and running to the starboard side as if we saw something we could make practically everyone on the deck come running over too.

Met one terribly nice lieutenant who is going to take me on a tour below decks if I can get permission to go. We are restricted to our rooms, the tennis deck, the dining room, and the lounge however, as they do not want us to get mixed with the men if anything happens both for their sakes and for ours. I would love to go below and see where the men are as some of the officer's descriptions are unbelievable.

Late in the afternoon Charlie came and got Kit, Doris and myself and we went to the wardroom for cocktails again. The same group and it was fun. Late for dinner and the whole table scolded me— "Well Fitje."

In the evening Connie McKenna and I played bridge with Major Black and a captain, the Canadian surgeon on board, in their quarters (M 42). Major Black, a Nova Scotian Dad's age, is simply wonderful. The doctor comes from Vancouver and is very handsome. Played for a 40th and the Dr. and I lost fifteen cents each. The doctor is a great skier apparently and told us a lot about skiing in the west. He and the major were very proud of their curtains, which they had made themselves! Went to our rooms about 11:30 where everyone was playing twenty-one for high stakes. Set watches ahead another hour.

Monday 6/28/43

The rumors on the ship are amazing. Have heard that we have been fired on six times, the first night we were two miles from Bermuda, Guy Lombardo's orchestra is on board, we have changed our course quickly any number of times because of subs dead ahead, the negro troops are very restless and we hear there have been a number of knifings and a white officer has been killed. There actually has been one appendix operation and one Negro was hit over the head with a bottle and badly wounded.

Sigmund, the Polish boy, is wonderful. He says "judy-bugging" instead of jitterbugging. Tonight he played poker and was worried at first because he won $20 and was afraid the American boys wouldn't like him. In the end it was all right though as he lost the $20 again and $10 of his own.

It was very windy and cold on deck this morning and even rained a little. Later it cleared up but was still cold. It was still light out at 11:00 when we had to go to our quarters. Tomorrow we may be able to see the coast of Ireland and we will be in the Firth of Clyde around 10:00. One of the ships officers said we would have to be below until land is sighted on both sides so we won't all run to one side and make the ship list.

Spent afternoon on tennis deck until 4:00 when Kit, Doris and I went to tea with the ship's officers. They were terribly funny, especially Benjy. None knew what a girdle was and Hugh thought it was "What you make mountains out of mole hills with". (Bra) Spent evening on deck with Harold Cross, a terribly nice lieutenant, from Phila, in the tank corps and with the Irishman John Buckley, who wants to live in Boston after the war! In the lounge tonight there was a movie, *Next of Kin,* and a Negro orchestra recruited from one of the Negro troops. Afraid the boys on deck will be cold tonight. Set clocks another hour ahead.

Tues. 6/29/43

Spent absolutely the whole day on deck. A beautiful clear sunny day, the ocean is quiet and calm. First sighted Ireland about 1:00, about ten miles away. I had almost thought it would be emerald green but it wasn't. All the Irishmen, especially Father Mullen, a Catholic chaplain from Cork, almost jumped overboard and swam ashore. We had a couple of alarms when unidentified planes approached but they were soon identified. Spent the morning talking to three Lieutenants in a tank destroyer corps, the only combat troops aboard. We compared rumors and originated a few new ones. (i.e. one of the men, a gunner, saw a mine, port bow last night; a steward named Hans was caught boring holes in the lifeboats, etc.)

Later in the afternoon we sighted Scotland and then turned into the Firth of Clyde with Ailsa Craig off the starboard side. About then we sighted a convoy moving in the same direction, which we passed very quickly.

Kathleen, Doris and I went to the wardroom for tea as usual, escorted by Charlie. I hate to think I may never see those men again.

Hugh Milley	Officers Ward Room
Benjamin Hector Davis	SS Queen Mary
Charles Townsend	GPO London
Duncan Drummond	British Security Office
Noel Robinson	25 Broadway, NYC

We made a wonderful plan to get things from the U.S. Our families can send them to NY and they can bring them over.

Rushed through dinner to get back on deck. It was lovely in the soft evening light. Beautiful rolling hills and little farms on either side. By 8:30 we were just off Grennock and had dropped anchor. I couldn't believe I was in Scotland. Blackout was not until 11:30 so we stayed on deck until then. The troops were so excited and cheered and clapped when a launch with an American flag came alongside. Most of them were comparing everything with the U. S. and deciding the U. S. much better. Even Brooklyn.

Didn't get to bed until nearly 2:00 and up again at 3:30 for breakfast at 4:00.

Wed. 6/30/43

Great confusion in the morning as we were the first to leave the ship. After breakfast went up on deck. It was quite cold and cloudy but lovely and almost light altho' blackout lasted until 6:30. At 6:15 we lined up in full equipment (helmet, two coats, gas mask, pistol belt, canteen, first aid kit, rucksack.) I was one of the lucky ones as one of the boys carried my suitcase. We waited on the deck of the lounge for quite a while with much yelling to the men were leaning our every porthole. There were some troops, a few nurses and the USO chorus girls on the launch. It took about a half hour to get to Grennock where we disembarked and got almost immediately on the train, where the Red Cross had two cars. The trip was a long one, as we didn't get to London until 12:30 that night. We changed once at Rugby where we had an hour and a half wait. Scotland was so lovely with rolling hills and little villages. All the people waved madly as we passed and made the victory sign with their fingers. We were all so tired as some of us had had no sleep in forty-eight hours that we laughed hysterically most of the way. We had been issued field rations on the ship and we ate some of them although in a couple of towns we got off and had coffee and sandwiches at canteens.

London was, of course, pitch black and we were loaded in trucks and some of us went to 12 Dover

St. and some to another RC club. Had tea and sandwiches there and fell into bed. Slept soundly until 12:15 the next morning. A nice room #43, single, right next to C. Luthrell, and K. Kennedy.

The ship certainly was wonderful and I hated to leave it. We saw Benjy and Duncan on the bridge and waved madly as we left.

7/1/43

London! I can't believe it. There seems to be more Americans here than Englishmen and you can't walk two steps without one stopping you.

CHAPTER 4

I Must Be Dreaming

July 4, 1943–July 7, 1943

Fitje arrived in London on July 1, 1943 and soon after wrote, ". . . it can't possibly be true that I am sitting 'somewhere in England. . .'"

Although the Blitz ended two years earlier, London continued to be a target for the Luftwaffe. Bomb damage was extensive and London was still under a blackout. She wrote two letters from London expressing how excited she was to be there.

She could not tell her parents where in England she was, but she probably spent the ten days before moving to East Anglia, in London. Much like any other tourist, she explored the city, taking in the sights and learning the subtilties of British English.

She wrote that she visited the Tower of London and St Paul's Cathedral, and went to Buckingham Palace where she watched the changing of the guard, and saw the Queen. She had tea at Claridge's and dinner at the Savoy, where she ate a "delicious dinner of omelet, chicken, beets, potato, and some dessert made mostly of ice cream."

Soon after they got to London, Kathleen Kennedy invited Fitje to attend a session of Parliament, as the guest of Lady Astor. She declined, saying she had an appointment. Years later she still regretted missing the opportunity. But the appointment was an important one. She received her orders, assigning her to the 95th Bomb Group in Horham, as the assistant director of the Red Cross aero club.

July 4, 1943

Dear Mother and Dad,

I feel I must be dreaming and that it can't possibly be true that I am sitting "somewhere in England" writing you. It is most peculiar to think of you all on the other side of the ocean instead of just a couple of hundred miles north of me.

It just kills me that censorship will not allow me to tell you the details of our arrival, as I wished so often that you could know what was going on. But I can say that I enjoyed it so much that when I left the ship I thought I could never be happy on land again. The last couple of days, however, have proven that wrong and I have come to the conclusion that I am satisfied anywhere with the American Red Cross. I did do my best to become a permanent part of the ship's staff but my services were not needed.

Regardless of what weather we were having we spent every available moment on deck and of course I have a lovely sunburn, even to the part in my hair. There were <u>no</u> dull moments with so much to look at and so many interesting people to talk to. Our quarters were crowded but comfortable and the meals were fine, although we only ate twice a day, at 9:00 and at 7:00.

Our group is really wonderful on the whole and thank God they all looked excited and happy when we left. I wish you could have seen us get aboard. I am going to send you a picture of myself in full equipment. I must weigh 200 pounds at least and my shoulders still ache from carrying it. A suitcase, knapsack, gas mask, two coats, helmet, pistol belt, canteen, and first aid kit is no light load. Everything is beautifully managed though and we are herded on and off trains and boats without us having to worry about a thing but what we carry. I have no idea where my other luggage is but I suppose I will see it eventually. It is wonderful to be relieved of all responsibility.

After disembarking we traveled a long way by train and reached our destination very late at night and so weary that I can't remember getting into bed. I didn't wake until 12:15 the next morning and then thought for at least five minutes that I was still in my upper berth on the ship. I could even feel it rocking. Those of us that couldn't bear to miss a moment of what was going on, including myself, of course, had not been in bed for forty-six hours when we finally got there. The train trip was wonderful as we saw so much of the country. I am very glad that you have seen it and I don't have to describe it, as I never could do it justice. We laughed hysterically most of the way and you wouldn't believe that all those girls, including myself, could eat Army ration consisting of cold stew out of a can without complaining and even with enjoyment.

Catherine Spaatz (General Spaatz daughter) and Kathleen Kennedy (Ambassador Kennedy's daughter) are both in the group, and we now have three nice rooms in a row. It is wonderful to have Kathleen around as she has lived in England before.

Of course, we went sightseeing the first thing and I can't get over how familiar everything is to me although I have never been here before. We were in London where we saw Buckingham Palace, St. James, Queen Mary's House, Hyde Park, and St. Paul's, etc. We went to Claridge's for tea and later to the Savoy for a delicious dinner of omelet, chicken, beets, potato, and some desert made mostly of ice cream. Even the coffee is good. Naturally there is not much variety but I guess, like at home, the restaurants get along much better than the housewife. There are really quite nice looking clothes in the shop windows, all rationed though and they are terribly expensive. We went to Liberty's but not having any ration tickets we could do nothing but look. I am beginning to understand the money and I am getting expert at getting around on buses.

It is amazing to be actually in a war zone and see the things that have happened which you could never quite believe without seeing them. I wish I could describe it all to you in great detail.

The English people are wonderful to us, particularly the Bobbys, whom we pestered with a thousand questions while we were sightseeing in London. It seems funny to be in such a small country. Even the newspapers are small, and no funny papers. Will you send me "Terry and the Pirates" from the Sunday papers? Everything is so much more orderly and we seem to be standing in line for something all the time.

Tell Anne that I will write her brothers as soon as I am permanently settled. We do not get our assignments until Monday, but I doubt if I will be in a Clubmobile, as we seem to be more badly needed in other spots. I have requested an aero club at a field and hope I will be, although I don't really care too much.

I know you have heard this before this but I have arrived safely, and am sure you were pleased to hear where I am, Mother. I don't suppose there was any party on the hill this year. This doesn't seem a bit like the 4th of July.

Much love to all of you,
Binni

July 7, 1943

Dear Mother & Dad,

Much excitement around here at this point as we are all getting our assignments. As yet I don't have mine but I have definitely been changed to an aero club, which pleases me no end. We will probably know very soon and by this weekend should actually be at work after all these weeks of waiting.

We have spent most of our time going to London to sight see and spending nights there so we could go out in the evening. People that we knew coming over turn up all the time. Last night I had dinner with an American Army Captain at one of the officer's clubs. When we started home we couldn't get a taxi, as it was well after blackout time so we finally got a ride with the newspaperman. He was so much fun to talk to that we ended by staying with him until he had delivered his whole load, as well as several other people that he picked up along the way. The English people are so nice to us. If you stand on a corner for one second looking bewildered someone will come up to you and ask if they can help you. Their directions are amazing though and I can't them at all. They always say, "It's perfectly simple. Go to the bottom of the road and take the first turn on the left." I have not yet found out what the "bottom of the road" is.

Yesterday was very exciting as we saw the Queen. We went to Buckingham Palace to watch the guard change and right in the middle of it the Queen drove out. I saw her very plainly. The guards no longer wear full dress but it is colorful anyway. After that we went to St. James Park and fed the ducks. I have never seen so many parks and the people seem to use them so much more than we use ours.

On my way home I bought a peach for five shillings sixpence, the cheapest I could find and just an ordinary peach. I couldn't resist it though and it tasted wonderful!

Monday we also went to London and saw London Bridge and the Tower of London and took a bus around the Houses of Parliament, Big Ben, and Westminster Abby. Near the Tower of London we met a wonderful "Bobby" who took us on a tour and showed us part of the old Roman wall, hidden way down a little alley, and the graves of the last two men hung in the city of London. In the alley where we saw the Roman wall, we met a street cleaner sitting on a fence watching a bright green parakeet sitting on a wall. He said he had watched it all day. We tried to catch it but it flew up in a tree. Neither the Bobby, nor the street cleaner seemed to think it was particularly strange that a parakeet should be flying around in the middle of London. We went also to the British Museum and saw lots of the plans for the reconstruction of London after the war. Some are really lovely. I was amazed to find that the pictures and stories in our papers of what London looks like now are not exaggerated in any way and I'm sure you would hate to see it now.

The latest package regulations are as follows. You can send me a package not over five pounds, or fifteen inches in length or thirty-six inches in length and girth combined. In order to mail it you have to show the postmaster a written request from me stating that I want the things. You can't send a package oftener that once a week.

This is absolutely all I will need but I will need these, as we were misled about civilian clothes and there are occasions where we have to wear them. Also it is cold and I need some of my sweaters.

1. Green wool dress
2. Heavy tweed, pleated skirt—the one I had made last year
3. Green sweater with initial
4. Orange sweater
5. Brown alligator shoes

Maybe if you sent a package now and another in a few weeks they would get to me before winder sets in.

Jane must have left her job by now. I am planning to look up Brian's wife as soon as I am settled somewhere. Has Lucy heard from him?

Love to all,
Binni

CHAPTER 5

I Couldn't Be Nearer the War

July 11, 1943–November 11, 1943

The Red Cross assigned Fitje to the 95th Bomb Group in Horham, sixty kilometers northeast of London, as the assistant director of the base Aero Club, which did not yet exist. She along with the manager, Jean Plageman and Red Cross district director Mac McGrath arrived at the base on July 10, 1943.

For Fitje, being on a bomber base with the crews that were "taking the war to the Germans," was intoxicating; it was a feeling that stayed with her until the end of the war. She wrote: "I am sure I couldn't be nearer the war than I am right now. This morning very early we were awakened by the planes taking off, and we watched them fly around the field and off in formation. It was a sight I'll never forget no matter how often I see it."

The 95th Bomb Group flew B-17s heavy bombers. It flew to England in the spring of 1943, as part of the Eighth Air Force and flew its first combat mission on May 13, 1943, bombing the airfield at St. Omer France.

Losses were staggering. In twenty-four months of combat the 95th flew 321 combat missions, lost 156 B-17s and suffered 1,774 casualties including 571 killed in action. In the four and one-half months Fitje was attached to the 95th, the group lost thirty planes, each carrying a crew of ten. Some crewmen were rescued while others were taken prisoner. Approximately one hundred fifty men were killed in action. The losses must have weighed on Fitje. While she never talked about them, she knew many of the men who never came back.

The first order of business for Fitje and Jean was to create the Red Cross Aero Club. They had to build and run a business, which meant hiring a staff, firing the ones who didn't work out, and managing payrolls. The job required them to procure what they needed to run a successful club even if it meant using guile to find furniture and other materials not supplied by the Red Cross or Army. It was difficult. She wrote, "Jean and I get terribly discouraged sometimes trying to make things run right and almost hope a bomb will drop on the place. Then at the very worst moment one of the men will come in and tell us how much the club means to them and honestly it makes any effort worth it because I really believe they mean it."

Fitje's letters provide a remarkable accounting of day-to-day life on a bomber base. This is what makes them so important. She writes about her job and what she and Jean do to decorate their quarters and the club. She writes about the staff and the men on the base. Her ability to capture details is remarkable. Other letters reflect her own tentativeness as she matures into her new role. In much the same way the aircrews learned the art of war through experience, Fitje and Jean learned by doing.

Today it's difficult to imagine a twenty-six year old woman, who had led a relatively sheltered life, thrust into a world dominated by men and asked to tackle difficult tasks with no experience and little training. This was unexplored territory, not only for Fitje, but also for many thousands of women who worked at jobs traditionally held by men before the war. It was as if they had stepped through a time warp and been given a brief look at a future that included women in leadership roles, which, once the war ended, would not become a reality for decades.

Fitje and Jean Plageman
serving coffee and donuts at Horham

⁂

July 11, 1943

Dear Mother & Dad,

Well, I can't believe it, that we are actually assigned and I suppose settled at last. And this is more perfect than I ever dared hope for.

One other girl, Jean Plageman, and myself were sent to a bomber base "somewhere in England," the location of which is so secret that I hardly know where I am myself. We arrived yesterday with all our baggage! I wish you could see our quarters—two beds and six chairs, a Franklin stove (named the Rose) and nothing else, not even a closet—really rugged after hotel life. So far the weather has been pretty typical, I guess, and we keep the stove lit all the time. It is the only heat we have and I shudder to think of the winter months. I am glad I brought I brought the "woolies." We eat in the officer's mess and the meals are excellent, elephant breast for dinner tonight (so we are told) not broiled or fricasseed (the common ways) but smoked! The English air makes me hungry all the time, and I am rapidly getting a ruddy English complexion and gaining weight.

To make the set up even more perfect we were sent here to start the club ourselves. The building is right next to us and is very nice. It consists of a huge kitchen and snack bar, a library, reading room, poolroom and Ping-Pong room. So far not much has been done and the walls are in the process of being painted. Today we spent unpacking kitchen utensils and cleaning a stove as big as a house with lots of help from the men. Monday we begin hiring a staff of twenty, from where we can't imagine, as we are not near any big center. Jean, who is about thirty-five, is the Director and I'm her assistant. There is also a nifty RC field director here who, so far, has done everything to get it organized. We hope to get it opened in a week if we are able to get kitchen help. I wish Bridget were here right now. I'm sure she would love making coffee in an urn big enough to sit in.

Johnny would go mad here, I know, with so many planes around. After dinner tonight we walked to the field to see at close range, some of the planes and they were fascinating. We have been promised a ride in one tomorrow but we are not quite sure whether we were being teased or whether we are seriously going to get it. Jean is getting cold feet about it and is afraid she'll find herself off on a raid.

I am sure I couldn't be nearer the war than I am right now. This morning very early the planes taking off woke us, and we watched them fly around the field and off in formation.* It was a sight I'll never forget no matter how often I see it. Tonight we ate dinner with some of the men who had been and heard all about it from them. Just think, these boys are doing what you are reading about in the papers and I am right here watching them go and hearing about it when they come back. I can't believe it!

I was so glad to get your letter, mother, written on the 20th and 21st. I didn't expect to hear from you so soon. Although they came by way of Washington they reached me on the 8th, which isn't bad at all. My new address is:

C/O ARC
Hdqts 95th Bomb Group
APO 634
C/O Postmaster, NYC

Send me Ann's brothers' addresses, as I am sure they have changed since I got them from her in February.

Tell Jones that I am on the lookout for a puppy to have one by next week. Everyone else here has a dog, practically.

Much love to all,
Binni

P.S. What is Jane doing? I forgot to say that one-day while I was in London I found the sort of ring I wanted in an old silver shop just off Berkeley Square. It is an old little finger ring, with three diamonds and two amethysts so I bought it for twelve pounds. It is awfully pretty. Also that day we went to Richmond and had tea on the Thames and then to Kew Gardens, which were lovely. The country is beautiful out here.

---

* The target was Le Bourget, France. Twenty-seven planes took off, twenty-five completed their missions, two were damaged and one was lost.

July 18, 1943

Dear Family,

I got letters from Mother, Hermie and Jane yesterday, which were most welcome. It doesn't seem to take the mail at all long to come. You can't imagine how often I think of you all & wish you could know more of what goes on here. It's all so interesting.

I wish you could see our quarters now. They are all fixed up beautifully. Some of the men painted our walls a beautiful light green and the quartermaster gave us some white bedspreads, a bureau, a table and a cabinet to hang our cloths in, and a coal shuttle. We made a bookcase out of a box, which we painted bright yellow and it really looks wonderful. We have absolutely no privacy as our dear boys poke their heads in the windows every time they go by.

I am going to be completely spoiled when I get home; we are treated so well around here. A couple of days ago we expressed a wish for a cat and just about an hour later we had one, a cute little black kitten hardly old enough to leave its mother. We named him Lieutenant Clark after the person who got it for us. It's terribly active and spends all its time jumping from Jean's bed to the desk and then to my bed. We're getting so afraid to say we want anything unless we're absolutely sure we do, because we're bound to get it.

This week we have really worked hard trying to get the club fixed up. We spend all our time in slacks and if you thought I was dirty when I broke my leg, you should see me now. I don't think I'll ever be clean again. Lately I have been painting chairs, unpacking dishes, brushing curtains, putting books on shelves, etc. We hope to open next week after we get our food permit and about fifteen more people as we have only hired five so far. They all live around here and arrive on bicycles to work and bring us eggs and flowers.

One day this week we drove to another aero club with an English officer to see what an operating one was like. It was a lovely day and we drove about forty miles in our little Red Cross car through wonderful farm country. I have never seen such lovely flowers. Coming back we stopped at a pub for a drink and then went to a wonderful old inn called the White Horse for dinner. Then we stopped to see some friends of the English officer who live on a farm just across a couple of fields from where we live. They were delighted to hear that theirs was the first English home that we had been in and gave us Irish

Unidentified G.I.
with Fitje's kitten, Lt. Clark

whiskey and a huge bunch of roses. Later on when we begin to crave eggs we are going to trade stockings and lipstick for their eggs. They have 500 acres of beautiful fields of wheat and barley and lots of cows and horses. Dad is looking in the wrong country for his ideal farm!

Another night we went to a tiny nearby village with a New Zealand officer on the post to see some friends of his about hiring people. The family was quite a poor English family with a house full of refugee children from London. The man of the house, and the rest of us, went to a little tavern and drank beer and played darts and ball billiards. All the local characters came in and it was wonderful.

Last night the officers gave a dance for which we arranged the flowers and to which we went and had a wonderful time being the only American girls there. It was nice to be clean and have civilian clothes on again. Some of the boys on the base have made up an orchestra, which is really quite good. As a result of the dance most people are a little tired today. Today being Sunday we declared our first day of rest. This afternoon we went to a baseball game right near our house between two groups on the field, and after that I went in a jeep to the field to watch the planes with some of the men.

I don't think my letters are very interesting. It seems to me that everything I think of to say is something I can't tell you. I wish I could describe some of the characters work in our building to you. We have a detail of men who spend most of their time standing around saying "Gee I like to see a woman work." Every afternoon at 4:00 we boil water on the stove in our office and drink tea sitting on the floor, as we have no chairs there as yet. The men drink it out of their mess kits. Now that we have maids they follow us around with tea all day long. The boys are terribly funny and we seem to laugh most of the time.

Now the kitten is sitting on my shoulder and purring in my ear. We were late to dinner tonight and all the other food was gone so we had two fried eggs. We'll probably be late from now on. I have taken some pictures of the club, the kitten and the quarters, which I will send you as soon as they are censored and developed. Tell Jane I have the picture of the monkeys she painted for me hanging over my bed.

Much love,
Binni

July 25, 1943

Dear Mother & Dad,

You have no idea how difficult it is to be alone long enough to write a letter around here. At this very moment there are two lieutenants, the food consultant, and Jean in our little room, supposedly having a conference, but the food consultant is filing one lieutenant's fingernails and the other lieutenant is talking to Jean about where to buy whiskey in London. And so it goes. Since I am sitting in a chair, which is unusual, I will seize the opportunity to write you.

At last the club is open and now we can look back and think the last week has been funny but I never thought we'd live through it. We were getting along all right until a chef was sent from London to help open the kitchen and we began to learn about the complications of the English rationing system. If you think it hard at home you should try it here for several hundred people. The trouble is we are supposed to have a manageress to manage that but we haven't gotten one yet so we have to do it all ourselves.

Not only that but when the chef came he brought with him his wife and three daughters aged seventeen, eighteen, and five thinking they could live here, which of course they couldn't. The only thing we could find to do with them was to deliver them to the police station in a nearby town where they spent the night. We couldn't keep them away thought and they spend their days here driving us all crazy. Finally one night with much clever contriving we managed to get the baby, and 1 of the daughters and the wife into town with no way to get back, all of which resulted in a horrible scene on the village square with all the towns people looking on and Mrs. Butler screaming that we were breaking up a happy home and she was going back to camp if she had to walk, so, of course, we had to take her back again. It was all exactly like one of the worst nightmares. We were all powerless in the hands of this damn family and I don't know what would have happened if the food consultant, a terribly nice girl from Cairo, Michael Philippe, had not come unexpectedly and seeing what a mess things were in is staying for a few days until we get things going. She got rid of the chef's family and the chef, who was only temporary anyway, is leaving Tuesday thank God!

The opening night was wonderful. Lots of people came, and the food, by the grace of god, was good. We are still short of staff though and Jean, Mr. McElrath, the field director, and myself and a couple of officers (who are only allowed in the kitchen) spent most of the evening washing dishes. The food bar is opened from 6:30 to 10:30. Last night was even worse as there was a Red Cross show, which we went to and nobody washed dishes because all the girls like to serve. So, Jean, Mr. McElrath and I washed dishes this morning from 9:00 to 11:30 and to think that I complained at home when I helped wash dishes for seven. Aside from everything else we have no one to light the fires and we have been getting up at 6:00 and lighting the ovens and the hot water heater.

Luckily Jean is very calm about everything, but you know me, I thought I was losing my mind. We seem to be lacking the most important things such as an accountant and you can imagine how little we understand English money. But god it's fun and you should see the men pack in. I know they are going to like it or I hope so anyway. We now have a piano and a wonderful big Victrola-radio combination. Packages arrive all the time and it's just like Christmas.

We have a little Red Cross car to drive around in and you should see the cute village we shop in. Mr. Palter, the baker, Mr. Hitchcock, the grocer, etc. For the opening Jean and I found a ruined house and picked huge bunches of daisies, poppies, roses and other flowers all from that one place. Honestly Dad, I have picked out lots of farms for you around here. Why don't you come over?

There are two boys from home here. One is Steve Stone, Dr. Stone's nephew who went to Brown and knows Hermie. He is one of the officers who helped us wash dishes. The other is Amelia Lister's brother who works in the officer's mess hall.

The meeting has somehow turned into a cocktail party and naturally I can't be left out. Tomorrow I have to go to London in an army truck to pick up some overstuffed furniture. We are the only lucky people with a private bathtub and hot water and people bribe us to use it. It is never vacant. I have taken some pictures and will send them when I get them censored. I am getting your letters once in a while now and hope you are getting mine. Tell Jane and Hermie I will answer their letters eventually but your letters are the only ones I've written since I arrived. I have really never been so busy or had so much energy. It really is wonderful. You should hear the names I'm called around here. "Fudge" and "Fife" seem to prevail. Maybe I made a mistake to insist on being called Fitje. I have a jeep named after me by the way!

We have added a lamp and an electric heater to our furnishings. Our cat is so wonderful. I never knew they were so clever. We are hoping to add a dog soon but I am glad we don't have it yet. You should see all the puppies around here.

Well, much love to you all. Hope to hear from you soon.

Binni

July 30, 1943

Dear Mother & Dad,

I can see you, Mother, trying to decipher this tiny printing[*] when it gets to you, but maybe it will be there a little quicker. I hope you are getting mail from me. Some of yours only takes ten days to get here. It seems to be ten days behind the Providence news, if there is any but I assume, as usual, there isn't much. Everything is fine here as far as we are concerned. The weather has been lovely lately and all the English people think it's hot.

Last night we had our first dance and Jean and I were scared to death because we got about 115 girls and then were sure none of the boys would show up. In the end too many came and the place was packed. I hope everyone had a good time, I certainly did. I have never been so popular in my life. The girls were Land Army Girls, Wrens,[†] and civilian nurses who arrived from around the countryside in Army trucks. You should see the wonderful food we have in the snack bar: tarts, cakes, cookies, donuts, sandwiches, hamburgers, Coca Cola, tea, and really good coffee. You know coffee isn't rationed over here. In spite of our terrible labor shortage we have plenty of volunteers, in fact we have trouble keeping the men out of the kitchen and there are now five of them washing dishes, and a lieutenant sitting in my bedroom fixing our invoices for us.

What a job to keep the stock straight. We have to account for every single thing used and we been checking it all day today, using our own method to make things come out right as we got a little mixed up last week. We haven't found a laundry and our sheets haven't been changed in three weeks. Lord,

---

[*] Fitje's letter was sent as V-Mail, or Victory mail. V-mail was used by the military during World War II. Letters were microfilmed in order to save valuable cargo space when they were sent home. The microfilmed copies were "blown up" at their destination before being delivered.

[†] WRENS refers to the Women's Royal Naval Service. The Land Army Girls was a British civilian organization created during the First and Second World Wars so women could work in agriculture, replacing men who had been called into the military.

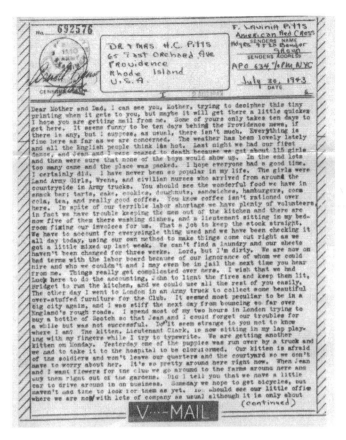

Fitje's letter was sent by V-Mail

but I'm dirty. We are now on bad terms with the labor board because of our ignorance of whom we could hire and whom we couldn't and I may even be in jail the next time you hear from me. Things get really complicated over here. I wish we had Lucky here to do the accounting, John to light the fires and keep them lit, Bridget to run the kitchen, and we could use all the rest of you easily.

The other day I went to London in an Army truck to collect some beautiful over-stuffed furniture for the club. It seemed most peculiar to be in a big city again, and I was stiff the next day from bouncing so far on England's rough roads. I spent most of my two hours in London trying to buy a bottle of scotch so Jean and I could forget our troubles for a while but was not successful. Does it strange to you not to know where I am?

The kitten, Lieutenant Clark, is now sitting in my lap playing with my fingers while I try to type. We are getting another kitten on Monday. Yesterday one of the puppies was run over by a truck and we had to take it to the hospital to be chloroformed. Our kitten is afraid of the soldiers and won't leave our quarters and the courtyard so we don't have to worry about her. It's pretty around here right now. When Jean and I want flowers for the club we go around to the farms around here and buy them right out of the gardens. Did I tell you we have a little car to drive around in on business? Someday we hope to get bicycles, but haven't had time to look for them yet. You should see our little office where we are now with lots of company as usual although it is only about eight feet by eight feet. One of the men

45

Pony and cart. Major Ed Russell is second from left.

form the hospital has just brought up a first aid kit, as our building is a first aid post, and is now telling us funny stories about the bicycle accident casualties. There are amazing things on this base. One of the gunners has a little black pony and a pony cart that he drives around everywhere in. I'm dying for a ride in it.

How is Ibby? Has the baby come yet? Have you heard anything about Trel and Tommy? I am sure there are lots of things I can tell you that I haven't so ask me all the questions you want and I will answer those that I can. It is really had to write letters as there is nothing I can talk about but the club and the cat and I don't know what I'll ever write about when the club gets running right, if it ever does. Did you ever think that I would ever like anything for five months though? I never did, and I still shudder to think that I might never have done this. It just amazes me that it never gets boring, and I seem to be able to go to bed at three and get up at 7:30 every day and never be tired. I am much fonder of Americans now that I see them in a different setting. There is a wonderful thing around here that we proudly refer to as "American ingenuity," as we have decided that Americans can do anything. The strangest thing we want done we just ask one of the boys and they think of a way in two minutes and do it in three. Isn't it wonderful? No other people are so clever.

Quite a bit of time has elapsed since I started this letter. I tried to finish it and listen to symphonies this morning from 8:30 to 9:30 before the club opened but just as I was listening to the 3rd record of Beethoven's Piano Concerto the electricity was turned off so I gave up. This morning we have been trying to get the larder straightened out; sorting the keys and marking them; locking the silver up so no more would disappear; trying to arrange to buy 566 lbs. of tomatoes, which of course is impossible; and trying to fix a schedule for our staff who to date have mostly been working from 8:30 in the morning until 11:00 at night, with no days off. The English certainly don't mind working. The kitten has learned to climb up on the windowsill where she sits all day staring at us.

Mother, you would be fascinated if you could see the food we get around here and were we get it from. Some of our cakes come all the way from London by train a couple of times a week, as we can't possibly cook enough here to meet the demand. The forms we have to fill out are much more complicated than anything Washington ever issued I'm sure, and all the boxes and containers that everything comes in have to be returned periodically, which is a tremendous job in itself. Our staff, which is mostly recruited from the vicinity; are all related practically. We have a mother and two daughters, and a mother and son. I seem to have come to the end again.

Much love,
Binni

August 3, 1943

Dear Mother & Dad,

Enclosed is a picture of me taken at our dance, which I thought you might like to have. I have taken a lot myself of the club and the staff, which I will send you as soon as they are developed.

At last things are fairly well under control. Although we still don't have enough staff we now have a manageress who is learning how to run the kitchen and fill out a lot of forms so we don't have to do that anymore. Today some woman came from London to put up some curtains, which are nifty and to rearrange all the furniture, which we quickly rearranged back again after she had gone. I am getting so used to the club the way it is that I can't stand any changes and neither can Jean. We feel that it is our creation, with a lot of assistance from a lot of people. I wish you could see the place right now. The snack bar is opened and crowded. All our help like to work at the bar and fight as to who has to do the dishes. Tonight we had hamburgers and one of the cooks stayed late to cook them, but the men said they were not American so now three of the men are cooking them and the cook has gone home. Aside from that all the cooking is done in the daytime, and the cooks are kept very busy frying eggs for the men who get them god knows where around the countryside. Beatrice the girl who serves the coffee is a scream, she is out there saying "at ease, at ease" to all the men who are in a hurry, and when she isn't saying that she is singing some peculiar song I've never heard before. The staff really are wonderful and have worked so

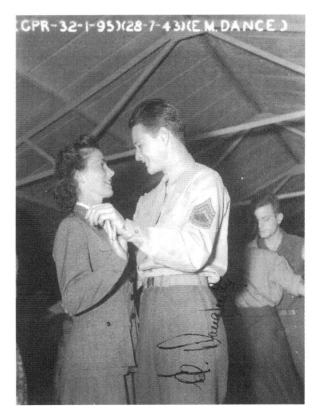

Fitje dancing with Sergeant Daugherty
at Horham, July 1943

hard. One of the cooks brings her young daughter to work as a volunteer every day until we get enough staff. I think Jean and I would have lost our minds if they hadn't kept telling us that everything was going to be all right. The woman who came from London today told us that we had the cleanest club and best spirit among the staff of any club she had been in so far.

We now have another kitten named Janie, which we got last Sunday. We thought Lt. Clark would be so glad to have company but not at all. He spent the first two days growling at her, and ignoring us and is only just beginning to be friendly again. She is terribly cute. They are both jet black and it is hard to tell them apart. The cat at operations, named Incendiary, was about to have kittens a few days ago and everyone had bets on what, how many, etc. The other night around dinner time an announcement came over the loud speaker that is attached to all the buildings on the base, and over which nothing but important things like air raids, locating people, etc. ever come saying "Attention all personal, Incendiary has just scored three hits; you will be advised of further development", which were at intervals. I think the final count was seven.

Sunday we went and had tea with the family of Mr. McElrath's secretary who now lives on the base but goes home on the weekends. It seemed most peculiar to be in a house again and very peaceful after this madhouse, but I like this much better. Her father is a Major in the RAF. They live in a cute little house with a high hedge around it and holly in the front yard as well as lots of lavender and a nifty victory garden. It was at her house that we got Janie.

Saturday night we went to another Officer's dance, which was nifty except that Jean and I couldn't go until about twelve after our club was closed, and the party was far advanced by that time. Of course we made up for it by not going to bed until six and having to get up bright and early at 9:30. Next Saturday we are going to another dance with a couple of officers from another base.

The cash has come and I must count it. It takes me hours to count this damn English money and I always get it all wrong.

Much love,
Binni

August 4, 1943

Dear Mother & Dad

Jean and I have decided the hell with the club this morning and are still in bed having just had our tea brought to us and held a conference with our manageress from our beds. The cats are stalking each other all around the room and I don't think Lt. Clark is being entirely playful when he jumps on Janie and almost pulls her ear off.

I was wondering if you could send me a couple of stockings now and then in a manila envelope. Mrs. Eberle sends them to Mildred and they can go as letters instead of packages. It would be wonderful to have extra ones to give away as people around here just don't any to wear. Send Belle Sharmeer, short length, if you send any.

You should see the intricate methods of salvage around here. All the boxes our stuff comes in have to be returned. Even envelopes are used twice. The rubbish and garbage has to be all sorted so we have about eight different containers for it. It is practically impossible to get wood to build anything and what we have we stolen from someone else. We are not at all above stealing what we can't get any other way, but just wait until after dark and paint it quickly before anyone notices. Everyone does it only they call it "borrowing."

Thanks for your letter from Maine, Dad. It sounded wonderful as usual. Early mornings around here make me think of Maine. It is usually quite cold and doesn't warm up until the middle of the day. I love having the evenings so light. Blackout isn't until about 10:45 these days.

Love,

Binni

⌒♫⌒

August 8, 1943

Dear Jane,

Honestly I'm sorry I haven't written you before this but I figure the family is keeping you informed and I really am busy. Thanks for your letters though. Have you heard from Tim at all? I haven't written him either and am afraid that he is pretty mad by this time. I think that you should definitely join the Red Cross after John goes. Once you get somewhere it really is nifty and you know how much I like it even when I was hanging around New York waiting.

This is the most wonderful and exciting spot although I seem to be in the minority for thinking so for it is quite a way from anything and there isn't much to do around here for the men except of course to go to our divine Red Cross club. We are having a wonderful time fixing it up and it really looks pretty nice. I wish you here to paint some murals on the wall. We have a wonderful Victrola and a huge stack of symphonies, but no time to listen to them. The picture of the monkeys that you did is hanging right over my bed, and looks wonderful against our light green walls, especially painted for us.

You are right, it is hard to work with so much going on, but you would be surprised how quickly you get used to almost anything and I can't imagine how I lived in dull old Providence for so long. Naturally there is a lot of social life connected with all this. We have had a few cocktail parties in our quarters, and we have been to a couple of dances at the Officer's Club and Saturday we are going to another base to a dance with a couple of officers who came over today to look over our club. You know, American girls and all that. We'd have a good time if we were sixty and cross-eyed.

You should see our two black kittens. We have had Lieutenant Clark for a couple of months and last Sunday we got another one named Janie. Lt. Clark was simply furious for a while and would do nothing but growl at her, but they seem to be better friends now. I'm dying to get a dog now that things are under control and I would have more time to take care of it.

You should see our kitchen staff. They are practically all related as they all come from the small town in the vicinity. We have Mrs. Shepard as a cook and her two daughters, Winifred and Joan as coffee makers, both very pretty and we can't keep the men out of the kitchen. When we need the men to help with the dishes we just send one of them out to entice them into the kitchen, and we get four or five in two seconds. Beatrice the coffee server is a scream and is now standing out there saying "at ease, at ease" to all the men who are in a hurry. Jean and I can't understand a thing they say and spend our time saying what. They are wonderful and have worked overtime so much that I should think they would all be dead.

The country around here is really lovely, and lately we have had wonderful weather. You should see Jean and myself driving out in the country with some of the soldiers to pick flowers, in our little car. Right now I feel like mother when she tries to write a letter. There are two boys in the office right now, one from Arkansas and one from Iowa. One is telling me about loading bombs and the other is telling me about someone stealing a pail from him and I am getting completely confused.

Much love,
Binni

August 10, 1943

Dear Mother & Dad,

Our efforts to sleep late in the morning prove very futile—so far we have seen three people without getting up—one, a cleaning woman who started work with us today, next the plumber, a soldier on the base, who came to look at a leak in the kitchen, and Clive the librarian who came to report that about half the books have disappeared. Naturally about this time we decide we might as well get up and I am waiting for Jean to take a bath so I can take one too.

This morning we have to go to a local Labor Board and interview eight women who we hope will come to work for us as cleaners and dishwashers. This afternoon we are going to start an exhibition in the club of things the boys have made. They really make wonderful things out of the plastic glass that comes from the planes—mostly rings and pins. I have a nifty ring that one of the boys made me with part of a green toothbrush handle for a stone. Very gaudy.

I haven't seen any vegetable gardens on the base with the exception of one full of lettuce gone to seed but I guess I've told you about the combat crew ponies and goats. They also had some chickens and ducks but I hear they have disappeared. Anything you want around here has to be nailed down. Even the chaplain takes our coal, and some of the linoleum. You call it borrowing though, although naturally they are never returned. Jean and I do it all the time and only a few days ago "borrowed" about 300 doughnuts from the officer's mess when no one was looking because we were short of food.

Have just come back from eating delicious ham for dinner, with tomato salad and apricot pie for dessert and Beatrice, the head counter girl who is noisier than Helen Dodd, has just come clicking across the courtyard to our quarters to tell us that the cat has been locked up in the larder all afternoon sitting on a box howling and eating cakes. We are having hamburgers tonight so the place is packed already.

Friday night we are having our second dance and so we tried to get some of the WAACS who are now at a base fairly near here. They haven't a free evening until Sept. 10th however, so we have reserved them for then.

The interviews this morning proved entirely useless and we only got one new person. We have got one awfully nice girl as a housekeeper who came yesterday though, sixteen years old and terribly pretty. We have to keep her locked in the storeroom to keep the boys away. She is an evacuee from London.

August 12, 1943

I have just eaten an orange! We got three each in the mess yesterday—the first I have had in England.

Lately we have been entertaining newspaper reporters. There is a girl here for a couple of days who is a war correspondent for some Middle Western papers and is here getting features and human-interest stories. She spent last evening talking to boys in the club, and is staying with us in our quarters. The night before there was a UP reporter here and a couple of the officers brought him down to see us after the club closed. We sat in our sitting room and dining room and talked about the war for hours. Jean and I sure got a collection of human-interest stories but we don't like to tell them.

Yesterday we went and had tea with the Soden's—the minister and his wife about whom I told you. You should

Jean with Goodan and Frenese at the opening of the Aero Club, July 1943

see the church. The doorway was built in 1066 and the rest of the church around 1635. Their gardens are simply lovely, full of Begonias (tuberous) and roses and the inside of their house is full of the most beautiful old furniture, china and paintings. They have two chairs made from a Jacobean bed, which used to be in what was an old manor house across the road but is now a post office, what is left of it, and dates back to James I.

Yesterday morning Joyce and I drove to a larger town about twenty-five miles away to get my auto license and do some errands and Joyce told all about the different manor houses around here and the families who own them. The Army now occupies most of them.

I have just gotten the first letter you wrote me after you had gotten my first. They seem to come a little mixed up as I have gotten several later ones. I am enclosing a picture of Jean in the door of our quarters. The window on the right is our bedroom. Much nicer than my apartment in N.Y. isn't it? Also another picture of Jean and two of our favorite boys, Goodan and Frenese, taken the opening night. The half open door in back is our office and the door on the left the kitchen. Doesn't the food look good!

August 13, 1943

Last night decorations were awarded and we forgot to go damn it, altho' we have been before. One of the officers came down later to show us his award—the Purple Heart.

Jean now has a ferret named after her. One of the soldiers bought it to hunt rabbits with. Lots of hunting goes on around here and the night before last we had a little bit of pheasant for dinner. Rabbits are especially prevalent and you often see someone on the road with six or so slung over his back. One of the men used to be an elephant trainer with Ringling Bros. before the war and the boys are trying to find an elephant for him.

Well tonight is dance night and we must spend the dance fixing the joint up.

Much Love,
Binni

August 16, 1943

Dear Mother & Dad,

At this moment I am staying at a terribly nice little inn in the small town of Roysten. The girl I have told you about, Michaele Phillippe, who came to the club to help us start the kitchen running, is living here at present, as this is sort of a central spot for her. She came to our base for the weekend as one of the officers asked her to the dance and yesterday I came back here with her. Michaele is terribly interesting. She is thirty-nine and looks twenty. She was married to André Phillippe the French auto racer who was killed about eight years ago and she has lived all over everywhere, was educated in France and Belgium and sent the last years before the war in Cairo where she is dying to go again as soon as the war is over. Here at this inn I have a huge corner room overlooking a lovely garden where I am right now sitting in the sun. It is so quiet after life on the army base. The only noise is a parrot here at the inn that the American boys taught to whistle, which it does continually.

It is kind of nice to be wearing civilian clothes for a change and terribly funny as the Americans naturally think I'm an English girl. Last night we had dinner with some American officers, friends of Michaele's, and they were telling me all about America, even as near home as Connecticut and how wonderful it was and how I would love it if I was ever lucky enough to get there. They described New York to me, and the differences between the north and the south and even told me I was well dressed for an English girl. I had to laugh at the picture they painted of America; just so ideal and wonderful that naturally no such place exists in the world, sort of like Dad's farm. You'd think they could tell by my accent that I was no English girl woman but I guess they just don't expect to see an American. Anyway, after an evening with them I began to see why some Americans and some Englishmen over here don't get along so well as all the Americans do is talk about home and what we have that they don't have in England. It is a hideous mistake, isn't it, and I hope I'm never guilty of it. If I had been an English girl last night I would have gotten terribly mad.

This morning I had breakfast in bed, a poached egg on toast that Michaele managed to get for me somehow. I feel guilty when I think of the good food we have. Lately there have been oranges at the base and the boys bring us three or four a day. We really have more than we can eat but of course they won't last for long.

It is terribly warm today, one of the warmest days we've had. There is a swimming pool right across the street and I am going swimming this afternoon. I will make this letter last for three days, as I can't mail it until I get back to the base. As you have probably gathered all our mail has to be censored there, which naturally means there are lots of funny occurrences I wouldn't dare tell you about, as I hate the feeling that someone is reading my mail and particularly someone on the base that I know. I guess that will make you wonder what goes on over here!

I have had a wonderful afternoon all to myself for a change. Late lunch at a little inn in town and sat at a table with a man and his wife and their little girl named Susan, about four, with blond hair and a Dutch haircut who looked exactly like Jane used to look. I was much amused, as her father wouldn't let drink water with her meals! The first time I've ever heard that happen outside my own home.* Then I shopped for Ping Pong balls and darts, which, of course, I couldn't find; went to see a service club in town, in the process of being built and not nearly as nice as ours and then went swimming in the pool and lay in the sun for a while. Then I came back to the inn and the man who runs it took me around the huge garden and gave me some apples and plums right off the trees. All around the garden are huge walnut trees with lots of walnuts which won't be ripe until November and also some mulberry trees and lovely flowers. All the gardens have lovely bright red geraniums. The owners are so apologetic about how run down they are since the war but they look wonderful to me. Across the road is an old 13th Century church, which Michaele and I are going to see when she gets home from work.

I am getting an English vocabulary now. Did you know that they call a telephone a "blower" (a wonderful word for them as they don't work nice and easily like ours and after trying to use them once or twice you begin to understand why the English seem to depend so little on these and go and see the person instead.) and a raid or mission is called a "flap". When you ask directions they always end, after giving them, with "you cawn't miss it." Since the Americans find you not only can but all too frequently do, this has become a big joke even to the extent of one of the Red Cross Variety shows being named "You cawn't miss it." I notice the English are also picking up American expressions and our staff go around saying O.K. and swell, etc. Being "thoroughly browned off", incidentally, means being mad as hell!

August 17, 1943

Today we went to Cambridge for the day and had a wonderful time walking around the different colleges and browsing in bookstores. I bought a copy of *Lamb's Essays*. What a wonderful town it is! I

---

* For some reason Fitje's father, Dr. Herman Pitts, believed drinking water with meals was unhealthy.

guess you have seen it, haven't you? I still can't believe I'm seeing these things and I'm sure the novelty will wear off. We had tea in a place called the Red Cow.

Last night before I went to bed I was wondering about Ibby's baby. In the middle of the night the air raid siren went off and I dreamed before I woke up that I was in the country and it was Ibby's baby crying. When I did wake up I couldn't think where I was and thought I was on the sleeping porch in the country. Isn't that funny? Imagine thinking that far back.

August 18, 1943

Back at the base again and glad to be here. So much can happen in our little place in three days that I really could hardly wait to get back. Nothing much occurred except the kitten 'Janie' has disappeared; they had ice cream for dinner in the mess; one of the soldiers brought us three baby rabbits, which Jean got rid of quickly in my absence and lots of other things, which I am gradually finding out.

I found a letter from Jane and one from both of you, which were very welcome. Yours were dated Aug. 3rd and 9th. I have stopped numbering mine but will start again. Enclosed is a picture of Lt. Clark just outside the door of our quarters with three of our dear friends. Lt. Clark was very glad to see me when I got home and has sitting in my lap ever since. I will never believe again that cats aren't affectionate.

I suppose Lucy is still a Recorder. I have to laugh when I think how serious we were about it at home and how calm we are here. It's amazing.

8:15 PM–I know you will be glad to hear that Janie has been returned to us.

Much love to you all

B

August 20, 1943

Dear Mother & Dad,

At last we have managed to get three truckloads of dirt for our front lawn and Jean and I have spent most of the day hoeing it and watering it with lots of advice from everyone who passes by and even a little help. Most everyone seems to think that grass isn't going to grow there and we sprinkling anyone who made any derogatory remarks with the hose.

Now we are relaxing before dinner with our bottle of sherry. There is a boy who lives on a dahlia farm in Virginia and is now a cook in the officer's mess leaning in the window! He is helping us with the lawn.

There is the most fascinating spot on the base where we spend a good deal of time. It's a little room in the decontamination building that some of our friends have sort of taken over to make things in. They make all sorts of painted boxes and plastic jewelry and some things for us at the club. One of them was an elephant trainer with Ringling Bros. before the war. They are the boys that own "Jean" the ferret and also a new addition "Polly" a baby rabbit, which we're scared to death they are planning to feed to Jean. They are going to take us rabbit hunting sometime soon. The farmer who sells us our green groceries has given us two black rabbits, which we are going to get as soon as they are old enough. If we accepted all our gifts we'd have quite a group by now—even a white mouse. The boys call our kittens "the girls." Last night we had a dozen eggs, which Jean got for a carton of cigarettes. We had fried eggs and pork, which someone brought me, with two of the officers after the club closed.

August 22, 1943

Jean and I are much amused by the soldiers who collect the garbage; only they insist that we call them salvage men, not garbage men. The procedure is this: there are three of them -they get the truck all ready to back it into the courtyard and then they send a scout out to see that Lt. Clark and Janie (the kittens) are out of the way. Then they back in. (one of the first times they backed a little too far to the right and took down the gate and part of the brick wall, which have never been replaced.) Then they send another scout out to look for us. If we are in bed, which we frequently are, we have to lean out the window and direct the procedure as they say every job has to have a boss and it would cause ill feeling if one of them should take that authority upon himself. As I've already told you we have about eight different containers each for a different thing. One man will take the lid off and look in as if he expected to find diamonds or a beautiful blond, then he beckons the others over and they all look in. then they all three sit down and discuss the contents for a while. This goes on every single day and takes hours. Everyday we have an argument about the coffee grounds, which they hate to take because it means looking for something to put them in. The garbage men call me "Red." The plumber calls me "Shorty" and the electricians call me "Rhode Island." Fitje seems to be practically impossible to learn to pronounce and only my better friends have learned it. It has become shortened to Fitch ("I" pronounced as in eye).

Jean and I get terribly discouraged sometimes trying to make things run right and almost hope a bomb will drop on the place. Then at the very worst moment one of the men will come in and tell us how much the club means to them and honestly it makes any effort worth it because I really believe they mean it. They seem to really take pride in it and are always making things for us and helping us.

August 23, 1943

Have just gotten back from taking Jean to the train as she has gone to London for a few days, leaving me to run a dance by myself and I'm terrified everything will go wrong. You have no idea of the little problems that arise—i.e., Last night while I was being cashier the orchestra leader came up and whispered in my ear "now Fitch, don't get excited but the orchestra isn't going to play Tuesday night."

Library at Horham

I notice everyone is beginning to preface their bombshells with "Now Fitch, don't get excited but. . ." I can hardly help getting excited, can I, although I do my best to control myself. Anyway that little matter has finally been straightened out.

Now, at this moment, there is a boy named Kurt hanging in the window who goes right on taking while I go right on writing. He is German, born in Germany, and his father was killed in the last war. He was a fireman in the railroad before he was drafted in Utah.

I wish you could see our librarian, Miss Scrivener, and very much the old maid, about fifty when she came. She just loves the boys and says they tell her she is "just like their mother." We notice she is beginning to wear lipstick and be very careful about the way she dresses.

One of our friends, Preswell, from Tenn. has been waiting for his wife to have a baby. Finally it came a month ago and a few days he got some pictures of it. Honestly you have never seen anyone so pleased. We call him "Pappy." Another boy, "Arkie", from Arkansas was also expecting a baby and he got a cable a few weeks ago saying his wife and the baby had died.* Isn't that sad. He's terribly nice and comes every night and sits in the office. We often leave him in charge if we have to go anywhere.

Pinkie just brought the mail, a letter from Mrs. Aldrich. Will you thank her for it? It was nice of her to write. Her family sounds as if they were having an interesting time.

You have no idea how many interruptions have occurred since I started the last entry. The latest, every night one of the boys parks his jeep in our drive while he goes to mess and every night for some reason or other he gets me to back it out for him, which I have just done. Another boy wanting to

* Pappy, Louis B. Ferency of Akron, Ohio, and Arkie, whose real name was not disclosed, were mentioned in an article written by Marjorie Avery, a Detroit Free Press foreign correspondent, who had a regular column titled London Diary. The column, which appeared on Friday, September 10, 1943, was titled "Right-Hand Men at the Aero Club."

Opening night: The "Horrible" Chef,
Fitje, Michaele, Mac McGrath and Jean Plageman

borrow two pounds, which I lent him. Rankin and Ogden, the two boys who wash dishes for us every night, reporting for duty. Never a dull moment!

We now have a fence around our lawn and everyone is making bets about whether the grass will grow or not. The boys call Jean "Mrs. Full Charge" because she is the boss. Honestly the names for people around here are a scream.

Well, time for dinner.

Much Love
Binnie

P.S. Enclosed is a picture taken of our opening night. From left to right—the horrible chef, since gone, me, Michaele, Mac, the nifty Field Director, and Jean.

August 25, 1943

Dear Mother & Dad,

Letters from Dad and Jane yesterday, which took only eight days to get here!

I will answer Dad's questions while I think of them. Yes the club is for enlisted men only, altho' officers can come in as guests of the enlisted men for something to eat. The officers on the base have their own club altho' there is no food served, and the enlisted men definitely do not like them to come in their club. Often, however, after a mission, the officers come in with their crews and they are, of course, very welcome and we love to have them there. Our office is at the back of the club and officers sometimes come there for something to eat or they come in after 11:00 when the club is closed and we cook, or eat what is left which is usually nothing. Last night one of the officers and I listened to symphonies until 2:00 o'clock. The first chance I've had and we have a huge stack of them.

The food is a terribly complicated matter. The rationing is divided into eight-week periods and we get permits for all rationed goods according to the number of people we expect to come and the type of base. We underestimated and hope to have our rations increased after September 19th when the period ends. We buy everything from local markets and cannot buy from the quartermaster, so have nothing from home. White flour, for example, is unheard of over here now. Only today Jean and I were in town looking for a little more variety and it is really amazing how little you can get. The towns around here are tiny anyway with just a few stores but we have had no better luck when we have gone to bigger places. We buy all groceries from out store where we order once a week. Apples, plums, lettuce, tomatoes, etc., we shop around the countryside for. We have apples and plums every night to make up for the shortage of other stuff. Up until lately I have taken care of the food but now that we have a manageress she is doing more and more of it. Bread comes from a tiny local bakery three times a week, fresh milk (only for the staff) every day, and meat for hamburgers three times a week. Yesterday I went to the bakery to increase our order and saw the ovens and watched them take the bread out. Mr. Patter, his wife and their two daughters run it and I think we practically support the place.

We have two cooks here from 8:30 to 4:30 who bake all day and make things like tarts, cheese squares, lemon buns and raspberry buns. Three girls come at 3:00 and make sandwiches by the hundreds and another girl makes the coffee and tea. The snack bar opens at 6:30 and we sell everything for a penny a piece except hamburgers, which cost three pence. We have practically no waste except the outside of the bread, which the staff takes home to feed their chickens. We are very proud of that. Our permits also allows us to order a few hundred pounds of fancy cakes from Lyons, a wholesale place in London, and they come by train where we order them for special occasions like a dance. We have long since used up our quota there, however. Also the officer's mess usually gives us about 400 cookies as a present once or twice a week when they make theirs. We are terribly short of sugar and can't use enough for coffee or tea. The boys often bring their own from the mess and sometimes give us donations for the cooking. What I don't know about buying food, now. Jean and I are going to run a hotel when the war is over.

Last night was dance night and I think it was a great success as lots of girls came and everything went very smoothly—ATS, WAAFS,* Land Army girls and nurses. Now, of course, it is harvest time here and every available person is working in the fields. There are lots of Italian prisoners in the fields too, that we pass when we go to town. The Land Army girls really work terribly hard.

I haven't been getting any real exercise except running around here so now every evening after din-

---

* ATS refers to Auxiliary Territorial Service, women's branch or the British Army. WAAFS is the British Women's Auxiliary Air Force.

ner some of the boys and Jean and I ride bicycles from the club all around the airfield, a long ride to me anyway. I have ordered a bicycle and should get it soon.

August 27, 1943

Ever since Janie got lost the soldiers have been bringing us more black kittens which we have refused to take, as we thought when Janie was returned that two were enough. One boy today brought one that we decided to keep so now we have three and everyone is teasing us about being old maids. We named the new addition "Mickie" after the boy who brought her.

We now have ordered two dachshund puppies from London. Isn't that wonderful! We can't get them for a couple of weeks until they are a little older.

We are getting awfully well organized now. Two more staff, which brings the total up to twenty-one. The other day we got a present of eighty-five model airplanes—U.S., Eng., German, and Italian, which, they use here for instruction. They were not only given to us but they sent three men to hang them on the beams in the snack bar and they look nifty. John would love them.

We have also gotten presents of huge photographs of the planes and others taken from the air which are now being framed for us; a radio and another Victrola and about 1000 new books all in the past week. The club is really beginning to look pretty nice. Of course, we think it's wonderful. One of the boys brought us a lemon yesterday, the first I have seen since I left U.S. We never ask questions about our presents so we don't know where it came from. The same boy also brought us a dozen eggs! At dinner the other night one of the officers gave us each a slice of white bread straight from the American air base in North Africa!

Mother, I have to laugh right now. When Jean came back from London she brought a bottle of rum and at this moment we are drinking rum and coke and lemon juice and arguing heatedly about the Catholic religion. Jean is a protestant about to become a Catholic—a fascinating transformation to me! Like father, like daughter, I guess. We have taken to resting in the daytime, as lately our sleep at night has been interfered with quite a bit, and this is the way we do it. We just this moment got another present of some ice which is also practically unheard of around here, and two boys are now at the window telling us that Janie the ferret has been lost. They are terribly upset!

Two patches of grass are now growing which everyone calls "Guam" and "Midway." We suspect that they have nothing to do with the grass we planted and would have grown anyway.

I wish you could see our two hired boys, Leonard and Guy. Guy is terribly cute. He is younger than John and half his age. He works from 7:00 to 3:00 and twice as hard as John ever thought of working. Leonard is sixteen and all the staff grumbles about him, as he never does a thing unless we are around and then he falls all over himself to appear to be busy. We call him "Beau Brummel" because if we ask him to do anything he usually says "yes, miss, I'd do anything for a lady!" We understand that he swears horribly at anyone else who asks him to do anything. He works from 3:00 to 11:00 and is supposed to keep the fires lit and wash the dishes. He makes our tea for us every afternoon and carries it all over the fort until he finds us. I am going to take pictures of the staff and send them to you.

August 28, 1943

Honestly, someone has just brought us another black kitten, which is now named Lt. Kelly after the officer and which I hope we aren't going to keep. Four is too many.

Today it's pouring rain. The chaplain had a party for the kids in the vicinity, which numbered about 100 when they all got together. Jean and I helped serve lemonade and cookies etc., they were awfully funny and everyone seemed to have a good time. The Catholic chaplain here is nifty. He is going to keep a church after the war and has extracted promises from all the Catholic officers for an altar, windows, etc. He's terribly funny.

The first package has come, the green dress and orange sweater. I will wear the green dress tonight to the officer's dance—it's that cold!

Mother, I forgot your birthday. Anyway, Happy Birthday, several weeks late.

Love to all,
Binnie

❧

August 29, 1943

Dear Jane,

Happy Birthday! I forgot Mother's but maybe I'll remember them from now on.

You are wonderful to write so often. Your last letter really looked as if the party was still going on. I was glad to hear where Mary T. and Gretchen are, although I'm really glad I'm not with them, as I can't imagine being any more contented anywhere else. Have you heard from John yet? I don't suppose you have. What would his troops be doing there anyway? Are they engineers or what? What exactly are you doing now?

Well Sunday again and although we actually never have a day off Jean and I are apt to relax. I don't know why it is so hard to work on Sunday. Perhaps because every other one we have a hangover, due to the officer's dance every other Sat. night. So far we have stayed here until 11:00 to close up the club and then gotten dressed and gotten there about 12:00. It's a terrible mistake as we go right to the bar and try to catch up with the group, which is terribly advanced by that time. Last night we went early, about 10:00, and it was never better, but I closed my eyes at 5:30 this morning and opened them again at 7:30, entirely the fault of our cats who wake us up bright and early. They are awfully funny. When they wake up we open the window between our beds so they can get out and they jump out but every ten minutes so they jump back in again and go to each of us making a queer noise that sounds like "B-r-r-r-k," just to be sure we're still there. We have to make the new cat, Mickie, sleep in the hallways because neither of the other will let him get on the beds and we have catfights all night. I will never believe again that cats aren't affectionate. Ours are mad about us and we have to lock them up to keep them from following us.

Last night the mess sergeant and one of the cooks at the combat mess asked Jean and I to go for dinner. We went about 7:30 after the mess was closed and they had fixed up a room for us, lit a fire and had a table all laid with a blanket for a tablecloth. We had the best dinner of steak, French fried potatoes, fried onions, sliced tomatoes, bread and jam, peaches and coffee. It was the best dinner I have had in ages. Everyone is so nice to us; it's just amazing.

I've been trying to write this all day but it's practically impossible. We have to stop and talk to everyone that comes in. In the last five minutes one boy wants to cook some beef in the kitchen and another boy who was at this fort but has been moved wants us to take him back to his present fort in our car, another boy looking for two other boys, and another boy saying he has ten letters to write, and that's exactly the way it is all day. Now some boys are outside the window with Jane the cat, pretending they are about to cut her head off with an axe and how they have put her on the roof of the car and gone off and left her and how, at this very moment, Loafer, another boy, has come in and seated himself on the stack of symphonies and announced that sometimes he wished he was buried under six feet of dirt! Honestly! It's so amazing. I could sit here all day and just about the people who come in.

I haven't seen Kenny but maybe I'll go to London sometime soon and will certainly look him up. I would love to see Brian's wife but I am not near enough where she is.

I wish you could see some of the nifty aerial photographs that have been given us—also eighty-five models of airplanes. They are nifty and make the club look much better.

Let me know when Ibby's baby comes in case Mother and Dad forget. Give my love to Pat and Dottie Deans.

Much Love,
Binni

September 2, 1943

Dear Mother & Dad,

It seems ages since I've written but I guess it's only been about a week. The time flies so over here. I can't believe it is September and the summer is over. Out room is like sleeping outdoors and poor Jean is so cold already that she wears a wool cap and sweater to bed. I don't know what will happen to her when winter comes. It doesn't bother me at all but reminds me of early morning in Maine, especially someone come in and light our fire before we get up and eat breakfast in bed of course!

We are now trying to work more or less on shifts instead of all the time the way we have been doing so we won't get so tired and disagreeable. This week I work from 7:00 to 12:00, and Jean from 2:00 to 12:00. Next week we change. Of course it doesn't work at all. Living so near the club we can't keep away from it. We are also allowing ourselves one night off a week and tonight is supposedly mine, but I didn't get it as we got a hurry call to serve coffee and donuts to a group and have just returned after disposing of 1500 donuts and 500 gallons of coffee. Lord how these men eat. Serving food away from the club is a new project we just started and something we have wanted to do. We are hardly prepared to do it yet though and luckily were able to get sugar and cream from the combat mess and got the doughnuts given to us. Jean and Mac and I do the serving. I guess I already told you that Mac is the field director here and the nicest person. I'm sure we never could have managed without him. Sometimes I can hardly wait to get home to tell you all the things I can't write and will probably bore you for weeks after I do. I don't keep a diary because I never seem to have time and I'm sure I'll forget most of it.

Jean and I had the most wonderful dinner the other night. The mess sergeant and one of the cooks at the combat mess invited us down there, after mess was over. They had a tablecloth and a nice fire. We had steak, French fried potatoes, fried onions, tomatoes, peaches and coffee—the best meal I have had in the ETO. After that we went to the dance at the officer's club, early for a change instead of waiting until the club closed. A brawl as usual but we always have a wonderful time.

The pets on the base are increasing rapidly. Two goats have been added and we understand some pigs are about to be. One of the combat crews has the cutest little black cocker puppy, which I admire so much that they accuse me of "sweating them out," waiting until they go down so I can get it. Not to be outdone, another have taken on a little boy about ten who lives with them and wears a sergeants uniform and is the club drinking coffee at 11:00 most nights.

Yesterday Jean and I drove to another town to shop and pick up a friend of Jeans to bring her back here for the night. She lives on a farm in the country and has everything—five dogs, pigs, horses, cows, ducks, etc. It's a lovely place. Her husband is overseas and her three kids seven, eleven, and thirteen were sent to the U.S. three years ago and she has not been able to get them back again yet.

The three packages have all arrived. Thanks a lot. I have practically run out of stockings and could easily use two-dozen, size 9 ½, <u>short length</u> Belle Sharmeer. I don't need any heavy ones as I have plenty of them when winter comes. Take the money out of the bank for them. I am accumulating more money over here as I never spend a thing and maybe I send some bonds home soon or save it to travel after the war. Has the Red Cross sent you any bonds yet? I should have one by now.

September 3, 1943

We have just gotten the news that Italy has been invaded! The news is so good lately. Now we have a radio so we know a little more quickly what goes on.

Yesterday we fired one girl, and hired three more so at last we really have a complete staff, I think. Jean and I are able to do much more with the boys, which is really what we're supposed to do and I spent the morning playing snooker, which I am getting quite good at and which is very much like pool except the table is bigger. We are fortunate in having two tables.

Must get this in the mail today. We are now allowed to censor our own letters.

Love to all
Binni

September 4, 1943

Dear Mother & Dad,

Have just gotten your letter, Mother, dated Aug. 23rd and enclosing Jane's letter and the Smith alumnae thing. I can't imagine what made you think we were near London. You are on the wrong track. Don't forget you can't get so terribly far from London and still be in England. I guess you got that idea from the day I went to London in the Army truck, but it was a long, long trip. I think we're as far from anything as we could be in England. I just love this independent feeling of you having no idea where I am so I won't even give you a hint. Our base is fairly new, although the RAF was here first and our building was originally occupied by the NAAF, which is a moneymaking organization, which runs canteens on RAF bases. Our quarters are in a separate building across a small courtyard from the club. There are four bedrooms and a bathroom in our quarters. Jean and I are in one, Joyce the secretary in another, Miss Scrivener, the librarian, in another, and Mac, the field director, in the fourth. We are the only ones in our organization who live on the base. The buildings on the base are all tan like ours and only temporary. The men are all American with a very few exceptions. The Englishmen are more or less liaison, I guess.

I wish you could see the heather that Jean and I picked the other day. After we picked up Jean's friend we drove a little farther just to have a look at the ocean and we passed a lovely place with lots of heather, gorse, and lime. We picked a lot and are going to try and plant it around our building. The grass looks wonderful and everyone admires it. We are going to landscape the whole post if we are here much longer.

We have lost another cat, Micky, and we are terrified to have anyone find out for fear we'll have another deluge of cats.

September 5, 1943

Last night we had a very good Red Cross show out here. The Red Cross has these traveling troupes of about ten people and they travel around to the different bases giving variety shows. The boys love them and cheer and yell. The cast is all English, but usually there is one American girl as manager. They travel around in a huge great van. Last night we went to the second show, which we usually do. Honestly I get more kick out of the animals around here—a boy sitting right near us in the front row had a large white dog sleeping calmly in his lap during the whole performance. There were four tiny puppies in the club, last night, three collies and a little black mutt. Major Russell wants to buy me a dog so I'm working on a collie. He's already bought me a large stuffed one, which sits on my bed. We ordered the dachshunds too late. They have already been sold.

After we closed the club Mac, Jean, Lt. Brickley, the special service officer Major Russell,* the adju-

---

* Base Adjutant, Major Edward Russell

Major Edward Russell, Base Adjutant, 95th Bomb Group

tant on the base, and myself went to an officer's dance for the officers on a nearby base held in sort of a private club down the road—after that we came back and made cheese sandwiches and coffee in our club. It was wonderful, except that we have to light a coal fire to cook anything. Lt. B. chopped wood and Major R. lit the fire while we watched. I had one egg, which I was going to eat until they got throwing it back and forth and broke it. It was rotten anyway I had horded it for so long.

There is an officer here who knows Mopsy Richardson and all that gang. I can't remember his name but he lives in Marion on the Cape in the summer and that's where he knew her. He's awfully nice.

September 6, 1943

Thanks for sending *Terry & The Pirates** but never mind anymore as I see it in *Stars & Stripes* the army paper, which we get over here. Why doesn't Ann send me her brother's addresses? They may be right on the next base for all I know.

Last night we had one of the dances we have every two weeks in the club. I think it was the best yet and went very well. There were ten WACS there who were naturally terribly popular. You should see the men when they girls start to come. They stand at the door and pinch their cheeks as they go through. We decorated the club with Hawthorne with lots of red berries on it and it looked very nice except of course it gets so trimmed that no one were here and were very flattering about how good the food looked and how clean everything was. They gave us lots of tips about other kinds of food we could have. I could have kissed one of the boys who came in the office while they were there and said, "You can take it from me that if it weren't for this club you could give the boys each a razor and tell

* A popular comic strip created by Milton Caniff in 1934. His last strip was published on December 29, 1946.

them to cut their throats!" Isn't that wonderful! Of course there's nothing like blowing your own horn and we know it's not that good but it's nice to have someone say that, especially in front of the right people.

Now it is evening and I have brought the radio into my room and was planning to have a nice quiet evening for a change. Now, however, Lt. Brickley, the special service officer is in here pressing his blouse. We are having great competition with him over our grass. He plowed up about an acre of land right beside the club for a tennis court, which of course was never built; at the same time we planted our grass. Grass is growing on his land much better than that which we so carefully planted. Today he said he's ordered a lawn mower but tonight he says he's going to have it plowed under because he thinks detrimental to our morals.

Joyce, the secretary, went home for the day and brought us back some honey from their own hives and some lavender from their garden. I am enclosing some of the lavender, and wish you could taste the honey!

Have just gotten a letter from Jane saying Ibby has a son. I'm so glad! Also enclosing two pictures of Jones and one of the Victory garden. It looks beautiful.

We are listening to the news all the time and I imagine you are doing the same thing. We are wondering what will happen tomorrow and where the Americans are.

Happy Birthday, Dad!

Love.
Fitje

September 8, 1943

Dear Mother & Dad,

Just a moment to at least start a letter while I am waiting for the manageress, Mrs. Upton, to finish her lunch so we can go to town and do the weekly marketing.

First of all to answer your questions, we get plenty of cigarettes, candy, etc., as we go to the PX once a week and get a weekly supply, also soap, gum and lots of other junk. We even get tomato juice and peanuts in cans. Yes, the base has a hospital and lots of doctors. We have a 1st Aid Post in our building and the only casualty we have had in the club so far is one of the cooks who got a bad cut on her arm. There are no nurses on the base (we are the only women) so I suppose if we ever get sick, which we naturally won't be, we could go somewhere else.

About my allotment Dad should receive $47.60 twice a month and a $75 bond every five months. If there are mistakes would you write:

American Red Cross
National Hdqrs.
Washington, DC

Yes I have plenty of money and not a thing to spend it on here.

Spent the afternoon shopping and filling out more of those damned forms. Sixty pounds of tomatoes, three-dozen heads of lettuce—we really do things in large quantities around here. This afternoon we found a wonderful truck garden and got fresh lettuce picked while we watched—also cucumbers and tomatoes, and lots of flowers.

We are still short on staff and are having a little difficulty with some who are definitely unfit in one way or another, like one of the cooks who threatened to elope with one of the men (both already married of course) and they still have us a little upset as the matter isn't exactly settled yet and we can't bear to lose the cook.

We had one very exciting evening this week; we went up in a plane. Jean, Joyce (the secretary) and I went as well as one of the corporals from the mess hall and a few of the crew, of course. They even brought a doctor along in case any of us got sick. It was simply beautiful seeing England from the air, exactly like lots of rugs and every inch of surface cultivated. Poor Jean got simply terrified even to the extent of sitting on the floor so she would be nearer to the ground and we finally had to go down on her account. For the next couple of days whenever we went into the mess hall the little corporal would rush around and tell all the officers how scared she was. She was terribly embarrassed about it.

Sunday we went to church in the little church right on the edge of the base. Joyce knows the vicar, Mr. Soden, so after church we were shown around. It's a lovely place. The church was built in 1631! Now Mr. Soden, an old man of about eighty-two, owns it and lives right next to it in a nifty house with the most beautiful gardens. The service was really funny. There were only about ten people there and the organ broke down and made horrible noises all through it. Mrs. Soden is the sole member of the choir. Only during the past month, now that the fear of invasion has past, have church bells been rung, as they were to be the signal if an invasion came. Also the road signs are gradually being put up again, which is nice, as we get lost practically every time we leave the base. We are going to have tea Wednesday with the Vicar and his wife.

Saturday night Jean and I went to an officer's dance on another base. It was a lot of fun but we are terribly loyal to our own group. Last night after the club closed we went and had a drink with some of the officers and naturally we never got to bed. We try to sleep a little later in the mornings now but the boy who chops the wood and likes the fires always sings while he's doing it and wakes us up. Every morning we ask him not to but by the next morning he has forgotten.

Poor Lt. Clark (cat) has been sick all week and we don't know what's wrong with her. We even had one of the doctors come look at her. No dog as yet, only a stuffed one that one of the officers brought me from London.

We have excellent food and I am going without nothing at all. It's hard to realize there is any food shortage until you talk to the local people who have a very difficult time getting almost everything. Sunday for dinner we had chicken, the first I've had and very unusual. It came from a special fund that the officers contribute to. We after had two fried eggs each for Sunday breakfast. Last night one of the boys brought a chicken into the club and the cook fried it for him. It smelled simply wonderful and he had the nerve to sit right in the middle of the dining room in plain view of everyone to eat it. Last night was a record night and we were cleaned out way before the snack bar was supposed to close. We are going to have to get more rations as we are serving more than we ever expected.

Jane mentioned how hard my mattress is so I thought I'd better mention again not to dare change it.

Am glad to hear news of every member of the family. Have you had any sweet corn or watermelon?

Much Love,
Binnie

⸎

September 13, 1943

Dear Mother & Dad,

What a terrible time we are having right now. No sooner do we get everything running smoothly, with plenty of staff to do everything, then the Labor Board comes along and takes our two dish washers away from us to send away to work because they are mobile. This means they are between eighteen and twenty-six and unmarried so have to be sent away from their homes to work. Our best sandwich maker's husband objected to her working here so she has to leave, so here we are back to cleaning tables at night and trying to hire more staff during the daytime. Also it has gotten so damp that no matter how early in the morning we wash the floors they will not dry before the men come in and the wind is so terrible now that some of the rooms literally have to be cleaned out with shovels in the morning. The floors are cement with linoleum over it, which, of course, makes it worse. We are trying to get the walk widened in front of the club and put up a fence so everyone won't walk across the field instead of along the walks. I suppose about the time everything is under control the war will be over.

I tell you about all the praise we get but I don't believe I have told you about all the criticism, and there is plenty of that too. If either of my brothers were tell me again that men aren't cattier than women I certainly will laugh. You should hear some of the rumors that go around about us. Since we are terribly careful not to do one thing that we shouldn't and none of them are true we just laugh at them. Someone yesterday told us our cookies tasted like G.I. soap. Last night I walked into the Snack Bar with a cigarette in my mouth and a tray in my hand and before the evening was over at least five of the boys had called it to my attention and informed me that American girls didn't walk around with a cigarette in their mouth. One day I didn't wear stockings and I don't know how many boys said, "Only Limeys go around without stockings." All English people are called Limeys around here. I have never had to be so correct in my life. If American girls were as wonderful as these boys even to think they are when they are away from them everything would be O.K.

The dogs around here are getting to be one of our big problems. Last night there were seven of them in the lounge alone when we closed the club. It takes us about forty-five minutes to get the men out, waiting for them to finish a game of something or other and no one ever seems to own the dogs. They are the worst to get out. There were three of them asleep on the couch last night and you get them out one door and they run in another. If we let them stay all night, which we have done, they start to howl about four in the morning and we have to go over and let them out. Once we found a dog and one of our cats asleep in the same chair.

Saturday night we went to the officer's club dance, one of the best yet. One of the officers found two goats in his bed when he got home and in retaliation lit a scrap basket on fire and put it under someone else's bed. It's a rough life! Last night we went down to the rifle range with three of the officers and shot for a while, which was fun.

September 16, 1943

We certainly have been busy lately. Yesterday we got up early and went to a bigger shopping center about twenty miles away to get hinges for lavatory doors, blackout material, records, our framed photographs and lots of other things, also to take our shoes and uniforms to be repaired, a process which takes weeks. While there we went to see a place called the Mansion House, an old house built in 1548 for a man and his wife and their nineteen children. It was fascinating, especially the kitchen with a fireplace as big as a room. On the way home we stopped at a nursery and ordered some cedar trees and other evergreens to plant around the place!

When we got back we found we were to serve coffee and cookies to the crews when they came back, so we rushed around getting that organized and took it down in the truck. Transporting forty-five gallons of coffee in three, fifteen-gallon vats is no easy job on our rough roads. It is the most beautiful sight to watch the planes land at night. The flares are like 4th of July. We got back just in time to close the club and wake up again bright and early to see the labor board representative who is going to get our dish washers back for us.

This afternoon just as I was about to rest for a while one of the gunners came up with his pony and brought it right into my room. The pony walked around and was so much at home that she even made a mass on the floor. We made Red, the gunner, clean it up and everyone gathered round and laughed and laughed, especially the staff, at us because we get mad when the kittens mess in the room.

The weather is better now so the club is cleaner and we are having the front walk widened in hopes that it will help. We are now dealing with the delicate trouble of firing our manageress who doesn't get on so well with the rest of the staff. The British caste system is what makes the trouble. She thinks she's much better than they are and doesn't know how to handle them at all. In fact she is absolutely no help to us and does everything the wrong way. Well, must get this in the mail.

Much Love,
Binnie

September 18, 1943

Dear Mother & Dad,

Drinking time again, usually the best part of the day because it's the only chance we get to sit down. Today, however, has been very leisurely. For once, we stuck to our schedule. I worked from 10:00 to 3:30 then went to sleep and Jean worked from 2:00 on, but spent most of her time sitting in the air raid shelter opposite the driveway talking to anyone who went by. On the menu for today: a bottle of sherry, which we talked out of the officer's club, a box of salted pecans from Jean's sister in Oregon and a basket of blackberries, which two of the gunners picked and brought us this morning.

Guess what just happened, one of the gunners, Sergeant Thomas, just came in with a knapsack and in it he had a tiny tiger kitten, which he gave us. We immediately named it "Hot Seat Thomas" after him, of course, because he is a tail gunner and some 20mm shells almost got him once. It's tiny and terribly cute. In his squadron they have a duck, a cat and a rabbit who are very good friends. There is a cute little puppy that hangs around here all the time named "Piccadilly" belonging to a gunner who went down that we are planning to adopt next.

September 19, 1943 Sunday

It seems to me that all I find to write about are our pets. Today we have lost Lt. Clark and Janie and have searched the squadron areas to no avail. Major Russell says, "Well, put it in the daily bulletin and they'll see it and come home." Lt. Kelly says, "Well, check with Major Russell, maybe they've gone on a 48 hour pass."

At present we are laughing at Mac who went away to Cambridge. To get there they had to change trains and the hopped of one train and on another and started playing cribbage. When they looked up about an hour later they were right back where they started from, having hopped on the wrong train. Also at Major Russell who when rushing out to the plane, picked his parachute up by the ripcord and pushed rushed out the door with it open and streaming behind him—now we call him "Ripcord Rus-

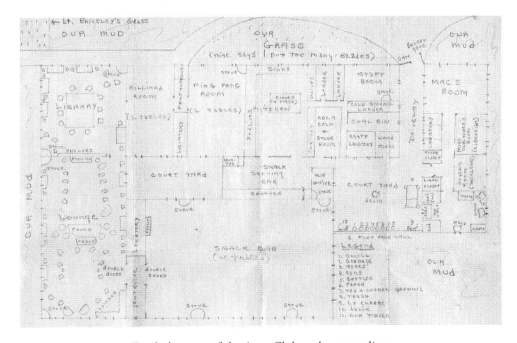

Fitje's drawing of the Aero Club and surroundings

sell" and to add insult to injury someone said to him, "Never mind Major, I don't know where the ripcord is either!"

I wish you could see the club now. The lounge, snack bar and library look especially nice, as we have gotten nifty photographs for the walls, lots of plants and a huge rug in the lounge. We also have had three maps put in wooden frames nailed on the wall, one of the U.S., one of England and one of London. Now that the weather is getting colder it is simply jammed every night. Last night we stayed open later than usual and sat and listened to one of the boys, Zaru, play the piano. He plays beautifully, all by ear, and can't read a note. There are a couple of artists on the base who are going to paint murals for us in the halls and eventually it should really look quite nice.

About Christmas, I really don't need a thing except stockings and maybe <u>warm</u> <u>nightgowns</u> and some Filene's F 828. I am not going to try to send a thing home, as I couldn't buy anything worthwhile and it seems silly to clutter the mail with what I could get. I will try to send you some more photographs, though.

Mother and Lucy, keep your eyes opened for a nifty dark red <u>wool dress</u> and buy it for me if you see it, with some of my money. I do wear civilian clothes to dances and only have that dark green dress, which will wear out before the winters over. Naturally I want something very nice up to $35. Ask Trelsie if you are uncertain. Size fourteen, not necessarily dark red, but not black or dark green. Maybe a mixture or purple—anyway a dark color, but colorful, <u>not</u> brown or dark blue. I should think Chez Elise would be best. Something dressy and really smooth. This is <u>not</u> a necessity—just if you happen to see something that you're sure I would like.

Enclosed is a plan of the club. Maybe you can get a rough idea what it is like.

Love to all
Binnie

September 24, 1943

Dear Mother & Dad,

I wish you could see the lovely spot I am vacationing in at this moment. It is very hard to think of any place to go besides London as there are so few places open now days, and Jean and I can't go away together. I started out yesterday to go to London but missed the train so came here instead. Anyway London is so crowded and it is terribly hard to find a place to stay. Jean had to sleep on a mattress in the linen closet when she was there last week.

Anyway, this is a lovely spot. I am at the Felix Hotel in Felixtowe, right on the ocean, huge, very respectable old brick hotel and terribly quiet. Before the war Felixtowe was quite a resort but now, of course, the beach is all barricaded and you can't go near. Still you can see and smell the ocean and it looks and smells wonderful. The meals are very good here and the dining room very amusing, as it is filled with old couples who never say a word to each other. All the men have a bottle of whiskey and a bottle of soda in front of them. The only noise is from four American Army officers who are staying here too, and even they are a little subdued.

In the back of the hotel on a bluff right over the ocean is a lovely garden where I am sitting right now in the sun. It is a beautiful warm day. What used to be flower gardens are now planted with potatoes. There is a woman sitting in another deck chair near me mending stockings, who has just told me that her grandfather owned a house that was torn down years ago so that this hotel could be built on the same spot.

I can't imagine how anyone from the base knew I was here and am dying to find out. No sooner had I gotten here than Joyce's sister who lives here came to see me and said Joyce had just telephoned and told her to look me up. Then Major Russell telephoned and can't believe I am here alone and insists on coming all the way down here tonight to take me out to dinner and check up, I guess. I am going back to the base on Saturday.

Jean was in London during the early part of the week and while there she went to head office to see Mr. Buford our supervisor. He told her that they would probably move me to open a new club, as Director, and give her a new assistant. Jean put up a good fight and said she thought it was ridiculous to move one of us when we get along so well and the club runs so well. Apparently they want people with some experience to open the new clubs but we opened ours with none so I don't see why others can't do the same. In the end he promised not to unless absolutely necessary and then not without consulting us. I would hate to leave where I am even though it means a raise and a promotion. Having started this club we feel that it is ours and I couldn't bear to have anyone take my place. Oh, well, naturally I'll go wherever I'm needed when the time comes.

The personnel changes rapidly. The day before yesterday was cause for celebration because three of the boys finished their twenty-five missions safely and will leave. I felt so happy for them and it reminded me of how relieved I used to be when I finished my exams at college, and think of how much more relieved they must be. Has Roger left the U.S. yet? I am waiting for him to come over here. Wouldn't it be strange if he did? I am enclosing an article about some of our boys that was published in *Stars & Stripes* so I guess its O.K. to send. Sgt. Thomas who is mentioned was the gunner who gave us Lucky.

The latest funny story: the night before last when we got to our quarters after we closed the club, Mac called to us after he got in his room and said "come and see the cat." Jean asked, "Which is it Lt. Clarke or Janie?" and Mac said, "I don't know, I never can tell them apart." We went in and there was a large white nanny goat, lying on the rug placidly chewing her cud she must have wandered in during the evening as all the doors are always opened. We had an awful time getting her out, as she was much too comfortable to want to leave. Mac goes around telling everyone that he is looking for new quarters, as we want his room for our animals. All the strays seem to adopt us and we have decided that the Red Cross is as it is called "The greatest mother of them all."

Well, to get back to Felixtowe, I spent the morning with Joyce's sister, Peggy. We walked up the road in front of the ocean for a long way. Most of the shops are closed up now and it was so quiet and deserted. Then we went to a little Swedish shop, Bonnet's, for coffee and I went with her while she bought her weekly rations, which didn't look like enough for one meal. I found another ring like the one I bought in London in an antique shop and would have bought it on the spot but the shopkeeper did his best to tell me I didn't want another. He even wanted me to think it over for a day and wear the ring while I was deciding. Can you imagine! These people don't seem to want to part with anything and you have to argue to buy it. I think I will back and get it this afternoon.

Monday night we had blackberry shortcake at the club. Jean and I have been trying to get enough blackberries for a long time and finally got enough from some little boys, some of the soldiers and an old man who "had never talked to American girls before." We had a hard time describing shortcake to the cooks as it means something entirely different to them but finally got the perfect thing although we had to practically make it. The staff thought it was awful but the boys loved it and have been bringing blackberries and asking for more ever since. We were a little worried about serving anything that required spoons as the boys love our spoons for their mess kits and we lost four-dozen in four weeks by just putting them on the counter to stir coffee with. Now we put one on the counter and tie it with a string. So we asked everyone individually to return the spoons when they were counted at the end of the evening, there were ten more than I had issued, and we can't imagine where they came from.

I wish you could see this ocean. It looks so calm and peaceful. There are a couple of ships going by with their balloon barrage trailing along behind. Except for them and the barbed wire I wouldn't believe I was in a war zone. This is about the first chance I have had to read anything and I have a book of poetry and *Crime & Punishment* with me. You must think we take a lot of vacations but you really have to get away to relax at all and you have no idea what two days by myself do for me.

Love,
Binni

September 30, 1943

Dear Mother & Dad,

Have just received your letter, Mother, enclosing the announcement of Ibby's baby. Wouldn't it be funny if Roger ended up here? I don't know what kind of planes he flies.

I am receiving congratulations today as the rabbit named after me has just had babies. The sign on her cage says "Mrs. Feitcher." You can see that people have troubles with my name.

I am enclosing a copy of a letter that Col. Gerhart wrote about us. Isn't it nice? I also enclosed a newspaper clipping, but censorship doesn't allow us to comment on them.

I am learning an amazing new vocabulary over here, most of which is unprintable of course. After five missions the gunners get a Flying Medal, which they call the "Spam Medal." You know how much spam they get over here—every meal so they say. Spam fixed so it doesn't look like Spam they call "Educated Spam."

We are now in bed at last. I wish you could see the cats. We now have five, four black adolescent ones and the tiny tiger tomcat, "Lucky." Two of them Ogden and Mickey live in the club and are wonderful mousers. Janie sleeps with Joyce and Lt. Clark and Lucky with us in a wooden box under my bed. Lt. Clark is very sensitive and quiet and Lucky tortures her all the time, he crouches on the bed and jumps on her back as she walks underneath. Did I tell you that Lt. Clark was kidnapped and we

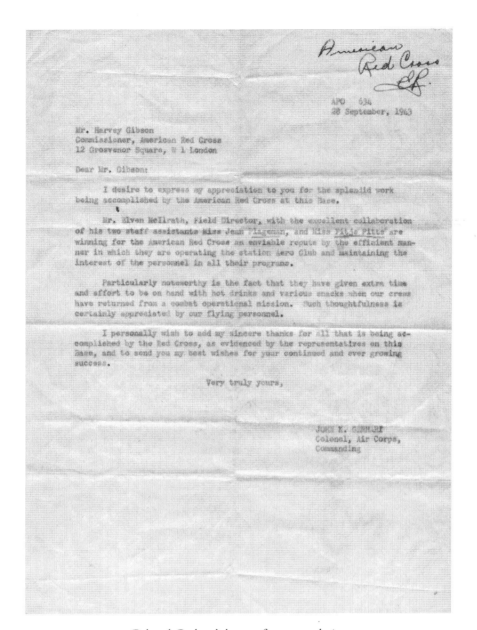

Colonel Gerhart's letter of commendation

had to give ten shillings to get her back? Lucky is now terribly busy pulling all our clothes off the chair. He woke us up this morning dragging a shoe around the room. He's just like a puppy he's so full of life. The gunners want to take him on a mission but since the temperature up there goes down to forty degrees below zero I'm afraid we'd have a frozen cat, as he has no heated suit to wear.

Nothing much new has happened around here. We fired one cook who immediately ran away with one of the soldiers who had an eight-day furlough. Saturday night we went to the officer's dance and I had a corsage of roses brought all the way from London by Capt. Abbot who took me. After the dance we came back to the club and had cheese sandwiches. Our telephone is probably the best addition and we talk over it by the hour.

Jean has the strangest dreams. Practically every night she dreams there is someone in the room and I wake up hearing her saying, "Who are you? What do you want?" Last night she said "Oh Fitje, there are three men in black uniforms here." We have to turn the light on and be sure no one is around. It' weird and makes shivers run up and down my back.

I wish I could describe some of the men to you. Freddy, for example, a very young, very nervous little gunner who borrows Jean's St Christopher Medal every time he goes on a mission, and Ralph*, a bottom turret gunner who is terrified that everyone will bail out and forget to tell him as he can't see what is going on. Lucky is a gunner who has had two brothers killed in the war and thinks it is quite a paradox that two years ago he was teaching Sunday school. Ralph and Scottie, who have been together in twenty-four different outfits and are now top and bottom turret gunner on the same plane, arrange it so one never goes without the other. Cyclone is a tail gunner who is growing a beard so his face won't freeze. The ground crews are wonderful too. Tonight Red, who works in the commissary brought us a chicken, which we had roasted in the club and Jean, Red, another boy and I ate the whole thing.

Mother, if you can't get the Belle Sharmeer stockings get any not more than thirty inches long. Will you send all you can, as we want them for Xmas presents for the staff? Could you send some cheese-cloth with them? We need it for coffee bags and can't get it without coupons. The coffee bags we are using are made of a costume that Joanie, one of the sandwich makers, wore when she was an angel in a Christmas play. We need about fifteen yards.

The weather is getting colder and I am wearing flannel shirts under my summer uniform. The trees are starting to turn and we are using an enormous amount of coal trying to keep the fires lit. It certainly goes fast and it seems to me we are always running out and have to steal it from the offer's mess.

Yes I do know the people who censored my mail. As far as I know it is not being censored on the base anymore as we were told it was O.K. for us to censor our own.

I spent the afternoon with one of the gunners taking all the empty boxes back to the stores they came from. I guess I told you that all empties have to be returned. These nights around payday are a little quieter in the club s everyone is playing blackjack in the barracks.

October 3, 1943

I thought this letter would be mailed before this but since it isn't, will add a few more lines.

Yesterday Jean and I went to a tiny town about four miles away to interview a cook who we hired on the spot. We went by short cut over a terrible, pretty, narrow country road. About a quarter mile off the road there is a tiny old church, which we had wanted to see so we drove up there on the way home. The vicar's wife was just walking out the gate so we asked her about the church and talked to her for a while. She told us she had two Land Army girls billeted with her. Last night she sent the girls up to ask us for tea so we are going there this afternoon. They are terribly nice, both from Yorkshire and they both work on a nearby dairy farm.

* Ralph died ten days after Fitje wrote this letter when his plane was shot down over Marienburg, Germany.

When we got back to the base we told our staff about the new cook and in two minutes had heard enough about her character so that I'm surprised she's not in jail. I guess she won't last long but we'll try her out and see what the men say about her. If there is anything really wrong with her the men will let us know before she has been here for an hour. They certainly know all about everyone for miles around.

This morning Jean, Lt. Brinkley, Major Russell, Sgt. Henley and myself went to get our weekly supply of apples and blackberries in the truck. Our apple-man has never talked to Americans before and thinks we're all crazy I'm sure. He could hardly wait to get rid of us this morning and said we'd wake the whole neighborhood up. Major R. and Sgt. Henley thought it was great sport to swing me in one of the tubs we put the apples in until I was so dizzy I couldn't stand on my feet.

We are now drying onions and parsley to use during the winter and having new stoves put in all the rooms, which we hope to be able to burn coke in it, as coal is scarce.

Our staff brings us fall flowers and they look lovely in the club. We certainly have a faithful staff. Mrs. Shepard worked sixty-eight hours last week and made 1000 cookies in one morning before 12:00. One of the boys worked from 7:30 in the morning until 11:00 at night yesterday. We tried to send him home but her wouldn't go.

It is Capt. Hopkinson who knows Mopsy Richardson and that group.

Must get this in the mail tonight.

Much love
Binni

October 10, 1943

Dear Jane,

Thanks for your letter. I haven't written the family for quite a while we have been so busy so maybe you'd better forward this to them when you finish. Your remarks about me getting laughs out of this war and you being glad everyone was so happy about everything certainly did sound like sour grapes and knowing you, I can bet it was. We certainly do get plenty of laughs. We do our best to because that's what our job is after all. But plenty happens that we don't laugh about and you have only to read the papers to get a general idea. As for being happy about everything, I have never been so happy in my life, but only because I'm doing something that I think is worth doing. The funny things that happen are all I can ever think of to write about, as most of them don't seem to be censorable.

Every Sunday, we have to go about eight miles to pick up our blackberries and apples for the week so we decided yesterday we might as well have a picnic. Major Russell, Major Alexander, Lt. Brickley, Sgt. Henley, Sgt. Thomas, Jean, Joyce and myself all went in our tiny truck with all our picnic equipment plus kettles for the fruit and had a wonderful time. It was a beautiful day and we played terribly active games so I can scarcely move a muscle now. All the local people gathered and peeked through the hedge at us and probably thought "those crazy Americans" as we seem to be the only people who make any noise over here.

It is getting really cold over here new, but we are trying very hard not to light the fires in the club until after Nov. 1 to save coal. Poor Jean has had a cold practically ever since we got here but I really like the weather and the cold doesn't bother me at all. I guess because it's a lot like Providence is really.

October 14, 1943

I am now in Felixstowe for a couple of days' vacation. You must think we go away a lot but it is only because you don't get any time off except while you're asleep on the post and about once every three weeks we try to go away for a couple of days. I seem to have discovered the quietest and most deserted place in all of England. It is lovely down here today—nice and warm and sunny.

About a month or so ago a woman reporter came out to the base for a couple of days and stayed with us. She wrote an article about us and the club, which appeared in the *Miami Daily Herald*, dated Sept. 6th.* One of Mac's relative sent us half the article but not all of it. Why don't you write for it?

We have a dance in our club every other Thurs. night at which we serve lemonade and for which we get ice from the officer's club. Jean always goes to get the ice around 5:30 and never gets back until the dance is about to begin—and then staggering. Well last Thursday I decided I'd better go with her so we both went. When we got there, there was no ice but lots of officers around who kept buying us drinks and we just couldn't get away. Finally we both staggered home after the first girls had arrived, and the staff though it was a scream when they found out we hadn't even gotten the ice. Next time Beatrice says she is going. This is the most peculiar place. Everyone is perfectly normal for a while and then for no reason at all everyone celebrates anything at all on the same night.

I wish you could see some of the things we have cooked in our kitchen at night. Now that the hunting season is open the men hunt a lot. They bring pheasant, rabbit, partridge, etc., into the club to be cooked and are they good! We are often to the feast. They say eggs are scarce in the ETO but not a night goes by that we don't cook quite a few that the boys bring in. Some of the boys have a ferret, Jeannie, that they hunt rabbits with and they have been known to get as many as fifteen in one night. They promised to take us someday soon.

I wish you could see the exhibit we are having now of the plexi glass and other types of jewelry and ornaments the men make. Some of the things are really wonderful. I have a collection of my own now of things they have made for me like a plexi glass ring, a nifty cigarette lighter made of a belt and two half-crowns and a bracelet made of tupences, etc. It is really wonderful what they can do. Someday we are going to get a photographer to take some pictures around the club as it really is beginning to look nifty now. On the 23rd we are having a huge big celebration, as it is the anniversary of the 95th. There is going to be an enlisted man's dance and an officer's dance on the base and it ought to be quite a night.

---

* The article, *Miss Avery Is Guest Of Two Americans* was written by Marjorie Avery and appeared in her regular column, *War Correspondent*.

Never mind sending this to Dad and Mother, as I will get around to writing now that I am going away. Give my love to Pat and E. May and everyone. I have just reread Mother's last letter written on Sept. 24th and which I just received yesterday. Mail is much slower now I guess because of the Christmas mail. Anyway I see by the letter that you are probably home now and I will be anxious to hear from you what you are doing. I almost made myself homesick the other night when I was showing Major R. the little book of pictures of the family that you gave me and telling him the last time I saw you all. He was highly amused! I have quite a few more pictures of the staff and of me serving coffee in the briefing room, which I will send as soon as I can get someone to censor them.

It is sad about Stephen D. However in the last three months that we have been here people have turned up that we never expected to see again and we hear some amazing tales so you never can tell.

Do you hear from Johnny often? I am so glad he isn't with colored troops any longer. Write me about Franny, Bobby and Rose, as I haven't heard a word about them. Is Charlie still around?

Just to show you how secluded this spot is, it is quite a hide out for Am. officers and their English girlfriends —there are about three here now. Remind me to ask Dad when I get home what he did during the last war, now that I have seen the way everyone behaves. I haven't one illusion left.

I haven't seen Kenny yet but got a letter from him and will see him if I ever get to London again.

Tell Mother and Dad that I just finished writing Mrs. Gage

We are in some suspense at the present as on Wednesday a new Red Cross girl arrived on our base with no word of instruction either to her or to us and we don't know whether she is here for training or whether one of us is about to be moved. I may be writing from China next for all I know. We think that probably she is here for a couple of weeks to see how it runs before she is sent to open a club of her own. Well time will tell.

Well I am going to write to Mrs. Gage and Brian's wife while I am here so will stop now.

October 15, 1943

I might as well add a little more to this letter in the fifteen minutes before lunch. It is a rainy day here and much like a northeast storm at home. I really hate to leave but am also anxious to get back to the base and see what has happened in my absence.

Joyce's cousin who lives down here is a WREN and one of the crew as a small boat manned entirely by WRENs. Doesn't that sound like fun? Do you know that here with practically no gas used by private individuals, they are allowed to have gas to go pheasant hunting? They say the pheasants become a nuisance it they're not kept down. I don't think they have to worry with the Americans here.

I am going to make you terribly jealous with all your cleaning problems, etc. One of the boys on the base cleans our uniforms for us beautifully in twenty-four hours. Another boy has a girl whose father is a shoemaker and he does our shoes in about two hours. (Ordinarily it takes two weeks.) All I have to do is talk Major R. into giving the boys a pass to take the shoes.

October 16, 1943

Got back to find letters from Jane, Mother and Tim. I suppose mail is very slow because of Christmas packages and letters. Christmas packages are already arriving here. Some of the squadrons give us packages of candy, cigs, etc., which arrive from the U.S. for boys who are missing. We give the stuff out in the club. Lately some has been coming in Christmas wrapping. Honestly it's terrible to see the stuff families send— what a waste of valuable space, as we can get all that here or most of it. And the quantities—we almost always have some on hand. I hope Roger doesn't come here. I would hate to have to "sweat him out" too.

Now Mother, don't worry when you don't hear. Naturally the mail will be slow around Christmas. I am fine and you would hear soon enough if I wasn't.

My love to all
Binnie

October 21, 1943

Dear Mother & Dad,

The rain is coming down in sheets right now and I left my raincoat at the club last night so I guess I'll have to stay here until it stops.

Jean has been London for the past few days and came back last night bringing lots of Christmas decorations for the club. It seems a little early to order those things but we wanted to get them while were still some around.

Things have been very busy lately. We got some paint the other day (you can only buy three colors here now—war paint—dark green, brown and black) and I have been painting large round boxes that powdered milk comes in to use them for scrap baskets. I also stained a nifty wooden bench we have for the food room—yesterday the boiler broke and the headcounter girl got appendicitis so we have been busy. Today Mrs. Shepherd, our wonderful cook is taking three days off to go to London. She says perfectly seriously that her mother hasn't written her for weeks and she thinks maybe she's dead and she's going to find out. Enclosed is a picture of Mrs. Shepherd. Her husband was wounded in the last war and she has supported her family ever since. She can make 1000 cookies in the morning and she chases the men out of the kitchen with a long wooden spoon.

Mrs. Shepherd, cook at the Red
Cross Aero Club, 95th Bomb Group

She won't even let us touch the food. Her daughter, Joanie, aged sixteen works for us too and her other daughter, Winnie, did until the labor board took her away. In the background are the windows of the Snack Bar and the wall. You will see me the bar.

Every morning now, when the "salvage experts" come they bring Janie and Lt. Clark each a live mouse. I wish you could have seen the confusion this morning. They keep the mice in a bottle and the cats almost went mad trying to get them.

We are having a big celebration at the club Sat. night, as it is the first anniversary of the 95th. Much to our horror we discovered that we sent out the invitation for the 24th instead of the 23rd so now we have to call everyone up and straighten it out. We have a nifty hillbilly orchestra that plays in the snack bar in the evenings now consisting of about five people and getting larger all the time.

October 22, 1943

Yesterday was Jean's birthday and we had a wonderful party in the evening in Lt. Brickley's Special service office. The five of us, and Lt. Brickley, Major Russell and about five other officers came. Brick had the office all decorated with toilet paper with "Happy Birthday Jean" written all over it. Mrs. Upton made her a delicious cake. After the party got well under way Major R. sent for the photographer of the base and he took pictures of the group. I'm sort of scared to see them.

The Salvage Experts just came in and a dirty hand reached in our window and handed us a calling card.

October 23, 1943

Well, today the weather is beautiful so I plan to go out in the courtyard and do some painting. Jean and I slept until 12:15 this morning without even moving. We sure were tired. Yesterday was the first anniversary of the 95th. Friday night the officers had their celebration and we went after the club closed. Got to bed at 5:30 and got up bright and early the next morning to decorate our club. It really looked nifty when we finished. We had an orange, blue and red pennants (made of mattress covers with 95th Bomber Group stenciled on some and 8th Army Air Force on others) hanging from the beams on the side of the room. We went and got a truck full of ivy, hawthorn berries and hay and autumn leaves and made great bunches of leaves which we put all around the 1216 coffee tins. We made streamers of ivy and red berries to hang from the pillars around the snack bar and had a huge sign saying Happy Birthday over the snack bar. Jean got three huge orange, yellow and red paper balloons in London, which we hung from the ceiling and we had blue practice bombs with 95th Bomber Group painted on them around. The boys did all the painted decorations and helped us put them up or rather we helped them. All day while about fifteen of us were doing that ten boys were putting in the new stoves and the hot water boiler broke so we have no hot water and Lord knows when we ever will again.

The mess baked a huge cake for us with beautiful decoration and a candle at 9:00 we invited the

Celebrating the 95th Bomb Group's birthday

staff officers over and Col. Gerhart spoke and selected two of the gunners and a WAAC to cut the cake. All the other workers of the staff made a short speech and there was much yelling and clapping.

We had about one hundred forty girls including fifteen WAACS and crowds of men and it really was a big success. One boy had just been married a few days before to an American girl living in England so we got there up in front of the microphone and gave them a carton of cigarettes and a carton of gum. Our staff is so wonderful. Most of the day-staff insisted on staying for the evening and helping us. After everything was over Jean and I stayed in the club celebrating with more of the gunners, one of whom has finished thirty missions (he volunteered for five extra) and is going home and another of whom had finished and been transferred and came back to the base for the dance.

We have also had reason to celebrate this week as one of the officers we liked a great deal who had been missing in action for a couple of months has returned and is back on the base for a few days before he goes home. Jean and I feel as if we had been with this group for a long time we have seen so many people come and go.

Last week I was away for a couple of nights and it was terribly exciting for a while both nights. Although I have heard the ack-ack guns often, never quite so close. These sounded right in my room and were very near. At one time the sky lit up where a plane went down in flames in the sea.

Jean and I spent the afternoon at the special service office organizing our program for the week. Tonight we have a Hillbilly orchestra and tomorrow night Bingo (very popular with eggs for prizes, fried in the club.) Father Nolan always comes and leaves it although he says he joined the Army to get away from it. We are getting so we have something every night. Lt. Brickley, Sgt. Healey and Pvt. Keyser (special services) are wonderful and run all the things we think of.

Someone gave me a chicken today so Mac plucked it and cleaned it and I stuffed it and it is now roasting. I am getting to be quite a good cook on a coal stove, although it is difficult with the staff and everyone looking on.

Am wondering where Roger is. Steve Stone knows him too.

Happy Birthday Johnny.

Love to all.

Fitje

October 29, 1943

Dear Mother and Dad,

While I am waiting for the fire to start burning so we can dry out the sheets before we put them on the bed I will try to get a few words on paper. The weather is very damp and foggy and we are told that will stay this way until December.

Today we went to an old cider mill to try and get some cider for Halloween. It was fascinating. The mill was built in 1728 and the apples are still crushed in a huge stone thing, round and about fifteen feet across with a horse hitched to a wheel that walks around in a circle moving the wheel around. The house where the people live who run the mill, is a lovely long, low house with a moat around it. They can make very little cider because of the sugar shortage so we couldn't get any, but they gave us a drink of hard cider and it was good. On the way home we picked many branches and autumn leaves for the club. Roses are still blooming over here and every day one of the staff brings some to us. Tonight, Barbara, one of the coffee makers, brought us a pheasant, which her mother stuffed for us and it is now sizzling in the oven.

Last night the seventeen workers of the orchestra had a party to which they invited us so we invited them to do the cooking in the club and use the staff room to eat it in. They had nine chickens to fry and about ten cooks doing it. What confusion and what a feast. We also had tomatoes, French fried potatoes and apple pie.

I don't think we'll ever have tap water again. The boiler has been welded three times and still is no good. We have been told that if we're lucky we may have a new one in two weeks away or so. In the meantime we are getting awfully dirty. No bath for a week! We are also having stove trouble, as the little stoves in the club are no good, and also burn coal instead of coke and we can hardly have enough coal for the ovens and certainly not enough for the stoves. We are now having new stoves put in but the pipes don't fit the old pipes so we are having no end of difficulty. I am confident that American ingenuity will figure out a way, however.

October 30, 1943

This morning we succeeded in getting forty-five gallons of cider in wooden kegs for the club. That is all we're going to have to celebrate Halloween. We're mad at our boys because they had a big brawl in the club the other night and we had to close a half hour early, because they wouldn't stop. There is now a beer parlor on the base, which closes at 10:00. Then they come to our place. Apparently the fight started there and was carried on in the club. Every time we'd get it calmed down some drunk would say "I can take on anyone here" and of course it would start all over again.

Got a Christmas package from Ann and Hermie, which I am trying not to open. Will write them immediately.

We fired one of our kitchen boys Lenny because he didn't do anything and have hired another fifteen year old, Ronny Norman. I wish Johnny could see all the boys—they really work hard for eighteen hours a day—keep the fires going, chop the wood and carry coal, clean the entries and lavatories and keep the outside of the building clean, run errands etc., more in a day than John has done in his life.

Is Jane home yet? What is she planning to do?

Love to all,
Binni

November 1, 1943

Dear Mother and Dad,

Well the sad thing has happened for which we have been waiting—I am to be transferred to open a new club as <u>Director</u>. You know how sentimental I am and I can hardly bear it when I think of leaving but then I suppose I will be just as fond of some other place in a little while. The worst part is leaving Jean and Mac, as I know I will never again be so fortunate as to be with two such nice people.

Jean and I had planned to go to Nottingham for three days and we are going tomorrow, then I will go to London to see what's what. I am going to ask for ten days vacation before I go anywhere else, as having opened one I know what a job it is. I got a letter from Brian's wife today asking me to come down there so I guess I will for a few days.

To make everything worse I am in bed with a cold but don't worry only a little one and am having excellent care surrounded by medicine and sympathetic visitors. When Jean told me the news we were terribly upset and then all of the sudden we thought of Lt. Clark and which one of us could take her and got simply hysterical over it. Jean told Beatrice to get the meat cleaver sharpened as we were going to cut Lt. Clark in half. I guess she'll stay with Jean, as Jean really likes her the best.

Major R. is coming down tonight with a bottle of rum and as Jean says it will be just like an Irish wake. Oh well, I get kind of excited when I think of doing it all myself because although I've worked as hard as Jean she has had the worry and responsibility being the boss and has had to cope with things like one of our fifteen year old girls being raped on her way home one night and three of the staff saying they were going to resign because we hired someone they considered not as good as they were. The caste system in England amazes me. Last night the truck taking the girls home hit a boy on a bicycle and hurt him quite badly. Well, never a dull moment.

Enclosed is a picture of the cake cutting at our party last week if I can get Major R. to censor it when he gets here. From right to left: Sgt. Fitzgibbons, gunner, Col. Gerhart, C.O., visiting RC girl and WAC, Sgt. Steele, gunner, Col. McKnight, etc.

I will try to write more often until after Christmas as I know the mail is slow due to the rush. I get all mixed up trying to remember the number of my letters but you know that I will write every week usually on Sunday or Monday so you can tell whether you are getting them all.

I will let you know my new address when I know it but in the meantime my mail will be forwarded from here and chances are I will only be a few miles away anyway.

Love
Fitje

November 3, 1943

Dear Ann & Hermie,

A few days ago your Christmas package arrived and I have locked it up in the supplies closet so will be sure not to open it until Christmas. Thank you so much. I hope you will all excuse me for not sending anything but really there is nothing around to buy without coupons and it seems so silly to send some stupid thing just to give you something.

Christmas seems so near now and I am terribly disappointed at being transferred right now as Jean and I had already ordered three Christmas trees and started collecting decorations for them. I almost decided to say that I'd rather stay where I was than have the added responsibility of being a director but actually, of course, it's very exciting and I couldn't turn it down.

Well, if I'd ever dreamed a year ago at this time that I'd be sitting in a hotel room in Nottingham, England, with three other girls, I don't know, I suppose that's what makes life interesting.

Jean and I traveled all day yesterday to get here and were terribly discouraged when we arrived as we expected it to be a very quiet little village with Sherwood Forest on the outskirts. Instead it's a large and dirty city with nothing in it but a castle restored in 1878, which we felt was hardly worth looking at. We came here because it was north of a meeting place with two friends of ours. One Mary Lincoln Denison, whom Jane knows, went to Julian's wedding in Bristol, said it was very sad and gloomy. Tell Jane his wife is very attractive, poised, worldly, strange and exotic looking. Maybe she'll like his blue suits. She's about ten years older than he is and Lucky thinks he's sort of lost in the army.

Today, being bored with Nottingham, we took several trains and finally ended up in Southwell, "a quiet little place" (according to *Baedeker's Great Briton*, which has become my bible along with *Suffolk Scene* by Julian Tennyson) where we saw a beautiful cathedral dating from Norman times and had tea at the Saracen's Head where Charles I surrendered to the Scottish Commissioners in 1646.

When are you going to send me your brother's addresses Ann? I see lots of Canadians around and maybe they are very near me. There are two kinds of American officers in the ETO, the kind that mention their wife in the first sentence they say to you and the kind who never mentions her no matter how involved you get. Well, it just takes some experience to learn a lesson.

Tomorrow we go back to the base and Friday to London to learn my new fate. I pray that it will be an operational base and chances are it will be.

Show this letter to Mother and Dad as I never will be able to write about Nottingham again and thanks again for the package and your letter, Hermie.

Much love
Fitje

◇

November 5, 1943

Dear Mother & Dad,

Well London again. I certainly have travelled around in the last few days. Yesterday I travelled from 11:35 until 8:00 in the evening getting back to base, not that we had so far to go, but we are in such an out of the way spot that we spend hours changing trains and waiting on platforms. Of course we forgot that you can't get anything to eat now on English trains and we talked so much about how hungry we were that another lady in the compartment opened her bag and insisted that we eat some sandwiches she had. We were terribly embarrassed but we ate them. I love these English trains. They poke along so slowly and give you a chance to look at the scenery. Of course they stop at every little village.

Nothing special seems to have happened during our absence except still no hot water and due to nearby occurrences all water, electricity and telephoning very scarce for the time being. Major R. came down at 11:00 with some rum and we sat around until 3:00 trying to make up my mind, as Mac and Major Russell seem to think that if I want to stay with the 95th it could be arranged through channels.

I know from previous experience though that I will probably never be sorry if I go and if I don't I will always wonder what I missed. I'm sure it's not wise to interfere with fate and it's certainly stupid to refuse a promotion isn't it? I'm sure Mac thinks I'm right to go. He's so nice I hate to leave him.

Up bright and early at 7:00 and almost missed the 10:44 train to London but somehow got here. It is so packed here that it is practically impossible to find a place to stay but finally got a room at the Brown's Hotel on Dover Street through someone who knew the manager.

Finally I got to see Mr. Buford who flattered me a good deal about the good work we had done with our club and said I had been picked for this important assignment because it was at Wing Hdqrs. and much of it has to do with getting along with all the stuffy old officers, all of which did not make me feel particularly elated as that's the kind of a man he is. When I told him I wanted a week's vacation he almost fainted but in the end gave me two days more than a week.

The air raid sirens are now blowing. I always seem to be alone when this happens.

Anyway, I think I'll stay around here for a couple of days and see a few people and then maybe go down to Palegate and see Brian's wife and maybe on the Bournemouth before I go back to the base to collect my things. One thing about the new base, it's not far from the old one and a truck goes back and forth almost every day. Also there will be no need for recreation in the club.

My new address is:

American Red Cross
AAF Station 358
APO 638
C/O PM, NYC

Have just had a nifty dinner of lobster and am trying to put a call thru to Jean telling her what my plans are. I will never get her, though, telephoning is so impossible and she will wonder what has become of me as she expects me back tomorrow. Next I am going to take my first bath in two weeks. I have been thinking about it all day. It is so nice to be all by myself for a change. I think I could spend a week sitting in this room.

Later

Haven't yet gotten near enough an APO post office to mail this so I might as well add some more.

Just to show you how much damper on the base it is than here—I can't write on both sides of this letter paper because the writing goes right through.

When I read this letter over I can see that you probably won't know what I'm talking about if you aren't getting the letters in the right sequence.

Anyway in the beginning I refer to coming back from Nottingham where Jean and I went on a three-day pass. Just before we left I was notified to go to London to see about being transferred.

Yesterday I had lunch with Kathleen Kennedy and saw Mildred Eberle in the afternoon. Mildred looks fine and seems to be enjoying herself. She and Kathleen are both in the same club.

Today I got up bright and early and walked down to St. James St. and through St. James Park to Westminster Abby to the 11:30 service. It was very impressive. Afterwards I walked across Westminster Bridge to get a better look at Big Ben and the Houses of Parliament. When you see the tremendous amount of destruction around it seems amazing that those places are almost undamaged. Today is beautiful and sunny, something that we haven't had for quite a while.

I telegraphed Brian's wife yesterday and got an answer a few hours later saying to come down to Eastbourne and am going there tomorrow morning for a couple of days and then back to the base to collect my stuff.

Jean must think I've gone to Italy, as I still haven't been able to reach her. Telegrams are no good, as they seem to send them by mail to an APO address.

Much love,
Fitje

November 11, 1943

Dear Mother & Dad,

Am trying to write you more frequently as you don't seem to be getting my letters due to the Xmas rush. I do write though and don't worry I am fine and happy. Please don't think of cabling unless important and then you can do it quicker through the ARC (Mrs. Calef) in Providence. As it takes cables practically as long as letters to get here and I'm sure the cabling dept. is much too busy for cables from worried parents.

Am now back on the base collecting my stuff and saying prolonged goodbyes as I'm still on vacation and don't go to the new base until Sat. If the weather is O.K., I am going to be flown over. The girl who is to take my place arrived this afternoon and is very nice thank goodness.

When I got down to Eastbourne to visit Jill Greeves I found that her grandfather had just died and her mother, Mrs. Ware, was staying at the Chalk Inn in Eastbourne with her grandmother, Mrs. Hinds. They were terribly nice and I had a very good time climbing around the South Downs with Jill and her dog and seeing the countryside. Jill was most concerned about Brian's contact lenses and I couldn't remember whether or not he had them when I last saw him. Maybe Jane remembers. Jill is crazy for a job in my new club so I may hire her as storekeeper or librarian after I see what the set-up is. She seems perfect for Brian and refers to him as "nice old Brian." She is only nineteen and very attractive, sort of Franny's type.

The inn was very nice. Filled with old people and drank tea until I thought I'd die. Just before we went to bed we'd go have tea in Mrs. Hinds room and one night we had an air raid and everyone said, "Oh goody, more tea" so we all gathered down stairs and drank tea until it was over. A plane was shot down about a mile and a half away and we went to see it the next day.

I got back to the base at the same time the new boiler arrived and we now have hot water again for the first time in three weeks. Believe me it has been no joke getting several thousand dishes washed with no hot water. It seems luxurious to have it.

I have spent all day copying the menus Jean and I have collected so I can have the same good food at my new club.

Your letter dated Oct. 10th with lots of news in it has arrived, Mother, also the one pair of stockings, which are perfect. I hear from Andrew and Tim regularly. Andrew is now a major and Tim is finishing his basic training and hoping to go to O.C.S. I never write to either of them so wonder why they bother. I never seem to have time to write anyone but you. Thank Ibby for her nice Christmas card.

Since we got our new stove it is so hot in our room that I can hardly stand it so guess I'll go over to the club and cool off.

You had better start referring to me as 'Fitje' as I am going to insist on it when I get home. No one has called me Binni since I left home last Feb.[*]

Much love to all
Binnie

---

[*] Fitje's childhood nickname was Binni. When she got to Europe she decided she'd rather be call by her given name, which resulted in a number of funny stories about men who had trouble pronouncing Fitje.

CHAPTER 6

Bomber Command

November 17, 1943–May 17, 1944

Fitje wrote her parents on November 1, 1943 telling them she was being transferred to another base and promoted to director of a new Red Cross Aero Club. She hated to leave the 95th and in subsequent letters mentions debating whether to refuse the transfer and stay in Horham. Realizing that the Red Cross needed her experience and expertise elsewhere, she moved on.

On November 13th Fitje transferred to IX Bomber Command at Marks Hall, a large estate between Earls Colne and Coggeshall in Essex. Four days later she wrote her sister Jane saying, "I came over here with great regret and an awful hangover on Saturday having celebrating until 4:00 the night before. Now that I'm here, of course, I like it a lot as I knew I would."

The mansion at Marks Hall was a huge brick Jacobean manor home built in 1609. In 1941 the British government requisitioned part of the estate in order to build Earls Colne Airfield. On October 16, 1943 Marks Hall became headquarters of IX Bomber Command under the command of Major General Samuel E. Anderson.

IX Bomber Command was one of four separate commands under the umbrella of the 9th Air Force. As a command unit it was non-operational, but commanded three Combat Bomb Wings. Only the 323rd Bomb Group, part of the 97th Combat Bomb Wing, flew from Earls Colne Airfield.

Once there, Fitje and her assistant, Martha Brush, from Zanesville Ohio, set about building a club. They opened on November 29th, sixteen days after they arrived. The club was smaller than the one at the 95th, but still required her to hire a staff and find whatever materials they needed to run a successful club.

Fitje's letters show that because this was not an operational base it was less stressful than what she experienced at the 95th. She no longer "sweated out" missions or met the planes at the field when they returned. Easier, however, did not mean it was without danger. On our trip to England in 1997, we visited Mark Hall. Although the manor home no longer exists, and the area built up since she was

Martha Brush, Fitje's
assistant at Marks Hall

last there in 1944, she provided a running commentary of her time with IX Bomber Command. As we walked, she paused and stared into a ditch at the side of the dusty lane. I asked what she was looking at. "I remembered the time I was watching a lone German bomber fly over the base," she said. "Just as the bomb bay doors opened, and the bombs started to fall, I was tackled from behind and thrown into that same ditch by one of the GIs." She explained that she though the man had less than honorable intentions. "Did it ever occur to you he might have saved your life," I asked. "Oh for god sakes," she responded in a tone one might reserve for a fool. "They were only little bombs, you know."

Her letters from IX Bomber Command reflect a different tone than the letters she wrote four and a half months earlier when she and Jean opened the club at Horham. No longer is she struggling to learn new skills, she is now a confident manager and leader. In a letter dated Thanksgiving 1943 she wrote: "I can see mother thinking there must be someone else around to do the advising and most of the work but there isn't and I am amazed to find that it can be done by <u>me</u>. I have learned more in five months over here than I would have in 100 years at home, I'm sure."

November 17, 1943

Dear Jane,

Your package arrived the other day and of course I won't open it until Christmas if I can resist but thank you so much for it. I hope you all will excuse me for not sending anything this year.

I came over here with great regret and an awful hangover on Saturday having celebrating until 4:00 the night before. Now that I'm here, of course, I like it a lot as I knew I would.

The set up couldn't be more different than the 95th. Much smaller, of course and being a headquarters, much rank. We were made to feel very welcome and everyone couldn't be nicer to us. My assistant, Martha Brush, is very nice and as there isn't even a RC field director on the base we really are on our own. We started today looking over our equipment, chiseling things from utilities and the quartermaster and visiting the labor board and the ministry of food in nearby towns. As before we are off in the country without many nearby sources of supply.

The club is very small so we won't need such as big staff. We now figure about fifteen. At present we are living with the three WAC officers on the base but we are going to have our own building for quarters as soon as some officers move out.

The officer's mess and club are one and the same, which makes it difficult as everyone goes to the bar before dinner. But never fear I have and will continue to restrain myself.

There is a very nice friend of Hermie's on the base, Roger Williams, who went to Deerfield with Hermie and who Hermie helped to draft. He is now a Lt. in Public Relations. I am going to some British officer's club with him to a dance tonight, and having a pheasant dinner with him tomorrow night as he recently shot a lot of pheasant.

It is sort of nice to be able to go to bed early for a change instead of sitting around talking to the boys all the time and also it's about the only warm place as winter has really set in and the club is freezing with no fires in it as yet. We are both too lazy to light our stove when we get home at night and of course there is no such thing as a fire in the bathroom so taking a bath is very discouraging and I am getting very dirty again.

November 18, 1943

Spent the day moving dishes around and generally directing traffic. We had a closet turned into our office and our own telephone installed, and we were presented with two brand new bicycles, so we are feeling pretty good. The pheasant dinner turned out to be quail and was delicious.

Have gotten two letters from Johnny and will write him soon. He seems to be O.K. and sure seems to like his new outfit.

Don't let Mother worry because she doesn't hear from me. I am fine; in fact I've never been healthier and happier. Cables take sometimes two months to get here and often never arrive. Even the Red Cross is finding it much quicker to write.

What are you finding to do in Providence?

Thanks again for the Christmas present.

Much love to you and the family.

Fitje

November 21, 1943

Dear Mother & Dad,

We are beginning to get terribly busy again so I had better write when I get the chance. Tomorrow night we have eight volunteers who are coming to paint the club at 7:30 so I imagine we will all be up all night working on it, as we want to get it done as soon as possible.

This club is very different from the last one. It is in a Nissan hut, which you probably know is shaped like this when you look at it from view. I am sure they are colder than a cabin in Maine would be during the winter, as there are air spaces everywhere and we no longer even bother to open our windows at night. I have pocketed my pride and am now wearing heavy underwear, as is everyone else.

You naturally can't get any kindling wood in England to light fires with so Martha and I have been saving wooden boxes (from the PX stuff as English ones have to be returned) and chopping them up with the meat cleaver as we have no axe as yet. We go home at night with our little bundle of wood and newspaper under our arms so we can warm the room up a little before we go to bed. Newspaper is also very hard to get and we hang on to any little piece and even burn some of the posters, which the RC sends around. I do think that it's healthy though. Living in the cold gives you lots of energy and you should see the food we both eat.

After much looking around I have hired two cooks and three cleaning women and a man to look after the fires. As yet no one to work in the evenings though and as we are planning to open on Thanksgiving, we are getting a little panicky. We will open anyway and I guess Martha and I will have to do everything for a while with the help of any soldiers who will volunteer.

Friday night we were invited to the Col's quarters for a pleasant dinner; Martha and I with four colonels and two majors. It was almost tragic, as we had thought it was Sat. night and were hauled out of the dining room by the adjutant after we had already almost finished eating. Luckily, he was walking through and saw us or we never would have gotten there. We had to wait about two hours for latecomers during which time I managed to get hungry again and ate three helpings of pheasant. The COs here are terribly nice to us and we have only to ask for what we want.

Last night the officers had a dance which we went to and had a good time. I went to dinner again at the Colonel's and this time had American hot dogs. This afternoon the adjutant, Major Styes took us to the nearby operational Base to see all the planes. It is a medium bomber group.

I do like it here a lot but am still homesick for the fortresses and the excitement of living there. I don't feel as close to the war now. I am hoping that maybe I can go back in a couple of months when this club is running smoothly. Maybe by that time I won't want to, but I have a feeling that I will.

Have gotten two letters from Big John and just finished writing him one. Jean telephoned and said she was forwarding two packages to me, which I imagine are from you. I am hoping that she will get over here next week for a couple of days.

We are going to be right after dinner tonight in preparation for next week, which will probably be awful.

Much Love
Fitje

Thanksgiving 1943

Dear Family,

I thought of you about 5:00 this afternoon while I was bicycling back to the base after interviewing a perspective manageress, and imagined that you were about to sit down to dinner then. I wonder how many of you were able to be there. We had delicious turkey in the mess, also cranberry sauce and pumpkin pie. Had it not been for that I would have never known it was Thanksgiving as it was just like any other day around here.

I was telling Martha last night that there is no use telling you because you would never believe that I am hiring and running a staff of about twenty, ordering food for their meals as well as the hundreds of snacks for the boys, and keeping them all happy, I hope. I can see mother thinking there must be someone else around to do the advising and most of the work but there isn't and I am amazed to find that it can be done by <u>me</u>. I have learned more in five months over here than I would have in 100 years at home, I'm sure.

The staff that we have so far is wonderful: Mr. Shinn who keeps the fires going and cleans the courtyard and lavatories, Miss Evers and Mrs. Slee the cooks, and Mrs. Wharton, Mrs. Joslin and Mrs. Eagle the cleaning women. I have hired four evening staff but they won't come until Monday. We also have Miss Tolbert (Mamie) the accountant, Mrs. Warton, the manageress, and Mrs. Jay, the recorder but they don't start until tomorrow. We open Monday, slightly short of staff and with the painting unfinished but we will manage. We were awfully lucky to get Mrs. Watson. She is fifty-two and terribly nice and will be able to do a lot of the things like forms and ordering that Jean and I had to do ourselves at Horham. Our Labor Board is excellent and has done an awful lot to help us get staff. One girl is only seventeen, married three years and is getting divorced. The boys are already saying she has a "classy chassis" so we anticipate trouble. Our accountant is very strange. She arrived two days ago and wanted to go right home. She was afraid she wouldn't do the work and was homesick and was having trouble with her boyfriend and all sorts of horrid things. After much arguing she was finally driven to the station and on the way changed her mind and came back. She seems to be practically having a nervous breakdown and we probably should have sent her back but she is so queer that she sort of intrigues me and I want her to stay and see what happens to her.

We are still living a long way from the club but we walk up for breaking in the morning and drop in the guard House and an MP brings us home at night. The mud here is awful and I have to wear boots everywhere.

We are trying to get the inside of the club painted and it is being done gradually. Did I tell you about our lovely office which was made from a closet with a window in it? We had the shelves taken out, a stove put in, painted the upper wall yellow, and the bottom dark blue, (Martha painted the stairs blue but it wore off) painted two big cans blue for coal and a scrap basket, and painted some of the furniture blue. It looks lovely. We also managed to get two straw rugs for it.

We have had huge bookcases built in the library and shelves all around the kitchen and the dishes, pots and pans are all clean and ready for use. We are exhausted at the end of the day and go to bed around 8:00. I can hardly wait for the club to be open and running smoothly so we can have breakfast in bed again.

Much love to you all

Fitje

December 11, 1943

Dear Mother & Dad,

I seem to write less and less often now that my letters don't seem to reach you anyway. Don't worry though it is just because we are so busy still working from 8:00 in the morning until 12:00 at night, but I don't know why since we have such a good staff.

Just to prove it: I was worrying about Christmas for fear they would all want the day off. I went out in the kitchen and one of them said "Miss Pitts, what about Christmas?" I told them that the club would be opened, of course, and we would be very busy and we hoped they would all stay and they all said of course they'd all stay and they were so happy with us they wouldn't think of letting us down on Christmas. Our manageress is wonderful and we are very fortunate to have her. She is about fifty-two and a very superior person. I feel very silly telling her what I want done and being waited on by her. It is almost like having you here Mother, and we have to fight to keep her from doing things for us all the time. She runs club beautifully and I hardly have to think about the kitchen at all.

This is really a very cute club. The snack bar and servery are yellow and the lounge and hallway are blue. We have lots of flowers around and plants and we are now making Christmas decorations and collecting holly, which grows plentifully around here. Today we bought bunches of Chrysanthemums and violets.

Chuck Williams is now in our office and Martha is sewing the buttons on his shirt. He just brought up lots of New Yorkers and sends his best to Hermie. I am glad he is here as he will be able to back up some of the stories that I can't tell until I get home and that you probably won't believe without another witness. He has been telling me about a lovely place called Lavenham where I am going on my next pass: "So peaceful that when bombs drop there they don't go off."

My dress has come and I love it. It fits perfectly except for the length. Also thanks for the night-gowns, which are also nifty. Thanks so much for sending them—also a package from Pat and two from the Tilghman Pitts'. No stockings so far but I guess they'll come in time. The nightgowns are plenty warm enough, Mother.

We now have two cats, a big white one that really catches mice, named Grace, and a little black and white kitten, Milo (Major Vega). They are very cute.

Martha and I are in our room about to go to bed. I have on your lovely flowered nightgown and the kitten is crawling around under my covers. I got a letter from you tonight, Mother, dated Nov. 6th and enclosing Mrs. Brown's, John's, and Twinkie's letter. That makes me mad what the Journal correspondent said. We have no coupons and can buy nothing in the way of clothing; even handkerchiefs cost coupons. The clothes are awful except in some very, exclusive shops in London and those are pretty bad. Most are utility clothes and the materials are awful. You never see any of the things like tweeds and sweaters that England is famous for. The people have forty-eight clothing coupons a year and everything but hats are rationed, even table and bed linens, towels, etc. A dress costs seven or eleven coupons, coat eighteen, shoes seven, stockings three, etc. We give our old stockings with runs in them to our staff and they are very glad to get them. Lots of women don't wear stocking even now that the cold weather had come. Naturally you can't very well dress at that rate and if the English woman can look O.K. in four year-old clothes I think they are doing all right.

December 12, 1943

We had bacon Mrs. Norman brought us with her ration book for breakfast.

Martha and I are sitting in our office. Martha is sewing insignia on a blouse for Beggs, the general's driver who is complaining about his wife. Every month when he collects his pay he asks, "Is the old lady still alive?" and when naturally the answer is yes, he says, "Well, I'll sweat her out for another month."

There are three other boys in here, Chic and Mac, two gunners, and Kit Carson, from Georgia. All three were on a binge last night and woke us up throwing stones at our hut at 4:00 this morning. They are a scream. They are arranging for Martha and I to steal a record they want, which is in the officer's club, having just gipped us out of threepence on some Coca Cola they bought.

This is the conversation, word-by-word, going on between the four boys in our office. Not much intellect around here.

"When I get home from this war I'm going on the most glorified drunk."
"Me too. I'm going to bed with a bottle on each side."
"Not I, I'm just gong to have a bottle on one side!
(Laughs)
"Well you can still have a bottle on each side."
"That constitutes a bottleneck."
"Who wants to neck a bottle?"

Joan, our maid, just came in and said, "Miss Pitts how many do you want tea for?" The boys held their breath until I said six and then relaxed and Chic said, "I knew we'd sweat it out."

I wonder if you even know I've moved yet and I've been here for a month now. I think it's nifty about Ann. Imagine being an aunt when I get home.

Merry Christmas and love to you all.
Binni

December 13, 1943

Dear Family,

Your package arrived today and I opened it enough to see all the little packages inside. You were so nice to think of Jean, Mac, Miss Scrivener and the girls and I will deliver the packages to Jean as she is coming here on Friday. The rest look awfully interesting and I can hardly wait until Christmas to open them. Thank you all so much.

Everyone around here has had the flu including myself but a very light case as being a sensible girl, mother, I went to bed immediately and I am practically well already. I have never had such good care. Mrs. Warman hovers around all the time and brought me two lamb chops (the first I've had over here) with her ration book tonight and cooked them and fried tomatoes for my dinner. I have company any all day long and find it just as easy to run things from my bed in fact easier because everyone seems to work harder.

This afternoon two of the English officers on the base came in to ask me if they could have our garbage to feed a baby pig they had just bought. Naturally I am delighted to have someone take it away. They went out and inspected the garbage and came back to say they had decided to sell the pig and eat it themselves it looked so good!

We are bothered with mice here and two of the boys have been telling me how they deal with them in the huts. One way is to balance a ruler on a table edge with a pail of water under one end and a piece of cheese over it on the ruler. When the mouse runs out to get the cheese the ruler falls into the pail and the mouse drowns. They say, however, that the mice are getting too clever and now one sits on the end of the ruler while the other goes after the cheese.

We have wonderful Christmas plans. The boys wanted a Christmas party on Christmas day as they have invited fifty kids from the vicinity. We have been collecting candy in the club and at the PX and it is coming in by the ton. I am sure they will all be sick. Tomorrow I am going to sit in bed and sort it into fifty piles and wrap it in Christmas paper. We are going to get a movie for them and are trying to get the mess to make ice cream. One of the huts here collects candy every week from their rations and the boys take it every week for a hospital for children near here, many of whom have been injured in the air raids. They love doing it and talk about the kids all the time. I'm sure no one but Americans would do that, and I feel so proud of them. The boys here, on the whole, are a much more intelligent bunch and there are many college graduates particularly among the WACS. May Marsh (Cpt.), Col Lewis' secretary, was at Smith while I was there.

Chuck Williams and May Marsh have just been in to see me. Lt. Williams bringing the Sept. 25th New Yorker (the newest around here) and a story he wrote about an experience we shared which is confidential right now but he has promised to send me a copy, after the war. I laughed and laughed when I read it and have come to the horrible conclusion that almost everything has its humorous side.

This weekend I am going to London with Col. Lewis (Pappy) and Major Styles, the Executive C.O., to see Alfred and Lunt Fontaine, and have a good time. It will be my first vacation since I got here. Col. Lewis is terribly nice and takes a great interest in the club. The other night he came up and I spilled two bottles of coke and a cup of coffee on his pants, so I'm surprised that we're still friends.

There are terrible disturbances in the kitchen tonight. First Daphne, one of the kitchen help, fixed a tray of the tea for me at the same time that Mrs. Warman was fixing my dinner and Mrs. W. forbade her to bring it over because my dinner was almost ready. Daphne came over here crying, because she couldn't bring it. Then Mrs. Warman kicked Joyce's (kitchen help) boyfriend out of the kitchen and Joyce came over here simply furious and swearing like mad. Think of me having servant trouble.

One of the MPs has just brought in a chevron for me to sew on.

Goodbye and thanks again for all the packages.

Much Love,
Binni

December 21, 1943

Dear Family,

Well Christmas draws near and I wish you could see our office.

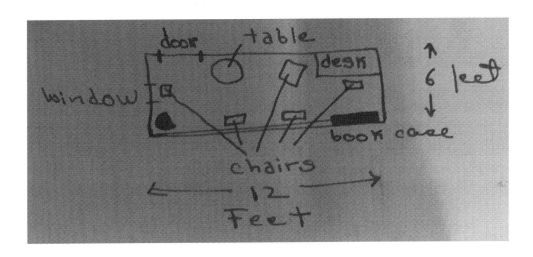

Can you imagine it full of men and Christmas decorations? We got a carton of stuff from the RC, bells, crepe paper, etc., and we have five Christmas trees.

As usual it has taken me a whole day to get so far. I started this morning while I was waiting for a telephone call and now Martha and I have locked ourselves in our office to have a little peace while we eat a <u>hamburger</u> (Dad) for dinner. The men are complaining tonight one of the staff put up a sign saying we were having "HAMBERGS." They consider the spelling a terrible sacrilege.

We are having more fun getting ready for Christmas. On Christmas day we are having a party for sixty children from the vicinity. The men have been saving candy for weeks and Martha and I spent the afternoon wrapping seventy-five packages of candy for them to take home. The GM gave us 150 oranges for them. We are having a movie and games, etc. The men are arranging all that and are most excited about it. We have been getting presents for our staff from the PX and from the men who have extra cigarettes. Everyone is so wonderful and we have so much help we are all stumbling over each other. I haven't had so much Christmas spirit for years. One of the boys brought us a whole truck full of holly and wreaths and we are going to decorate Thursday night after the club closes with lots of volunteers to help. This club is so small and cute; it is easy to make it look nice.

I finally went away for a weekend to London and had a nifty time. I went with Col. Lewis and his assistant Major Styles and we had a neat suite at the Grosvenor House Hotel. I wore my new dress and I love it. The only thing wrong was the length and Martha shortened it for me. Sat. night we went to see *There Shall Be No Night* and Sunday afternoon to a concert at Albert Hall and then to some friends of Col. Lewis' for cocktails—Peter and Betty. Peter is a Canadian was very badly wounded at Dunkirk and is now in the British Air Ministry and Betty is his American wife who has been here with him since the beginning of the war. They are terribly nice and live in a part of London that is sort of like Greenwich Village. We got to London early Sat. morning and I went shopping and got a new uniform. We have nice new RAF blue winter uniforms and very heavy winter coats—I also tried to buy things for the club but the stores were packed and couldn't find a thing or get near a counter. Monday morning Martha came in with the car that came for us and got her uniform so we are both well dressed for Christmas.

That was a pretty good guess about my home prior to this one, but now you'll have to start all over again, Mother. I am not so far though, although I haven't had a chance to see any of the old group yet, but talk to them over the telephone frequently.

December 22, 1943

Am waiting for Martha to take her bath so we can go to bed.

I wish you could see the way we live. Times have changed and I am no longer neat and orderly. We literally get up and go over to the club before it is light in the morning and don't get back until 12:00 at night and often later, altho' our quarters are only about fifty yards away, except to dress for dinner. Our clothes are everywhere as there is no place to hang most of them. Our beds are never made unless the boy, Fred, who takes care of our fire, feels sorry for us and makes them during the evening. I never get a chance to wash clothes and now send everything to the laundry. I really don't know what we do all day but everything takes so long because you have to spend so much time talking to the boys and being diplomatic and you would be amazed how good I'm getting at that.

Today Martha and I took a Christmas tree up to the general's quarters and trimmed it. We had fun and fixed the room up beautifully with the help of Mattex and Curly, the two orderlies. We even succeeded in getting them to take our white cat, Grace, who is going to have kittens (we didn't tell them that) and who we couldn't keep because she is too dirty.

Christmas Eve

We have decorated all day and I wish you could see the club. It looks wonderful. We have huge paper balls hanging from the ceiling and red and green paper streamers running from them. We have a

Christmas tree in each room, which we decorated after the club closed last night with the help of some of the boys. We decorated then mostly with candy, painted Ping Pong balls, cotton and colored paper. We have evergreen branches and candles all around. In the front hall we have a fireplace, which we made of wood and covered with red paper, which looks like bricks, with candles on the mantle piece and a wreath over it. All the doors have wreaths on them. It really looks swell and it's amazing how American ingenuity can make something out of nothing.

We are serving hamburgers, chicken salad and apple pie as specialties tonight as well as the usual sandwiches and cake. There is a USO show on the base and we are having dancing after it.

We had more fun decorating with the help of three MPs (one of whom used to decorate store windows), a gunner, Chic, and his WAC girl, Pinky, the nicest couple, George, a Greek boy who we call "The Greek" who has the most amazing facility for getting anything and even brought us a ventilating fan, though God knows where he got it, Mac from Boston, who played professional football before the war, John, who went to Dartmouth, and Kit Carson a very nice boy from Texas. We saved a huge carton of candy for a nearby, crippled children's hospital and the boys took it this afternoon. I wish we could have gone but we were too busy. We wrapped up cigarettes and soap for our staff and also save candy for them.

We are now drinking Martha's brandy, which we have saved for today and getting dressed for dinner in our new uniforms.

Today I go a whole batch of envelops, a total of twelve pairs of stockings and I think I have received everything you have sent; also two nice notes and red handkerchiefs from Mrs. Aldrich. They are lovely and I will use one tomorrow. Thanks so much for all you have sent. I am celebrating the Xmas season by wearing my red woolies!

Christmas Day

Am taking this moment while the movie is going on to wish you all a <u>Merry Christmas</u>. I have thought of you all, all day and wish that you could be here much more than that could be home.

This is really one of the best Christmases I ever spent. We closed the club at 3:00 last night and I know everyone had a nifty time. This morning we got up bright and early, distributed the presents to our staff, got lots of presents from the boys, patched up our decorations and rearranged everything for the children's party. We went to mess and had turkey, but it was gloomy in the officer's club compared to our place, which is anything but gloomy.

The kids arrived (50) about 3:00 and lot and lots of men. They seem to be having a wonderful time and the men and the WACS are taking complete charge. I wish you could see it. It really is quite a sight. There is the cutest little red head, a son of one of our staff who cries every time a soldier speaks to it.

Many interruptions and now party is all over. Martha, The Greek, and I are sitting in our office with the door locked drinking some sherry that Major Sayles gave us for Christmas. It really was a big success and the kids apparently had a swell time as the officers went back on the trucks with them have called us to say how enthusiastic they were. Lots of officers came too and even a general but I can't tell you which one, and we were terribly flattered after the party, everyone, officers and all, swept the floors

Christmas party at Marks Hall, 1943. Martha Brush is back row center.

for us and fixed things up for the dance tonight, which has started, but Martha and I don't have the energy to go out.

In the middle of the afternoon some of the boys took a huge box of candy over to the crippled children's hospital. All the kids see them coming and yell, "Yea, here come the Yanks."

Well I suppose Jane won't approve of the fact that I'm happy making Christmas a little pleasanter for the boys, but it makes it especially worth it when you see them so anxious to make it nice for all the kids who really have so damn little these days.

We have opened our presents from home at last and thank you all so much. It was fun to open so many and such useful little packages.

I almost forgot to say that at last I had a goose. I bought it for two pounds, Martha stuffed it and Mrs. Warman cooked it. Martha, Mrs. Warman, two WACs, four of the boys and I ate it tonight. It was delicious. So you see, this Christmas has been worthwhile in more ways than one.

Much love to you all. Wish you were all here.

Binni

December 26, 1943

Dear Jane,

Thanks so much for the Xmas box. It was wonderful, especially the films and the stockings, both badly needed. I am taking pictures, but it is harder, in fact impossible to get them developed here as they are much more strict about that sort of thing so I don't know when I'll ever be able to send them home.

Wish you could have been with us this afternoon. I went with one of the men, Sgt. Petrohilos and a WAC, Pinkie, to a children's hospital about ten miles from here to see the kids. It is more fun. The wards are all open on to a long sort of courtyard and as you walk past the kids all yell and scream, "Here come the Yanks." They call me "The Yankee Nurse" and Pinky, "The Lady Soldier." Some of the men go every week and take them candy and gum and magazines. They know all the men by name but I guess they will never learn to call me Fitje.

The club is packed tonight as usual and the Victrola is playing *Paper Doll* and *I'll Be Around* constantly. There are lots of jitterbugs among the WACS and it is really quite a sight to see the snack bar in operation at night.

Your job sounds very interesting. Do you like it? Who do you see around Providence?

One of the WACS who went to Smith just brought in the *Alumnae Quarterly*, and I see that Vicky Schrager died. You knew her didn't you or must have heard Dottie Deans speak of her.

Much Love,
Fitje

December 31, 1943

Dear Mother and Dad,

Received your letter today dated Dec. 8th with the picture in it, Mother. The mail seems to be coming in a little faster now. I hope I have told you everything about the club and where we are living, etc. It seems as if we had been here for so long now and everything is running so smoothly that I may have forgotten to tell you a lot.

We do have our terrible days though and yesterday was one of them. Martha has been sick so I have been working doubly hard. Yesterday I had to do the shopping, and everything went wrong. The rolls weren't baked and I had to wait at the bakery while they did them; then the hamburger meat wasn't ground and I had to wait at the butchers while he did that; when I got back in about four hours later everything was all wrong at the club. So many of the staff had flu that everyone is tired and cross. Mrs. Warman came into my office and said, "I'm sorry to trouble you, dear, you look so young and so little to have so many worries, but I can't stay here any longer if Mrs. Lake is going to stay." For a little while I felt so sorry for myself and that I was definitely too young to have so many worries; however, everything is all fixed up now, mostly because the next morning all the members of the staff who had been sick showed up and everyone is less overworked. These damn women who can't live with each other sure give me a pain.

Well, tonight is New Year's and we expect that most people will probably be drunk in the club tonight so we are sticking around instead of going to the dance at the Officer's Club. One of the boys brought us a bottle of whiskey, but we are going to save it until Monday because Jean is coming to visit me. You should have seen us this morning making a personal loan of thirty pounds so some of the boys could buy wine for a party.

January 7, 1944

I am spending a lovely afternoon in our room for a change making blackout curtains and fixing pillows for our couch, which we have made from a bed. We bought a copper teakettle for the stove and turned our extra bureau in which we keep linen into a bar with nothing on it but a bottle of sherry and some glasses, which we stole from the officer's club. If it weren't for the extra bedsprings and the telephone booth it would really look nice.

Mrs. Warman is away on a week vacation and the staff who don't like her threaten to leave in a body when she comes back. I'm not very worried that they really will. I can't understand why they don't like her. Last night they were grumbling about her so I told them that she was coming back on Sunday and that both Miss. Brush and I would hate to lose anyone of them but if anyone really thought they couldn't work with her they could come into my office and resign immediately. After that I was terrified but no one came and I haven't heard a word since so I guess everything will be O.K.

We have a new little fourteen-year old boy, Dennis Cobbold, who helps with the fires and is very cute.

Well here is Martha and we must get dressed and go to dinner. (After four months of living on and Army base I haven't learned to call it mess.) I understand we are having pork tonight. It will be nice after C Rations for days.

Much love,
Fitje

P.S. The flannel nightgowns are nifty. I hardly have to have a blanket over me.

1944

January 6, 1944

Dear Jane,

I thought I'd die laughing when I got your letter yesterday describing the Christmas Party and Mother trying to say "red ribbon." Your description was really much better than being there. First I read it over here in the office and everyone thought I was absolutely crazy I laughed so much; then I read it again over in my room and laughed some more.

I came storming over here at 9:30 this morning in a terrible mood because we had been waked up twice between 5:30 and 7:30 by the boys on their way to mess throwing stones at our hut or doing what we call "buzzing the hut." At night if they are out late they have a habit of running their flashlights along the side of the hut which is which is rippley (you know like a Nissen hut would be) just to let us know they are back. Martha and I invariably wake up thinking we are being machine-gunned and Martha even rolled over our bed on to the floor one night before she realized that we were not. A few nights ago they not only did that but then shined their flashlight right in the window on my face and I woke up thinking the hut was bombed and on fire. It's a rough life. Anyway when I got over here this morning, there were four of them over here eating breakfast because they didn't want to get up early enough to eat in the mess. Of course all the staff were standing around watching them and nothing had been done. Was I mad! And the only reaction I got was "doesn't Fitje look cute with that fire in her eye." You can see what authority I have around here.

Roger Freeman

I wrote Ibby a letter yesterday telling her that I had talked to Roger over the telephone and that he is very near me and is coming over when he has time. He has been very busy lately because the weather has been so nice but it will change soon. I can't get over how much warmer the winter is in England than at home. It is damp and muddy over here but it is damp in Providence too. Half the time we don't wear coats when we go to mess and are still riding miles in open jeeps without freezing. We have a Sibly stove in our room now and just have a fire at night so we can go to bed in a warm room. It is a wonderful stove and we keep water boiling on it and have tea before we go to bed. Last night we had four lemons that someone gave us and had hot lemonade. We have moved into the larger room in our quarters and it really looks quite nice except for a telephone booth which is stored in there because there isn't any other place to put it. We have made lots of candlesticks out of whiskey bottles because the electricity is always going off, and even have a great patriotic poster hanging on the wall saying, "We shall win, or we shall die."

Jean came and spent Tuesday night with me, and I drove her back on Wednesday and saw Lt. Clark and Jane, Major Russell and all of the others. Lt. Clark is expecting babies in about six weeks and I am going to have one of them. Jean made fun of my cat Milo and said she looks like Ramses II. Right now she is playing with a Ping Pong ball on the desk and making it very difficult for me.

The staff are all down on their hands and knees scrubbing the floor of the snack bar and I must go to see how they are progressing as the club opens at 12:00 and it is almost that now.

Do you hear much from big John? Thanks for your letter.

Love,
Fitje

January 14, 1944

Dear Family,

Just a note to let you know that your Christmas package containing the weather gloves, powder, pins, needles, earrings which I have on, etc., was waiting for me when I went to the Mess tonight. I opened it in the bar with crowds gathered watching. They were much amused by Johnny's message to bring home a flyer, and you can tell John that several volunteered. I gave the package marked to Jean to the only other girl present, the WAC officer, Mary Jo Black and she is going to wear it on her night-gown. Thank you very much for this one and for all the others. You have no idea what fun it is to open so many little packages, and to see all that Christmas paper because we have none of it here. One of the boys tied one of the bells around Milo's neck when I open the package again at the club and she is now is sitting on the desk watching me type. Typewriters fascinate her. She loves to stand on the keys and play with the letters as they pop up.

Martha is now in London taking a three day course in driving army trucks and I am going on Wednesday when she comes back to take the same course. Roger is also going to be there on leave and I am going to see him Wednesday night.

The joint is very quiet tonight, mostly because the Victrola is broken and usually it is on all day and all night. We have had to stop serving hamburgers because the English meat like the English milk is not considered pure enough to serve to Americans. Damn it! They were our best feature. We are now serving delicious powdered eggs sandwiches, which Martha and I invented ourselves one afternoon, we were so sick of spam and cheese. The most exciting thing that has happened lately is that only two of the staff showed up the other afternoon and Martha and I and four of the boys ran the place from 4:00 on. What a mad house it was.

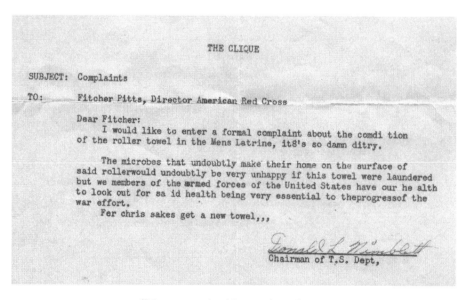

"Tongue in cheek" complaint letter

I can't get over how warm the winter is in England. No snow as yet. It hasn't been nearly cold enough. Rain, fog and mud though. We sleep with the front door of our hut open at night because our Sibly stove makes the room so hot that we can hardly stand. We have now trained one of the boys to shut the door and our windows from the outside as he goes to breakfast in the morning so we wake up in a comparatively warm room although it is cold early in the morning. Now that we live right next to the club, of course, we don't have to worry about the fire, as our little man Mr. Shinn takes care of it. Sometimes I think I live in more luxury here than I did at home. We even have our beds made in the morning.

I am sending you our first complaint because I know it will amuse you. The Clique is the group that I have told you about; Kit, Chic, Mac, The Greek, Mike, Kremkau, etc., and you probably know what the TS Department is.

January 15, 1944

Don't want you to think that our roller towels are always dirty, but Mrs. Warman, who usually takes care of changing them, was away at the time and I forgot.

Spent the morning doing the shopping and looking for teacups so we could have some nice ones when we have company for tea instead of the usually mugs. Couldn't find one; and was told that they are not being manufactured anymore and are practically impossible to find. There is nothing but utility furniture and china to be had.

I may send home some of my unnecessary stuff, so don't be surprised if you get a few packages. I want to have as little as possible around in case I move from here soon.

Tell Ann that I got a letter from Warren and may see him in London next week if he is able to get there while I am there. Jane, I will look E. May up immediately. Am so glad you have heard from Big John.

Much Love to you all and thanks again.

Fitje

January 23, 1944

Dear family,

Please excuse the mail but do not have the time to write much more than this so thought it was better than nothing. Everything is about as usual. Martha has just gotten back from taking a four-day driving course in London and I was going this week but things at the club were such that I couldn't get away. A lot of the staff have been sick and at last they are all beginning to get better and are coming back to work. I am going next Wednesday which is really better anyway as Jean will be there then to. I got a letter from E. May who is now in London so naturally I will see her. Also there is the possibility that one of Ann's brothers might be able to get there.

The office has been crowded with boys all afternoon as one of the boy's brothers who is a B-17 pilot has been visiting him and they have been up here. I wish you could see them eat. Poor Mrs. Warman keeps bringing in plates of sandwiches and cake, which go in two minutes and we have to go back for more. Sometimes I wonder how we ever have enough food to serve in the evening. One of the boys is being transferred so last night after the club closed we cooked French fries potatoes and onions and ate for hours. I went out to dinner last night and had oysters. I ate eighteen without John and Dad to heckle me. The first I have seen in I don't know how long.

We have been having cold foggy weather lately so things have been very quiet. Today is lovely though but I suppose we will have to pay for with another week of rain. Last night the boys filled our stove so it would burn all night and it turned red hot and made the room so warmed neither of us could sleep and we couldn't put the damn thing out. We spent all night getting up and drinking water and opening windows and even the outside door. Steam heat that you can regulate must be wonderful.

Our cable address is FL Pitts MGASU Platform. That is all. However cables take at least five days to get here and more often weeks and weeks and sometimes never arrive. If you should cable me and shouldn't hear from me you would worry so don't do it. Chances are that a letter would always reach me in a shorter time than a cable would. Don't worry I will write every week unless for some reason I can't and then a cable wouldn't get to me anyway.

Am still trying to see Roger as I missed him since I couldn't get to London. He will probably come over Sunday evening soon as I know he can always get a ride. I am anxious to see some pictures of the baby as he says he has some.

Today is Martha's birthday and we are trying to think of some wait to celebrate tonight.

Much love to all.

Fitje

February 1, 1944

Dear Family,

Have just come back from spending almost a week in London taking the Truck Driving Course partly, but mostly having a good time. I went up last Wednesday, and got there in the afternoon in time to buy a few records and go to the OWI* to see W. May. She seems to like it a lot. In the evening I went out with Lt. Cross who I met coming over on the boat, a very nice boy from Philadelphia. We went to a couple places for drinks and then went to the Grosvenor House for dinner.

Thursday the course started and it was funny. We went out to Wimbledon to a racetrack and drove these huge two and a half ton trucks around and around all morning. In the afternoon we went to London and drove right through the middle of the city. Another girl, Ruth Kniep, at least three inches shorter than I am and weighing about 100 lbs. was with me, and we had an instructor named Mr.

* Office of War Information

Cook. The first day he spent all day telling us that since we were little we were used to letting other people have their own way but to remember that we were now driving a big truck and everyone would watch out for us. He made us cut in and out of traffic and tear along and scared us to death. The second and third days when we got more used to it he sat us on the edge of his seat with his hand on the emergency brake most of the time. And we would say, "Relax Mr. Cook, we know what we're doing," but he didn't seem very confident. Friday we drove in London all morning and in the afternoon we went out to Epsom and drove around the racetrack where the derby is held. It was lovely out there. It seems to me that spring is coming here already. Saturday we had our test and that was the funniest part. We were each supposed to have our own truck to go on a convoy, but at the last minute they discovered that I have the instructors truck so they took it away and I went with Ruth. Unfortunately Ruth had picked a defective truck that stalled all the time. First Ruth drove and it stalled about five times, and all the eight trucks behind her would have to stop while she got it going. Then I drove and that was even worse, because we went us a hill much longer and as steep as Meeting Street Hill and it stalled three times, and the whole convoy has to stop. On the hill it really took both of us to navigate. Ruth would pull on the emergency break so hard that she wouldn't be able to let it off and one of the men would have to come and help us. Of course we got laughing so neither of us knew what we were doing. Finally one of the men drove it home and it stalled four times with him driving so we passed the test. Anyway I think the whole thing was pretty silly, as I can't imagine that most of us would be of much help as truck drivers.

On Thursday Major Russell came up and stayed until late Sunday night so we had a wonderful time. I went to all the places in London in the evening that I haven't been in and wanted to go. Thursday we went to the bar at the Ritz and the Mirabelle for dinner; Friday we went the L'Abri bar and the Bagetelle for dinner; Saturday we went to Meurice's for dinner and then to the Embassy Club. Sunday was a beautiful day and we walked around down in the vicinity of St. James Park and then went to hear the London Philharmonic, and then to the L'Abri bar until Adj* had to go catch a train. We really had a wonderful time. I stay over until Monday because there were some things I wanted to get for the club. Monday morning I went and got a very good permanent, went to the PX and got some flannel PJs and went shopping for the Club. About all I could get was a case of peanut butter, but we have been trying to find that for months so we're very glad to get it; also a few pictures, maps, and vases. Got back to the hotel just in time to get a telephone call from Roger while I was waiting for someone to come for me. He really looks very well and seems to be enjoying himself. He has a mustache. Did he have that when he left? He brought about a million pictures of the baby and Ibby and the baby looks awfully cute; he thinks Lucy should not think of doing the lady Marines.

I wrote you a letter on Dec. 6th describing in detail our set up here, and I just got the letter back today because I had violated a censorship regulation, by mistake but stupid of me, although it was very obscure.

I am not sure whether or not I have told you about our living quarters in any other letter. In case I haven't, we are living in a little Nissen hut about seventy-five feet from the club. It has two bedrooms,

* Major Edward Russell, Adjutant, 95th Bomb Group

a bathroom with a bathtub and a linen closet. Mrs. Warman lives in the small bedroom and Martha and I have the big room. We are the only three. There was a fourth, but she didn't fit in so well so I fired her. Can you imagine me firing anyone? If she had known how scared I was when I decided that I couldn't put it off any longer and had said one word to dissuade me, I would have changed my mind, but she didn't. It really is a nifty setup. Although just as near the club as our quarters were at the other base, we have much more privacy, because the windows are high and the kind of class that you can't see through. Our quarters aren't pretty but they are comfortable and we like them.

Right now we are in terrible difficulty. We had an accountant who was here for two days a week doing our accounting, but we share her with another club because we don't have enough to keep her busy all the time. Well, the other club fired her so she has to leave us too. We fired our recorder thinking we had someone better to take her place and at the last minute that fell through, so we are without a recorder or an accountant. Martha and I are desperately struggling to do all the accounting and keep track of all the food, without knowing too much about it, but we are learning fast. Six months ago I would have been awful worried, but now, honestly, I don't worry about anything from minute to minute because I think I would go mad if I did. Tell Jane I have also learned to make up my mind in hurry; in fact I don't even hesitate for a minute anymore.

Send me some Anthony's gumdrops sometime if you can get them anymore. How I would love some orange juice, bacon and eggs.

I wrote you didn't I that the stockings have all come. Thank you very much.

Much Love,
Fitje

February 18, 1944

Dear Mother and Dad,

I will try and do a little better by you this week, as I know there was a long lapse between my last two letters. Before I forget, some more stockings came in a box. Thank you very much.

We have had a couple of busy days. Yesterday morning Martha did the shopping while I made out with the payroll. For a change it came out right. In the afternoon we invited the four flight nurses who are temporarily on the base up for tea, as well as the three WAC officers and "Doc" Jones, the doctor on the base and a wonderful guy. We had tea in our recorders because the office is much too small for so many people—all home made food and it was really very good. The flight nurses are very nice and very interesting; one of them was an airline hostess before the war. We felt very lazy in the evening and I spent most of in the office playing solitaire with one of the boys, the Greek. At 11:00 all the boys who have been pubbing come in and it always creates lots of excitement as they are often covered with mud and scratches from crawling through the woods on their hands and knees.

Today we got up bright and early and, in rain and a flurry or two of snow, rode to town (about a mile and a half) on our bicycles with the money for the week, to deposit it in the bank and cash our pay checks. One of the WAC officers and a Lt. went with us and we had a wonderful time pretending we were flying in formation, and contending with all sorts of enemy opposition. We were supposed to go to the dispensary for our shots this afternoon but put it off again as we have been doing for weeks. Instead we started serving tea about 2:00 when a courier came in from another base and wanted something to eat. He was about twenty-one and has been away from home for four years having been in the Merchant Marine before he joined the army. He comes from Buffalo and said, "I haven't seen my mother for four years and I would give anything to be back there now." After he left two of the nurses came up to bring their laundry to one of our staff to do so we had tea again; then some officer came up to see about cashing a check so we had tea again; then some of the boys came in to use our typewriter so we had tea again; then we paid the staff and said goodbye to a cook, Mrs. Slee, who is leaving, and then two officers came up from personnel and so we gave them tea. And so the afternoon goes on. Now Martha has gone over to wash her hair, and things are getting quieter.

I have not heard from Roger for a couple of weeks so I am going to call tonight just to check up on him. I may go to his base for a dance for a dance Saturday night if I can get away from here, so maybe I will see him then.

Next time you write let me know how Hope McConnell is. I hope she is better. Got Jane's letter from John. His experiences don't sound very pleasant, but the letter was very interesting wasn't it. Got a letter from Carol yesterday, which I will someday get around to answering. I sure am glad that the WAVES fell through. She admitted that she was jealous and well she might be.

Mrs. Warman is leaving on Wednesday, I am sorry to say, in some ways, although we will be glad in others because life is rather difficult for her here, on account of her age and the fact that she is a little lame, so it will be sort of a relief not to have her around. We haven't yet hired anyone to take her place. Even the labor board is so short of labor that there is no use going to them when all I get when I do is a cup of tea. They are very nice!

One of the boys is sitting in the office trying to do a little work and he keeps going to sleep. He is asleep right now. Four of the boys went to London on furlough this morning early and they have telephoned three times in the last hour to see how things are going here. We tell them they might as well come back if they're that homesick.

I have been away just about a year now and I can't believe the time has gone so fast and so much has happened. Maybe in another year the war will be over.

February 19, 1944

Got up this morning and went over to the dispensary to have our shots before we had a chance to change our minds. Each had four, and this afternoon they told us that they have been using us as an example all day to all of the officers who didn't want to have them all at once! We spent the afternoon trying to figure out whether to raise our prices or cut down on our staff to get our expenses down a little, and also writing the weekly paper, which was started by Special Service but which would've petered out so we have taken it over rather than given it up. I wish I could send you a copy but it is restricted.

Late this afternoon I went to the dentist, a delightful experience; only two minutes walk or less from our front door, no waiting for trolley cars anything, and everyone keeps coming in and watching, telling jokes and generally keeping your spirits up. I quite enjoyed it.

Last night we had an unexpected visit from the Supervisor of Aero Clubs, Mr. Igan. Everything was running very smoothly; the club was jammed with men and WACS; there were no men in the kitchen; the place is clean, and the food was particularly good. He scared us to death by talking about moving us and asking me how I would like to open a great big club, but in the end told us not to begin to worry yet, so I guess everything is alright for a while anyway. He said he was very proud of our Club, and naturally we allowed as we were too.

Martha and I are trying not to go to the bar every night because it has gotten so damned expensive so we went right down to mess tonight and ate steak, corn, potatoes, and chocolate cake with the two flight officers on the base. After dinner I did go to the bar with one of the Courts and Boards Officers who is being very nice to me because he knows that I have some cigars and he wants them. In the end he offered me free legal advice and walked me back to the Club so I gave him four. Tonight the club is comparatively quiet because there is a movie on base. Only excitement so far—Mrs. Warman caught the cook drinking in the back hall with one of the men, and I, just back from the bar, had to tell her that we would not tolerate that sort of behavior. The cook is quite elderly and runs two pubs in nearby town. She only works for us, because she lives alone with her granddaughter, who also works for us, and does not like to be alone tonight. I know that we should get rid of her, and Mrs. Warman keeps telling me that I'm cowardly because I don't fire her, but I still haven't reached the point where I can do that easily, and I lie awake at night worrying about it.

February 20, 1944

Sunday again, and for some reason we always relax, even though it's just like every other day. Last night we kept the club open much later than usual, as the movie wasn't over until 11:00, and everyone comes here after the movie. The staff went home and Martha and I, and a couple of the boys serve the food. Luckily the water was suddenly turned off so we didn't have to wash the dishes.

Today we slept until 12:00 and had lunch at the club instead of going to mess—pot roast, potatoes, and brussel sprouts—not bad; and walked down to the Post Office to get our eggs for the Bingo prizes, which one of the boys who works there gets for us. It was quiet afternoon—only seven for tea, two of the boys, two of the flight nurses, and three pilots from a nearby base. Martha went off to London for couple of days in a jeep, and I am sure she will freeze to death before she gets there as the weather has suddenly gotten quite cold, and it is a long ride.

Now the Bingo is going on, with one egg, one package of cigarettes, and a cigar as the prize for the first game. Kit Carson is running it tonight. He is, at present, in difficulties with Mrs. Warman, because he and one of the other boys, Mac, a huge Irishman from Boston, sat one of the staff, Daphne, in the sink this afternoon and then ran water on her, and got her very wet. Mrs. Warman said to them "I shall tell Miss Pitts and she will be very angry," and was terribly put out when I laughed.

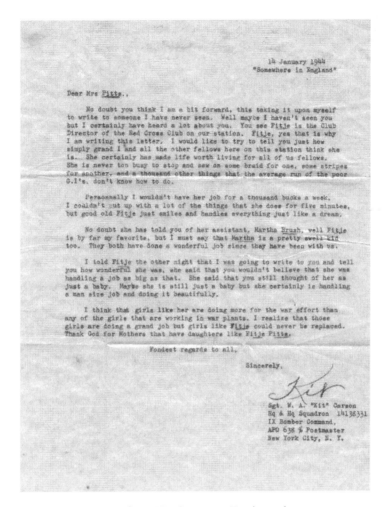

Letter from Kit Carson to Fitje's mother

The group that is in London on furlough just called for about the twentieth time since they left the day before yesterday, and somehow Martha happened to be with them. How I don't know as she started out with the three pilots who were here for tea. They were all very incoherent over the telephone.

One of the staff, Mrs. Peters, brought her mother with her to work today so she could see the Club and her mother (an old lady) has been sitting out in the snack bar observing everything all evening, and looks very bewildered. I just went out to see how she liked it and she said, "They all sound very happy, don't they."

By the way, tell Ibby that the three pilots who were here today, came over with Roger, and speak of him as a wonderful Ping Pong player. Did she know that; they also say that he is a wonderful guy. I had meant to write her about seeing him in London, but have never gotten around to it. Anyway I knew that you would convey the message. If you see Grace will you thank her for the nice long letter? I was so glad to hear from her and will try to get around to answering it.

Got a joint letter from John, Ann, and Jane. I am so glad that Ann is so well. Tell her that I'm sure that my nephew (naturally) can help but be good-looking with such handsome parents. Isn't it sad that Pat is really getting divorced? What is the matter with them anyway?

Kit and Mac just apologized to Daphne and she has forgiven them so all is well. Mac is furious because Mrs. Warman blamed it mostly on him as Kit is one of her favorites, and he swears that Kit was the instigator, which I can believe. I wish you could see the assortment of soldiers in Hut 3, our favorite. The names are enough—Kit, Mac, Hump, Pop, Murph (a Jew, we call them all Murphy) Shag, Chic, Walker, The Greek, Hilary (whom we call Freddy McGurgle) Kruckok (who we call Crew Chief) Mike, etc.; What a group. I wish I had a picture of them to send you.

Kit says to tell you, Mother that he is still "Sweating out" your letter.

Hope you had a good time in Atlantic City, Dad. I suppose that John is in Yale by now.

Much Love,
Fitje

March 6, 1944

Dear Mother and Dad,

It has been on my conscious all weekend that I haven't written for over two weeks so I will try to make up for it. I have just gotten back today from London where I went for the weekend with Major Styles and Col. Lewis and a WAC, Capt. Von Stein. We had a very nice time. Drove up on Saturday arriving in time for a drink and a play, *While the Sun is Shining*, a very funny play about an American bombardier, a French Navy officer and an English Earl, an ordinary seaman, with a butler whose son is a Lt. Commander; very complicated and terribly funny. As you probably know plays start about 6:00, or sometimes even at 5:00 in London now, because of the raids and the blackout and the difficulty in getting around. The tubes stop at 11:00 and you have to depend on them pretty much for getting around after dark. It is a dismal sight to see the people sitting on their blankets waiting for the trains to stop so they can go to bed, although there are not so many now.

After the play we went back to the Grosvenor House for dinner and danced until the place closed. I wish you could have seen the lovely suite we occupied, two big bedrooms with mirrors all over the walls, two bathrooms and a lovely living room. I have lost my sense of perspective a little and it probably wasn't really so hot, but it looked nice after a Nissen hut. Col. Lewis and Major Styles and Capt. Von Stein are all about forty, and very nice. Von worked in Hollywood writing script before the war and is terribly interesting. Sunday we slept late and then went to the apartment of some more WAC Officers for tea. Their apartment is nifty. Formerly occupied by the Countess of something or other, it is just like a house in Boston, with the kitchen in the cellar, etc., until you get about six flights above the street. Late in the afternoon, we went to a cocktail party General Anderson had at the Governor House where he was also staying. It was very nice, and lots of interesting people, including three Generals. After the cocktail party, our group, plus General Anderson, and a few others went to the Ambassador and dance for a while.

This morning before we drove back I went to the Officer's PX and bought myself a nifty nurses interlined raincoat.

Our new Manageress has arrived and seems very good. She has so much energy that she practically does all the work herself. Apparently Mrs. Warman, who interviewed her for us so that we didn't have to go to London, told her that we are careless about the money and about airing the sheets before we put them on the beds. Ever since she arrived she has been airing the sheets and asking me if the money is O.K. Since we have to go to the bank on bicycles we don't go more than once a week, but I think that where we hide the money is safer than in the bank.

I wish you could hear the shortened language that has developed around here. Here are a few examples:

Seet	Did you eat
No, Jew	No, did you
Squeet	Let's go eat
Squash	Let's go wash
Squ-up	Let's go up

Warren was here last week on a 48-hour pass. I'm afraid we worked him awfully hard, as we had to get the Coca Cola so he helped load and unload 175 cases. He went to a U.S.O. show on night on the base and the next night we all went over to the beer parlor for a little while. He stayed in one of the huts with some of the boys.

March 7, 1944–News Flash

Jean just called up to say that Lt. Clark is now the mother of four kittens, born this morning, three girls and one boy. I am going to have one of them when they are old enough. Milo is a scream. A few nights ago we let a stray dog sleep on the spare bed in our room. Milo was simply furious and spent the whole night sitting on the end of Martha's bed watching the dog. She is not the least bit frightened of them and they are scared to death of her. She has an annoying way of walking behind them looking very ferocious. The other day we watched her chase one away from the garbage pail and she is always chasing them out of the club. The other afternoon I was in the back office looking in the filing cabinet for something. Milo jumped into the drawer I was looking in and then crawled down the back into the drawer beneath. When I finished I completely forgot her and closed the drawer and left the office. Late in the evening about six hours later I went back for something and opened the drawer and heard this little pathetic meow and there she was. She was mad at me for a long time. Right now she has been missing for 24 hours and we are terribly worried.

There has been a basketball tournament going on at IX Bomber Command, and we were the only group that wasn't in it. Finally the tournament was over and one of the groups won it. Next they were to play the 9th Air Force Hdqrs. Five of our boys thought that was too bad so they decided one day in our office to challenge them. The next day they played and to our amazement won, since none of them had played for a year or more and had never practiced together. I guess it was just good luck. Now we are the champs of IX Bomber Command. It was really funny, all the fuss it made. Some of the boys were mad because they weren't asked to play and one of them even cried in our office because he was so disappointed. They are still not all on speaking terms. We have decided that we are sort of a clearinghouse for all that sort of thing, as being non-partisan we hear both sides of every argument. I wish you could hear some of the funny fights the WACS have with their boyfriends. It seems as if everyone on the base is on one side or another. Martha and I get so mad at them, as often it never would have happened if everyone minded their own business.

Our new manageress, Mrs. Thompson, is from Lancastershire and has a wonderful accent. We like her very much and so do the boys. They call her Tommy, and there is nothing she won't do for them. She has traveled a lot and is very interesting. Her husband was killed at Dunkirk and her son during the Battle of Britain. Our cashier, Mrs. Camp, had two sons. One was killed in the RAF and last week she heard that other, in the Fleet Air Arm had been killed. One of our cooks, Mrs. Wootton, who is married to an American gunner, is leaving us because she is expecting a baby; and one of our cleaning girls, Joan, a terribly nice kid, has just informed us she is engaged to one of the drivers on the base, a very nice Italian boy who lives in Brooklyn. Somehow I feel sort of sorry for her leaving this nice quiet English village to go live in Brooklyn, but she is terribly excited. Our staff is really wonderful and very loyal. They are so pleased when anyone from the Red Cross comes around to see the Club and says that it is that it is very nice I always feel like asking them to go out in the kitchen and say it in front of the staff, as usually they get the information second hand from us.

Really I wish you could know some of these boys. Maybe you will meet Mac when the war is over as he comes from Boston. We call him "Big Barnsmell" when he is sober and "Lenny" (from *Of Mice and Men*) when he is not, which is about every evening. He is six foot three and weighs 215 lbs. He is so strong that he has been known to push down brick walls with one hand. The other day he wanted to get in here and the door was locked so he just pushed it slightly and broke the lock in half. Last night he had a plate in his hand and sort of subconsciously broke it right in half. He also bent my flashlight at a fifty-degree angle. Every night he goes to the beer parlor with a gallon can and drinks beer from it. When he gets back here he is usually in a fighting mood and wants to throw everyone out of the club. He is the only boy who gives us any trouble and we wouldn't let him bother us except that we are afraid that if he did hit anyone he would kill them. We have scolded him so much that now he keeps saying, "Am I making any trouble, do you want me to go up to the hut." If we do tell him we think he should go to bed he goes, and the next day is always very remorseful. He eats like a horse and doesn't care what it is. We often give him cold baked beans, which he eats right out of the can. He is fond of an awfully nice WAC named Mary but most of the time they are not on speaking terms.

I am enclosing a picture of myself, and Major Russell walking down the Strand, taken by one of those candid camera people unknown to us.

The weather has gotten much nicer lately and we ride our bicycles around quite a bit. We can hardly wait until the flowers start coming out as there is lots of lovely country around here and they say that it is lovely in the spring. Right now Martha is at another club, as there is only one girl there alone and it is a much bigger club and needs two people. I am praying that she won't be taken away from me for good, but am afraid that she will as this club is so small and if there is a shortage of girls naturally it isn't right for two of us to be here. She comes back here at night so I don't have to live alone anyway. She is so nice that the club that gets her as a Director will be very fortunate.

I telephoned this afternoon to check up on Roger, and although I didn't talk to him found out that he is fine. A friend of mine on the same base is keeping track of him for me, and will keep me informed of anything that might happen, but isn't very apt to.

Wish I could see Franny and Ann together. I am sure it was very amusing.

Spent another pleasant hour at the dentist this afternoon and taking one of our staff to the dispensary to have her finger dressed as she cut it quite badly the other day cutting bread. She is terrified to go alone so we have to go hold her hand while the doctor is fixing it. Mrs. Thompson is a nurse and very useful when anything happens.

I am wondering how John likes being away from home. I guess he misses the icebox most of all, and I must confess I think of it a great deal of the time. When I get home I am going to spend lots of time eating, although our food is perfectly O.K. I can't help thinking about orange juice, eggs, and meat! Also milk, which, as you know, I never drank but I haven't had a glass since I left N.Y. and bananas, which of course we haven't even seen. When I remember trying to buy Spam at home and being mad because I couldn't get it! Spam and C-Rations comprise a good part of our diet.

Much Love,
Fitje

March 14, 1944

Dear Mother and Dad,

I have started a letter to you several times this week but have never gotten any further than putting the paper in the typewriter. Just as I started this one the dentist called up to remind me that I had forgotten my dentist appointment at 2:30 this afternoon and as a punishment he is coming up to tea. So I guess he will arrive any time and I will have to stop again.

March 15, 1944

Have had a busy week. Martha is still working at another club most of the time, although she is here at night. The weather has been nice and much warmer. Sunday I went for a walk in the woods with Mac, who I described to you in my last letter. We walked a long way and it was lovely. Our objective was to pick something green for the club, but all we could find was lots of Pussy Willows, although things are starting to come out. I can hardly wait for spring to really start to come. People who live around here say that it is lovely. You should hear the birds around here, Mother.

Last night we had a wonderful three-man orchestra in the club to entertain, a pianist, a trombonist, and a drummer. They also brought a singer who was really good. After the entertainment we had a party in our quarters for one of the WACS, "Pinkie" Jones, because it was her twenty-second birthday. She is engaged to Chic who, I guess, I have told you about. Mrs. Tompson made us a beautiful cake for her with white frosting on it.

Our staff is so wonderful. I at last got around to firing Mrs. Robinson and things have been running very smoothly ever since. One of our cooks has left. She is going to have a baby so poor Mrs. Tompson has been doing most of the cooking. She is wonderful. We cook about 600 cakes a day so it is no easy job. Our food recorder, Mrs. Joyce, is a wonderful person. We asked her to pick up some meat for the staff and bring it to work with her the other morning. When she got to work she had forgotten the meat so instead of saying anything about it to us, she borrowed one of our bicycles and rode a mile and a half to get it. She is about your age mother and hasn't been on a bicycle for years. The only way she could get off was to fall off. We heard about it from the M.P.s because when she went out past the pickets she said, "If you want me to stop you will have to shoot me." She runs a sort of boarding house for combat boys who are on pass, and several of the boys who I know at the other base come down there and always come up to see us. One of them is now missing in action and another is on his way home having finished his tour of operations. I think that I have told you about those two before—Scottie and Ralph, who have been together ever since they got in the army. Ralph was the ball turret gunner who was afraid that everyone else would bail out and forget to let him know. Ralph is the one that is missing now.

I am writing this letter with great difficulties. Mac, Greek, Kruckok and Reilly, are all in the office. Mac keeps putting his finger in the workings of the typewriter, which accounts for all the mistakes.

G.Is at IX Bomber Command, 1943. S/Sgt. John Kruckok (The Russian) is far right.

Kit got your letter today mother. It had been all over everywhere because you forgot to put IX Bomber Command Hdqrs. on it. He was very pleased to get it. Well, Martha is trying to get Kruckok to go up to the supply room and get us some thumbtacks, Greek is trying to work a deal where he can get some candy to take to the children's hospital; Reilly is agitating that we all go to eat; and Mac is asleep in the chair; I guess I will stop and get dressed for dinner.

Love,
Binni

March 27, 1944

Dear Mother & Dad,

Again a long time that's gone by since my last letter. The time just goes too fast that's all. It is now light here until almost 8:30 and some of the boys have built a baseball diamond and a badminton court right in a field in front of the club so we really spend most of the time outdoors, watching baseball (and even playing) or playing badminton, raking our lawn and mowing the old grass in preparation for our garden.

Much to my surprise Roger Freeman walked in last week while we were having tea for two other flying officers. He looked very well and seems to be fine—told me lots of news and talked mostly about Ibby and the baby. Am keeping close check on him through another friend of mine on his station, a ground officer.

This weekend I took a couple of days off and went back to the base I was at before mostly to see Lt. Clark and the kittens. They were so cute. Two of them died, but the two left are lovely, grey with blue eyes and Mrs. Clark, as we call her now, is a wonderful mother. She sits in her box and talks to them all day long (noises such as Brrrp, Brrrp, Brrrp). She is really awfully cute. Went to a dance there Sat. night and how the place has changed. So many new faces and so many of the flying people have gone down since I was there. It was sort of depressing to hear about them all at once, whereas, being there, you hear from day to day and it doesn't seem so bad. Major Russell and his Sgt., Sgt. Allen, drove me back on Sunday and it was a lovely day. We stopped on the way to walk around the ruins of an old castle way up on the wall and it was lovely. Major Russell and Sgt. Allen were very impressed with the club and I was flattered when Major R. told me I was really doing a good job because he isn't inclined to flattery usually. They kept saying "It's so clean" which pleases us like anything because both Martha and I are terribly particular and almost drive the staff crazy making them keep everything unnecessary out of the kitchen, etc.

Mrs. Tompson had made a delicious chocolate cake in honor of my home coming so we had chocolate cake and tea before they left.

This afternoon I went to the dentist and brought the dentist and the two "Docs" back to the club for tea. They are so nice to us and we keep them very busy as our staff are always sick or hurting themselves.

While I was at the other base I boasted so much about our basketball team that their team challenged ours, so they are going to play next Tuesday and since they are the 8th Air Corp champs and our team was defeated in the IX Air Force tournament I am a little worried as to what will happen.

Now that the time is drawing near I can hardly wait until June to see whether Ann or Franny wins and what the result is. Just think only two more months till Ann to write Warren, as he never hears from home. Maybe it would be quicker if she sent me the letters and I forwarded them, as our mail seems to be so much quicker. Write me how Hope McConnell is and what Luckie is doing if you think of it.

I wish you could see all the primroses blooming around here, they are so pretty and we have the club full of them now.

Isn't it sad about Dinnty? What happened to her anyway?

Much Love,
Fitje

March 31, 1944

Dear Mother and Dad,

We have done nothing all evening but talk about how often most people write to their parents and I am put to shame as most people seem to do it at least twice a week; they're probably boasting, but still I know I am getting worse and worse. Anyway yours are absolutely the only letter I do right now; I really don't know where the time goes. This evening Chuck William was up with the latest manuscript by Ben Ames Williams for me to read; it is called *Leave Her to Heaven*, should be published soon and he says it is excellent; I am going to read it tonight.

It is now 11:30 and only a few people are left in the club. Today was payday so probably the ones that are left are gambling, as I have been breaking up crap games all evening. Martha is in London for a couple of days but is expected back tomorrow. This morning I woke up hearing a great pounding on the side of our hut right about where my head was. Thinking it was one of the boys I ignored it as long as I could but when it didn't stop I looked out. Mac was standing about twenty-five feet away throwing snowballs at the hut. I couldn't have been more surprised; no snow all winter, and then the ground is covered just when you think spring is on the way. It didn't last for long though as is all gone now. It settled on the roof of the club just long enough for us to find out that the roof leaks in two places. Oh, well, I guess we won't have to worry about that until next winter.

Mrs. Tompson is furious tonight. She is so particular about balancing the food made with the food served, that she even gets mad if Martha or I take anything as we walk through the kitchen. This afternoon the morning staff (for an April Fool's joke) hid a tray of tarts that she had just finished making (twenty-four delicious tarts) and she up first thought that I had taken them to give away, and when she found out that I hadn't, walked all through the club to see if any of the boys had. We finally found tucked away in the corner of the larder with a little note attached to them. I pity the morning staff when they come tomorrow.

She really is wonderful, and is really proud today because she got a letter from Major Russell thanking her for the nice reception he got when he brought me back last Sunday. She has been here for four weeks without a day off, and we can't drive her away even over night. It is terrible. Instead of setting an example for our staff they seem to be setting us an example.

Nothing very special has happened since I last wrote. I had one wonderful day when I went to another base with two of the boys who had to go there to collect some supplies, and saw the Red Cross Club there. I would like to get a chance and some transportation to go around and see some other clubs, as I know that ours might improve with a few new ideas. At least it is cleaner than some and I'm proud of that. We now have a lovely file of recipes, that conform to all the Ministry of Food regulations, etc., and really have quite good food, although I have been eating it for so long now that I have sort of lost my sense of perspective, I think.

Well must go to bed and read my book.

Love to all.

Binni

April 3, 1944

Dear Mother and Dad,

A lovely day, really spring, I guess. Our clocks have been set ahead an hour now so it is still light at eight and after. We have had quite a bit of rain lately so it is nice to see the sun shine.

Last night was an exciting night in our little club. We have a wonderful three piece band here complete with singer, which we now have every Sunday night. There was also a U.S.O. show on the base. Since it is always quit here when there is a show or a movie, we decided to let all the staff go see it, and Martha and I went mad serving behind the snack bar, clearing tables, etc.; and in between times jitter-bugging with the boys. After the show the whole U.S.O. troupe came over here and we gave them refreshments and they put on a sort of impromptu show here. It was so wonderful and everyone enjoyed it. I have never heard such yells, and applause. We were very glad that we thought of the good idea of inviting them.

Mrs. Tompson has been away for a few days, but our staff are so well-trained and so good that they operate beautifully without her, and we hardly have to do anything extra. We miss her mostly because she cooks the best of our food. When she isn't here, we just don't have those little things. Can you get margarine and lard at home, or is that rationed? It seems to me that every good recipe that we get uses too much margarine and we can't make it. We have been trying to improve our pastry, but since we have lard and not much margarine and can't use any butter for cooking, there is not an awful lot we can do about it.

I am about to send $100 home in the form of a money order when I get around to getting it. Will you let me know how my bank balance stands? I started to figure out my income tax and decided that the Government owes me money so I wouldn't bother about it until I got home. You should have at least two war bonds from the American Red Cross by now as I should get one every five months beginning last march. I should be quite rich by the time I get home.

April 4, 1944

Have just been consulting with the plumber who was here to fix our drains, which are all plugged up. Thank goodness there is coke again on the base. For a while we had only coal, which stuffed up all the stovepipes and we seemed to be spending most of the time up on the roof trying to clean them out. Yesterday I sent John, our sixteen-year old handyman, to clean out the ones in the snack bar. Hearing a little confusion in the snack bar I looked out to see the boys in there desperately trying to hold the stovepipes in the stoves with flames shooting out all over the place. John was standing happily on the roof beating the pipes as hard as he could to knock the soot out with no idea of the confusion he was causing inside.

Mrs. Tompson came back last night, a day earlier than expected, bringing Martha and I each a lovely Wedgewood plate, and a bottle of scotch over a hundred years old which she had stored away in a friends attic as she has rented her house. She was much the youngest in a family of three boys and three girls. Her mother died when she was born. Her one sister lives in the U.S.A.; another went to China as a medical missionary, and died of typhoid on the boat coming back to England after thirteen years over there. Her three brothers were all killed in World War I, and now her husband and son. I guess she is about forty-two. The boys just think that she is wonderful. She brought back a lovely pewter mug to Mac, although she swears that she has no favorites, but says that he is a lot like her own son, so she wanted him to have it.

Received your letter today, Mother, in closing the clip about dad which I proudly showed "Doc" Jones. "Sweating out" over here means waiting for something like "sweating out a promotion," or "sweating out" your wife who is having a baby. We say it so much that I can't believe there was ever a time that I didn't use the expression. Kit finally got your letter and was very pleased.

I can't imagine Johnny at Yale, but I bet he's having a good time. Yesterday I got a lovely red handkerchief from Mrs. Aldrich for an Easter present. I am going to write her when I finish this. I guess I told you about Chuck's father's book, *Leave her to Heaven*. I am now trying to finish it. It is quite good, so watch for it. It should come out this month, he thinks. He is very nice about bringing newspaper correspondences down to see us. Mostly I guess, because he knows he can get them something to eat down here. A New York Times reporter the other night asked me if we "Salvation Army" girls got much competition from the Red Cross. I retaliated somewhat by telling him that I admired him because the *Daily Mirror* was my favorite paper. Did I tell you that Robert Preston (of movie fame)* is on the base and one of the other officers brought him up to tea the other afternoon?

---

* Robert Preston (Meservey) was best known for his portrayal of Professor Harold Hill in The Music man (1962). At the end of the war in Europe he was with the 386th Bomb Group stationed in St. Trond, Belgium. His job was to receive intelligence reports from 9th Air Force headquarters and brief the bomber crews on what to expect on their missions. Fitje was also with the 386th in St. Trond.

One of my big regrets is that I will never be able to bring any of my cats home for you to see. Milo is so funny. Yesterday Martha and I walked around the base, to the post office, the officer's mess, the PX, the valet shop, etc., really quite a long walk with Milo running along behind us just like a dog. She now has lots of boyfriends who meow outside the door. The staff loves her and for some reason calls her Tiddlywinks. When they bring our breakfast in the morning, they say, "Good morning Miss Pitts, Good morning Miss Brush, Good Morning Tiddlywinks (With lots of feeling). May we take the kitten over, Miss Pitts?" By that time we are very glad to get rid of her because she spends the hours from 7:00 to 9:00 jumping from bed to bed and purring around our ears. Mrs. Smith, the cook, who is just like Helen Dodd, loves her the best and worries about her if she is out of sight for a minute.

What I love about it over here is that in spite of the war being so much closer, it is for some reason so much more peaceful, and I think it is because the people are so calm no matter what happens. Having known them as well as I do now I can see how they got through the first two years of the war so well. Honestly when I think of the things that have happened since I got here and how it would have bothered me at home, but seeing the way our staff reacts to it, sure has taught me something. I will always remember some of the things different ones of them have said to me at various trying times. The way of living over here sure is in contrast to our mad dash at home, not that I won't be glad to get back to it when the time comes.

Much Love,
Binni

April 11, 1944

Dear Mother and Dad,

This will be just a note to let you know that I am still alive. We are resting for a minute having just loaded a truck with one hundred cases of Coke in town and we are about to go out and unload it.

Milo greeted us when we got back by rushing out and climbing up on the axle of the two and a half ton truck and Martha had to crawl under it on her back to get her down.

We have had a very active week, doing several things. We are planning a big dance next Sunday so the invitations had to be gotten out. Then we decided to clear out one of the store rooms to make another office for people to paint in as there are several artists on the base and they have been using the back office as they were afraid someone would see them if they came out in the open. It is wonderful for the purpose as it has a sink in it and everything. The only trouble is it necessitated moving all the junk in the storeroom over to our rooms, but since we only sleep there we decided that we didn't care. Also since spring is here we have started our garden. When we started digging we found that the soil was all gravel, so we had to steal topsoil all over the base for it. Also you seem to strike water about a foot down around here, but I refuse to be discouraged and I hope things will grow. So far all we have are sunflowers, bulbs, lettuce, cabbage, and Sweet William.

We suddenly found out that we were about to be very low on rationed food, especially margarine, so we are now worrying about that. We have such good cakes here and we hate to have less, but six and a half pounds of margarine per day is not very much. Nevertheless we manage to make about five hundred cakes a day with it. We have only two pounds of butter per day, eight pounds of sugar, and four pounds of cheese; and then the boys get mad when we tell them that they cannot go out in the kitchen and eat great slabs of bread with about a quarter of a pound of butter on it. I really get tired of explaining about how our food is rationed to them.

I wish you could see how pretty it is getting around here now. Did I tell you that this base used to be someone's estate although you would hardly know it now except for the house, which is now the Hdqrs. building? There are lovely rolling fields all around and the approach to the base is really lovely with an iron fence on either side of the road and great trees over. Behind our club there is a huge field, which has now been made into a baseball, football, badminton, and volleyball field. Every nice night there is a baseball game. Behind the field there are lots of woods with brittle paths all through them where we walk to pick flowers for the club. This morning Mr. Shinn brought us a big bunch of pink violets, and this afternoon Mrs. Camp brought me a little bunch of different colored primroses to wear in my hair.

How are Ann and Franny? Give everyone my love.

Much Love,
Fitje

April 13, 1944

Dear Mother & Dad,

April 17, 1944

As you can see I didn't get very far the day I started this letter.

A lot is happened in the past week. First of all Martha is to be transferred. She leaves on Friday and we are all very unhappy to see her go. I am to be here alone, but I guess I'll manage okay. This is such a small club and it really runs beautifully.

Last night after a hectic week of planning we had our first big dance and it was a great success. We invited twenty-five civilian girls and twenty-five Land Army girls as well as the WACs. We made it awfully cute invitations on red and green paper. We turned our quarters into a dressing room for the girls and Mrs. Joyce, our decoder. All dressed in flowered chiffon, stayed over there and helped them, sewing on buttons, etc. At 5:00 we turned everyone out of the club and Martha and I, with the help of two WACs and some of the boys, took all of the tables apart and all the chairs out and decorated the whole club with laurel colored light bulbs and lots and lots of daffodils. It really looked wonderful. We had huge colored eggs and rabbits made of paper pasted on the end walls of the snack bar.

The food and servery was wonderful. We had purple, yellow and red crêpe paper streamers over the back table and a lovely white tablecloth over the front—and the food. We got a dozen eggs and made one hundred real egg salad sandwiches, we had sardines on little strips of toast with potato chips and watercress on them. We had all sorts of little cakes, and apple and custard tarts all made in our kitchen, and vanilla and strawberry custard (all individual) with foam on top. When the food was all put it on the table with lots of flowers and stuff around it sure looked good.

One of the best things, we got five dozen camellias from the greenhouse, which used to belong to this estate, and Jones, one of the staff, stood at the entrance with a basket and gave one to each girl when she came in. They were very pleased. In the middle of the evening we had a jitterbugging contest, which was a scream. We got a little Jewish boy who used to be a hawker at Coney Island to do the announcing etc. The nearby town won. We had a carton of cigarettes and a box of Elizabeth Arden bath powder for the prizes.

The staff all came dressed in their best clothes so of course couldn't do much manual labor, but we got it done somehow. After they went home Martha, Mrs. Thompson, myself, and some of the boys washed most of the dishes we were exhausted by the time it was over and I have been biting everyone's head off all day today.

We have been talking about that all week so I can't think of another thing that has happened. Got a letter from Hermie enclosing a plan of their new house and it looks awfully nice. I am glad Ann is so well. Also got a very nice letter from Ibby. Terry must be awfully cute.

Much love,
Fitje

April 22, 1944

Dear Mother & Dad,

Well Martha got off early yesterday morning amidst under confusion and about fifty boys helping her roll her bedding role and closer trunk while I lay comfortably in bed and watched. The staff gave her a cute little red alarm clock for a farewell present and Mrs. Thompson was so upset that she pretended that she was asleep so that she wouldn't have to say goodbye to her. Anticlimax though, because Martha just telephoned to say that she was coming back this afternoon for the weekend, so I'm now racking my brain to think of a way to get to the station to pick her up. When Marlow heard the sound of the typewriter she came tearing in saying meow, and is now sitting watching the keys go up with great interest, purring like mad. She is just like Jones with the vacuum cleaner. She has a big black boyfriend that keeps hanging around and who she ignores so far.

It seems very strange to be alone here. Last night I left the club for the evening for the first time with neither of us in it. One of the WACs and one of the soldiers on the base got married last Thursday and are just back from their honeymoon, so the medical department for whom the soldier works had a party for them. It was really very nice. An orchestra and about fifty people, beer to drink, and potato chips, sandwiches and cake supplied by us. Everyone seemed to be having a nifty time when I left about 11:30.

Today I went to do the shopping and bought the flowers. Pretty soon the woods will be full of them and we will be able to pick them ourselves. They're terribly expensive now, but are getting less so all the time. Every week Martha and I treat our selves to a carnation to wear in our hair in the evenings. Today we had a passenger, one of the technical experts on the post not in uniform who had to go to the same town to do an errand. He had a wonderful time carrying all my bundles and said he felt as if he were home again and shopping with his wife. He gave me more good advice about the shopping than anyone has been able to give me so far.

Before Martha left of course we had a number of parties. This is the strangest base because the boys were been transferred out to the groups keep coming back. Some of them have come back here every time they have a forty eight-hour pass. This week, several have back, all of whom have transferred since we've been here, to be gunners. One of them is just finished gunnery school and is waiting to go up on his first mission. He is from Boston and what a character. He is a terrible drunk, and will drink anything that he can get his hands on, even vanilla extract, but he is always nice and never even so much as swears in front of us. He was broken from sergeant to a private for being drunk and disorderly in London about four months ago but is hoping to get his stripes again now that he is a gunner. Sometimes he wanders around the base all night and keeps waking us up at intervals to see if there's anything we want him to do. I hope he will make a good gunner. It is sort of pathetic because every once a while he tries to pull himself together but he just can't.

There is another boy on the base, Leo Arsalanian, who comes from Providence and his parents own one of the store right next to the Osteopathic Hospital, on Warwick Avenue I think. The little store that advertises John's homemade ice cream and used to have a sign front of it saying "curb service." His family has Americanized their name and call themselves Lyon. I told him that I was going to ask you to stop in and see them sometime when you're driving past. He is a very nice boy. The other afternoon there were a lot of boys in the office and we got talking about what nationality they all were and how many different languages they could speak. It really was amazing. They all told about how their parents got to the U.S. and why they came. One was a Polish Jew, one a Serb, Leo is Armenian, and another was Italian. Leo's father came over when he was seventeen and doesn't remember crossing the ocean to get there. He still insists he crossed the channel to England and then took a train to the United States.

I have been meaning to tell you but I keep forgetting that I have never gotten Mrs. Gage's letter. It must've been lost in the mail or something. I hope she won't think I am rude because I don't answer it.

I wish you could've seen me the other night defending my club. Everyone had gone home about 11:30 but two drunks just in from pubbing, two new boys on the base and Kit, Leo, and the chronic drunk Hillary. I was trying to ease the strangers out the door so that I could lock up and was having trouble doing it although they were getting there gradually. Kit and Leo were waiting for me to lock up, as the boys are very nice about seeing that someone is there and we aren't left to lock up alone. Finally a bottle of gin dropped out of the back pocket of one of the drunks and smashed on the vestibule floor. That was more than Kit could stand and he came tearing out and push them out the door. Naturally everyone got mad and before I knew what was going on, all five of them were beating each other up. I, not being able to think of anything I would hate worse than a fight in the club, got right in the middle of it and finally pushed the strangers out the door and locked up. I was so mad at Kit for interfering, and I really told him off. The next day I felt very badly because I knew as soon as I thought it over that he was only trying to help, so I apologize to him, he apologized to the two strangers, and the two strangers came and apologized to me, and now we were all the best of friends.

Can't think of another thing to say except that I wish you could see our garden, which is progressing beautifully. I am now getting ready to plant some flowers around the other side of the club. Sunday night we are having another dance, cabaret style with tables all around the edges of the broom and colored lights. Tuesday night we are having a WAC, Headquarters softball game, which promises to be exciting. The Hdqrs. boys are going to pitch and bat left-handed.

Where did Andrew go, do you know? Haven't heard a word about Roger so he must be okay.

Much love,
Fitje

April 26, 1944

Dear Mother & Dad,

It is getting towards the close of a lovely day—warm sunshine and I even got lots of freckles and some sunburn. I had the best afternoon. One of the boys, John Daly, and I bicycled about three miles to a little town to see if we could buy some grass seed. We couldn't, but did get some paint and some dish rags both of which I have been looking for a long time. John is an awfully nice boy, very artistic, the son of a butcher. He paints all our signs for us and has been helping with the garden. While we were exploring the little town we came to a house with a little green house attached to it and lots of geraniums in it so we stopped in to see if they would sell us some. A Mr. Mann and his sister live there. They had never talked to an American girl before and were so nice. They insisted that we stay for tea and showed us all over their lovely garden and their tiny lumber mill right next door which is been in their family for 150 years. One man, Fred, who we met, had worked there for fifty-seven years today. I wish you could see the gardens now. They are lovely. The owners keep apologizing for them because they are not like they were before the war, but I think they are even prettier because they look less cultivated.

The day before yesterday I went down to the field with some of the flight section boys. When I got there some of them were about to take off in a C-47 to a place up near Liverpool to pick up some supplies so I went with them, and just left the club for a change. We had a wonderful time. About nine of us went. I navigated on the way up and flew a little on the way back or rather sat in the copilot seat with my hands on the controls. We flew over Liverpool and I got my first glimpse of the Atlantic Ocean since I landed in England last June. While we were waiting there for Chic to pick up the supplies we plugged in an electric coffee percolator and heated water, and opened some K Rations and made coffee and ate crackers and passed such remarks as, "It sure is rough in the ETO" and "If only our families could see us now." When Chic came back all he had was too little boxes about the size of

C-47

a tin of coffee. We thought that was pretty funny, eight men, one girl on a big plane, all that way for two little boxes. When we got back to the base Capt. Gillespie said, "Sergeant, go get a truck and unload those supplies right away." We must have flown near the Gages and thought of dropping in for tea. I told you didn't I that I have never heard from them? I am now trying to hitch-hike a plane ride to Ireland and hope to go on very soon for a couple of days.

Martha came back last weekend and is coming again this weekend. She is now taking a driving course and is to be in a Clubmobile. I miss her a lot and I guess she misses it here as she calls up about every night. Milo keeps me company at night and she is so cute. I have the door open while I am getting undressed and she comes home about 12:00 regularly. With three soft beds in the room she now chooses to sleep on the top of the hard bureau. I am very sorry you haven't been hearing from me so regularly and will try to do better in the future.

Love,
Fitje

May 4, 1944

Dear Mother & Dad,

For four nights now I have been trying to remember to bring my pen over here so I could write you a letter as you can see I have still forgotten.

This week I took off for two days and went down to Salisbury with the Greek while he picked up supplies. He started out Monday morning early in the Jeep with the top down and by the time we got there Monday night I was very sunburned. Salisbury was packed and I spent the night at a hotel in a bathroom complete with bathtub and bed right next to it. Usually occupied by Lord someone-or-other's batman,* so I was told by the maid. Pinky Dennison, whom Jane knows is at the ARC in Salisbury so I saw her and we went to visit the lovely cathedral there together. We came back to the base Tuesday stopping in London for dinner on the way.

Since I got back I have been full of energy and repainting the club, as most of it is light yellow and beginning to look like a little dingy. Luckily we have lots of paint leftover. Today we spring cleaned the kitchen and it was fun Mrs. Thompson had to go to London on business so we did all the cooking for today, yesterday and the cook had a day off. Joyce, fifteen with terrible asthma, Jean who engaged

* Valet

to one of the boys is seventeen, and Dennis, fifteen, very shy, and a wonderful worker, cleared up the kitchen and did a wonderful job. Every inch of floor, wall and shelf was scrubbed. I tried to fry an egg for my lunch and they said, "Get out Miss Pitts you're in the way." I always thought the kitchen was clean but it looks very differently now.

In the afternoon I dragged one of the boys, Paul Cassidy, out to help me pick flowers. Although he helped while we were out of sight he wouldn't have been caught dead helping me carry the branches home. The fields are all full of bluebells now and we keep the club full of bluebells, tulips, daffodils, and apple and cherry blossoms, as well as lilac and iris, which the staff brings from their gardens. I wish you could see the snack bar when we open it at 6:30, not that the food varies much from night tonight but Mrs. Thompson fixes it so nicely with flowers and parsley and watercress as decorations, and don't think it goes unnoticed because we have had many, many compliments on it. Why I say we I don't know. I don't do the work but I sure will praise my staff to anyone who will listen to me, and to them to. Now that summer is coming I know that we will have to get rid of at least one of them, as we won't be so busy, and it keeps me awake nights trying to decide which one as they are all so nice.

I got the picture of Johnny and I love it. It is very good of him isn't it? Tell him I thought of him the other night. I washed my hair and then went over to the club before I put it up. What comments! "Hey Fitje sure you forgot to plant the corn." "I never noticed all those gray hairs before but you still don't look a day over forty," etc. My morale suffered considerably.

Well it is 1:30 and I must go to bed, as Kit and Snuffy, two GIs, woke me up this morning at 6:30 swinging my bed around. I have a promise to get up for formation and eat breakfast with them. Mrs. Thompson was furious at them for coming in, which they shouldn't have done, and she got up and threw them out in no uncertain terms while I pretended I was still asleep.

May 5, 1944

I repainted the whole front of the snack bar while some of the boys took turns trying to throw a Ping-Pong ball in the paint can, which they finally succeeded in doing. Mandage, one of the boys, who transferred from here to one of the groups, is back on pass. He's been on thirty-seven missions and for some reason expects to get home on furlough in a couple of months. He is going to call you up if he does.

Why are you so fond of Mac, Mother? I forgot what I told you about him. He is mad right now because his two WACs finally got together and started checking up on him. Now they won't speak to him or each other. He calls Mrs. Thompson mom and she cooks him a powder egg omelet every night. She leaves a special can of beans on the shelf near the door for him, which he eats cold out of the can.

Martha is temporarily only twelve miles away and is at present spending the night here. She is very fond of Kruchok, the Russian, who is a wonderful boy.

I am in closing a note to Jane, as I don't know her address I am very excited at the prospect of her coming over.

Much love
Fitje

May 10, 1944

Dear Mother & Dad,

To say that I was surprised to hear about Lucy is putting it mildly.* You forget that I don't know any of the preliminaries of those things and had no idea such a thing was in the air! Write me about the wedding. Lucy must've been a very pretty bride. You two must feel very strange to be alone again. I suppose very soon I will be hearing about Ann and Hermes baby and then there will be two strangers in the family that I don't know. I feel very remote from it all. A year away from home makes more difference than I would have thought it would. If Johnny gets married before I get home I will feel as if there had been some changes.

Things are about as usual here. It is kind of lonely without Martha but I am busy so I don't really mind at all. She still isn't far from here and will be back this weekend, but after that she's going to move again, and will probably be farther away. The club is running smoothly, but we have to reduce the staff still more to make expenses meet and we can't decide who to get rid of.

Last night I went pubbing with a WAC and two of the boys, Mac and Snuffy. We walked for miles (so it seemed) and it was very pretty, but all the pubs were out of beer. We spent hours leaning over people's gates wishing someone would invite us in, but no one did, although we could see the people peering around their curtains probably thinking we were very strange. In the end we came back and fried ham and eggs on the stove in my room.

Did you get my letter enclosing a note to Jane? I can't remember mailing it but guess it must've been gotten mail because I haven't been able to find it around. Tell her to bring some Ace Combs if she comes. Combs are very hard to get and mine is in terrible condition.

Much love.
Binni

May 17, 1944

Dear Mother & Dad,

Today the little matchboxes from Jones arrived and they are so cute. The English staff admires them and is sure that only in America would you find little gadgets like that. I have already given away half of them for souvenirs, so you can tell Jones that he is very popular.

---

* Fitje just received news that her younger sister Lucy married Bill Grosvenor on May 1, 1944 when he was home for a ten-day leave. Bill was a flight leader who flew P-40s in China. He flew 132 missions with the 75th Pursuit Squadron, 14th Air Force under General Chennault. He later flew P-51s with the 2nd Air Commando Group. Bill flew 60 missions in India/Burma/Thailand area. Bill was awarded a Silver Star, Distinguished Flying Cross, Bronze Star and the Air Medal during the war. He was a Major at the end of the war.

Milo is not at all popular at present she has suddenly learned how to catch mice and young rats. Yesterday she caught three but never kills them as I guess we give her too much to eat and she isn't hungry enough. She brings them right into the kitchen or on Mrs. Thompson's bed and someone else has to kill them. Today she jumped up on the baking table and walked right across about a dozen tarts, which were all ready to be put in the oven. Mrs. T. was so mad she almost cried. We try to keep her out of the kitchen but it is very hard to. The other day, while someone from the medical department was inspecting the club, she walked right into the kitchen with a wiggly little rat in her mouth. It was terribly embarrassing.

Well the time has come again as it seems to come only too soon in this business when I am going to move again. I just heard about it this afternoon so not breaking the news to Mrs. Thompson yet, as she was practically hysterical when Martha, left and swears that she won't stay without one of us. Anyway I asked for a weeks vacation before I go to the new base and they are going to see if it can be arranged and let me know definitely tomorrow. If I can have it I think I will go down to Cornwall for a few days. Anyway I will let you know my new address in a couple of days as soon as I know it myself. The base that I am going to is operational anyway, thank goodness. It is a permanent base and the club is much bigger and already operating so I won't have to open it. It will seem strange to go to a place that I didn't start myself and very sad to leave this little place as I feel that it belongs to me especially since I have been here alone. I don't know what to do with Milo yet but I guess I had better leave for here she is doing so well with the mice.

Now that this club is running so well I know that I would get in a rut if I stayed here much longer and a big club will be something different. It has a first and second floor and I don't know how long it's been since I've been in building with two stories. I hate to think of some stranger in my little office.

Well nothing particularly exciting has happened lately that I can tell you about. Martha was back last weekend and we had the usual party and stayed up all night as usual. I had to fire two of the staff that very evening and was so upset that I couldn't enjoy the party at all. I guess that I told you about Daphne and John, the two kids who wash up in evenings. I hated to see them go, but as Mrs. Thompson said, we couldn't afford to be sentimental, and we had to cut down on expenses.

Mrs. Aldrich wrote me a nice long letter about the wedding and will you thank her so much. It really was a wonderful letter telling me all the details about what everyone wore and so on, and I almost felt as if I were there.

Well a couple of boys that were transferred to another base have just come in so I will finish this tomorrow.

May 18, 1944

Well it looks like I didn't get any leave right now and I'm going to have to leave here Saturday. I will write you soon and let you know where I am. It will take me at least two days to pack all the junk I've accumulated in six months here.

Love
Fitje

CHAPTER 7

Home of the Memphis Belle

May 21, 1944–May 27, 1944

Fitje transferred to the 91st Bomb Group at Bassingbourn on May 20th, but was only there for eleven days before transferring to the 386th Bomb Group. Her letters don't say why the Red Cross transferred her so quickly although it must have felt her experience was needed elsewhere. According to her letters the Aero Club at Bassingbourn was one of the largest clubs, with a large experienced staff that ran "very smoothly." She wrote her parents saying she knew they would ". . . wonder why I was transferred again so soon. I promise you that it wasn't because I did anything bad."

Activated on April 14, 1942, the 91st Bomb Group moved to England in October of the same year. It flew its first mission on November 7, 1942, bombing a Luftwaffe air base at Abbeville France, and it's last, to Pilsen, Germany, on April 25, 1945.

The 91st flew 340 combat missions and lost 197 planes. 887 crewmen died in action and another 123 were listed as missing in action. Another 959 airmen became POWs. In thirty months of combat the 91st Bomb Group suffered the greatest number of losses of any heavy bomb group in World War II. Only seven divisions (all infantry) had killed-in-action rates higher than the 91st BG.

Fitje never talked about the loss of the men she knew. A cloud of death associated with the operational groups moved her to write on May 27th that being ". . . back on an operational station is sort of depressing but I will get used to it again I guess. The gunners seem so much younger and I feel so sorry for them."

The 91st Bomb Group was best known as the home of the Memphis Belle, which was one of the first B-17 Bombers to complete twenty-five missions, after which it and the crew returned to the US and flew around the country raising money for war bonds. Pilot Robert K. Morgan named the plane for his girlfriend, Margaret Polk. In 1944 the War Department produced a documentary, directed by Billy Wilder, called *Memphis Belle: The Story of a Flying Fortress*. The movie, *Memphis Belle*, starring Matthew Modine and Harry Connick Jr., was released in 1990.

May 21, 1944

Dear Mother & Dad,

Well, here I am at my third new home in a year, and what a set up.

This is a huge big base and much different as was a permanent English base before the war, and the first to be taken over by Americans so this group has been here for a long time. The buildings are all permanent, no cute little Nissen huts, and we even have steam heat, something I haven't seen for a long time. It is much too grand and I am home sick for my rough life at IX Bomber Command. You must go see the movie *Memphis Belle* when it comes to Providence, as it was about a plane and pilot actually on this station and a lot of the movie was even taken here. It will give you an idea of what it is like.

I was driving over here Saturday morning after the usual parties, etc., and it was very sad. My successor was there and is very nice and I was happy to leave my little club in such good hands. I did not mean to celebrate my departure in any way as I knew it would make me very unhappy, but Friday night the medical department and the special service department, "Doc" Jones and Major Lindsey, and some of the boys came over to my quarters with two bottles of scotch and we had a good time. The boys packed my clothes for me and it was very funny.

The club here is tremendous (two stories). It seems funny to go up and down stairs to get to my office, which is on the second floor. It has been running for year and a half and runs very smoothly. The girl who started it just left before I came for a new and entirely different job. It has the reputation of being one of the best-run clubs in England, and I hope it will continue to be with me running it. At present I have a staff assistant* but I don't think that she is going to be here for long. She is very nice, by profession a diver. She was in the Aquacade at the World's Fair and in Vaudeville in New York before the war. Her husband is a special service officer also over here. Our quarters are not far off in the officers club and quite nice. There are even tennis courts on the base.

The funny thing is that I visited this club sometime during the first two months that I was here and went away once with Micheal Phillipe, whom you probably remember. I remember very clearly going back and telling Jean that I was glad I wasn't stationed there! It is sort of cold and forbidding, if that's the right word. Thirteen of the staff live right here at the club and there seems to be about twenty-five more that come in during the daytime although I'm not quite sure yet. As a matter of fact I'm very vague about the whole thing is I've only been here for two days. Today we went over to get some flowers at another part of the station which is an old estate taken over by the Army. You would love the vegetable gardens, Dad. Captain Marshall is in charge of it and he showed us all around. They grow lots of the vegetables eaten at the station, tomatoes, lettuce, celery, etc., even watermelon, melons, grapes, nectarines, peaches, sweet corn, raspberries, strawberries, etc.

* Jean Gureasko

Well, there is a dance tonight and I must go help decorate the joint.

I am wondering about Jane. Does she know yet what her plans are? What do you hear from Lucy?

Much love
Binni

❦

May 27, 1944

Dear Mother & Dad,

Well another day at the 91st bomb group draws to a close and it is a nifty one too, warm and sunny. We have relaxed all day, as last night was the night of the show that Jean has been working on and thank God it is over. It was a big success and brought the house down. Everyone forgot his part of course, but the ad lib was marvelous. There was one pinup scene in which there were six of the fattest men on the base dressed in red crêpe paper skirts. They were very funny. We sweated out what the Colonel would say about the unrehearsed dirty jokes, which the two masters of ceremonies outdid each other in telling, but so far nothing has happened.

Jean is very nice and really wonderful at her job. She is twenty-six and has a son eight years old. Her first husband was a pilot and was killed at the very beginning of the war. In fact she thinks that he probably was flying from this base. She is now married to a 1st lieutenant in special services who is also over here, but I don't think she likes him very much. She has done a lot of work in photography in New York and takes wonderful pictures.

I am beginning to know the staff, having concentrated on it all week. There are three girls in the officer snack bar, Sasha, Mary, and Greta. Mary is married to a Colonel who is stationed in Yorkshire. Her six-year-old daughter is in a boarding school in the south of England. Greta was on a ski team before the war, was in France when the Germans got to Paris, and left just ahead of them. She had a very exciting time getting back to England. Sasha is Canadian. Her husband is American but joined the RAF before the war started. They were married over here the summer before war broke out when she was here traveling. She has never been home since and now has two children. Her husband was on this base before it became an American base, and was shot down over France about two years ago, and is a prisoner of war. She is awfully nice. Mrs. West, the manageress, went home to London about a month ago and found that her home had been bombed the night before and her sister killed. Mrs. Webb one of the cleaning women just got a telegram here saying that her son in the RAF was missing in action.

This club is really very elegant. The last was the smallest Aero Club in England, and this one is one of the two biggest. It is quite a change and I still feel lost. The boys at IX Bomber Command are so nice. One of them has called me up every night so far as they think that I must be lonesome. My friend Hillary, about whom I've told you, was very badly hurt in a plane crack up recently but I guess is going to be alright. I forgot to tell you that this club has a real soda fountain and we serve fountain cokes. As far as I know it is the only Aero Club in England that has one.

Being back on an operational station is sort of depressing but I will get used to it again I guess.

Warren "Red" Farwell, Fitje, Jean Gureasko, Fitje
and J.C. "Hinkie" Hinkle, Bassingbourn, May 1944

The gunners seem so much younger and I feel so sorry for them. Hinkie and Red are the two I know the best so far and they are so cute. When they're not flying they are always around. The other night Hinkie, Red and I took coffee and donuts down on the line to the ground crews on their two planes. They were so nice and insisted on taking me all over the planes. Although I have heard it all before I never get sick of having the mechanics explain everything to me. They feel such a responsibility for their planes and the men that flying them and very proud when their planes never have to turn back because of some mechanical defect. The crew chief of Hinkie's plane is named Mack. He and six mechanics take care of that plane and another on the hard stand right next to it. Naturally it is practically a twenty four-hour job patching them up, etc. Hinkie says that when they are already to take off the ground crew, one by one never fail to stick their heads in and say good luck. The other day we went down to the hardstand to sweat in the mission with the ground crew and it was terribly exciting with all the crew chiefs kidding each other if one of their planes landed with a feathered engine which of course meant a lot of work for that particular ground crew, and watching the crew chief guide those huge things on to the hardstand.

May 28, 1944

Two of the boys from IX Bomber Command dropped in to see me this afternoon and were much impressed by the set up, especially the Coke machine. Pinky, Red and I took them down to the combat mess for dinner.

, I just got the envelope today containing the white gloves, bobby pins, and picture of Jane. Thanks an awful lot they will be useful and I like the picture of Jane. Mrs. Thompson, by the way, just loved the picture of John and wanted me to leave it behind when I left.

I very badly need more stockings so will you start sending me more in envelopes—no cotton ones as I don't like them, and anyway, it is too hot for them now. See if you can get some rayon mesh, as I think they might wear better. I am dying to hear what Jane's plans are. I expect to hear every day now that I am an aunt. Hope Ann is well. I haven't heard from Warren for a long time and I'm wondering where he is now. Does Anne know? How is Franny?

Love to everyone.
Fitje

CHAPTER 8

Warren and Hinkie

During her brief stay at Bassingbourn, Fitje met Warren "Red" Farwell and J. C. "Hinkie" Hinkle. Red and Hinkie were tail-gunners and best friends. Red, born in 1922, was from Eagle Rock, Missouri; Hinkie was from Bell Buckle, Tennessee. By the time my mother met them they'd both survived over twenty-five missions. Some might consider their longevity a miracle, as the life expectancy of a tail-gunner in World War II was nine missions.

The authorship of the story is a mystery. While it is written in the first person, suggesting Fitje wrote it, and is unquestionably her voice, the writing style differs from that of her letters. The style she would have used to write her letters most likely differed from the style she adopted in more formal writing, but it is a mystery. It is possible she wrote it with someone else, perhaps a journalist was on the base looking for a personal interest story. Whoever wrote the story, it is important as it is the only mention in any of her letters of the terrible stress the crews were under when they were on missions. The fifth paragraph in particular seems to capture the adrenaline that must have surged through the crewmen even after the mission was over and they returned to base.

Warren "Red" Farwell and
J.C. "Hinkie" Hinkle, May 1944

A war puts strange personalities in strange places and the fact that it should have made Warren and Hinkie tailgunners on fortresses to fly thirty missions over Europe, sweating out weather, and flak and occasionally protecting their planes against enemy fighters seems one of the strangest. Warren, with very red hair, is called "Red" by most of his friends but we feel that his personality deserves a more distinctive nomenclature so we call him by his middle name. He has brilliant red hair, almost white eyebrows, blue-blue eyes, freckles and rosy complexion, made rosier by the fact that he blushes easily and most of the time. He has a soft-spoken drawl and a slow, lazy way about him, but his slight stammer and an expression he has when he is daydreaming reveal the inner turmoil of his mind. Often the talk is of his pilot, Lt. Curr. "Boy, I felt sorry for that kid today. He flew almost the whole trip; the copilot was so scared he couldn't take the controls. Boy, was he tired. He's only a kid you know." This makes us smile, because although Lt. Curr is only just twenty-one, Warren is not yet quite twenty-two.

Hinkie is shorter and slighter than Warren. He is extremely muscular, brown-haired and brown-eyed. He, too, has a southern drawl but a quick manner and unbounded energy. Most of the time he dresses in an old sweatshirt and his shorts, which stick out, over the tops of his pants are usually plaid or bright orange. He looks for all the world as if he had just stepped in from a game of schoolboy football, and as a matter of fact left college in his freshman year just after the football season to join the army.

On the days that they are flying we have a code with the chaplain and he never forgets to let us know. At briefing Warren and Hickey tell him and later he calls us. "ETA 2130 hours. OR-T Tommy and OR-Q Queenie." At 9:30 we are in front of the control tower sweating them all in but particularly OR-Q Queenie and OR-T Tommy. We hear in the distance the monotonous grinding of engines carrying the big bombers home. Several groups fly over and finally our own with the large triangular "A", which identifies them. Everyone counts and watches for feathered props and other battle damage. They peel off and begin to land. Our two always seem to be among the last, but they are safe again. We go back to our office and wait until interrogation is over.

Finally they come in, glowing outwardly from the period at high altitude and inwardly from several shots of scotch in the briefing room. They are very tired, and their faces still bear the marks of the oxygen masks. They are dirty, but have hurried over without stopping to wash. Most of all they are glad to be back and a little surprised that they are. We listen to the happenings of the day and although we don't say so we can't believe they could have seen all that horror and come back still looking like two kids. We are glad that their mothers don't know what they go through, and we think of those addresses that they have given us and thank God we don't have to use them.

Sometimes it is a milk run; no flak, no fighters but still that fear, almost worse as there is no relief for it. "That old weather man was wrong—we couldn't see any of the targets. We came back with a full bomb load. Boy, did I sweat that one out—cumulus clouds all over the place. You could see them standing up behind the pilot. They thought it was a milk run—Boy, did I sweat out those fighters. I guess I've had it. I had two drinks and then my pilot said I guess we'll have to have one on our 25th—twenty-five for the U.S. and now five for General Doolittle. I'll have one if you'll have two more—Whoo! You know I was on that Sweinfort raid and those guys weren't and I know what it's like to have the fighters come out of those clouds. You haven't got a chance. They dart out one after another and you've had it before your fighters can get back to protect you. Look where they routed us today—right over Germany—over all the fighter bases to try and make the fighters come up. I'm telling you Fitje I really was scared. Boy, did I sweat that one out. Only five more to go and I'll never fly in a B-17 again—five more for General Doolittle. Why weren't you and Jean down to sweat us in? We can see your smiling faces a hundred miles away. We only had four P-51s with us today. I kept watching them and did they look lovely, almost as lovely as you look, Fitje. Maybe I'm a little drunk and shouldn't talk, but I'm telling you, before I ran around with the boys and did a lot of things, everything in fact, but not anymore, not if I live through the next five. I really think that when your time is up, it's up, no matter where you are or what you're doing. But I go see the chaplain every time. Good old Chaplain Biggs. It's just like he says, it might not do any good but it makes a guy feel better! You and Jean are going to celebrate with me aren't you? I'm going to be four times as drunk as I am now. Boy, I'm going to pass right out on the sidewalk. Hey listen Fitje, if I don't get back you and Jean can have the scotch because I'm going to give it to you to keep for me, like you said. I'm going to get it this weekend. I promised my ground crew a drink so I'm going to take a bottle right in my bag on that last one. Boy, will we be flying low. You know the 323rd dispersal area—we've going to buzz right up those trees. My navigator says 'I want to see those trees over my head.' I hope these last five are all milk runs like today. I'm telling you, Fitje, I sweat out Berlin every time I go for a briefing. I don't know—you're in flak for about fifteen or twenty minutes steady. Sometimes I wonder—like those guys bail out over London just because the flak is so heavy. The other day a guy in our squadron bailed out over Leipzig, and the ship wasn't hurt badly, just part of the wing or aileron gone, and they

Hinkie, May 1944

can set the automatic pilot and get back okay. The rest of the crew got back. Poor guy—I'll never forget it. Right over the target. If I had a cigarette and a light I'd smoke now. Only five more for General Doolittle, and then we can all sweat Hinkie out. He started with me, but I don't know, he sure got behind. It seems to me they send the pilots to Berlin who don't believe in evasive action. They should fly like this—boy that flak. I guess I'll go sack it for a while. Hey, Fitje, what time is it? Will you call me at 7:00 and be sure they wake me up? Then I'll shave and shower and be here by eight. I have to shave every day—Boy, my skin's tender and that oxygen mask rubs my face if I don't—Boy. What time are you going to wake me up—7:00? Don't forget now. Be sure I'm awake. You don't think they'll make me fly tomorrow just before I go on pass do you? I'll tell them Fitje says I can't. I guess I'm just not the combat type. I feel sorry for anyone who's more scared than I am."

Often the planes land late in the evening and we wait in our room for a knock on the window that tells us they are safe. We hurry into our coats. Those long walks in the rain while we hash out the days work. I say rain because it usually is raining in England and often it is welcome as it hides the tears that you try to keep back as you listen to the fears and troubles that cannot be loaned in the barracks where all have the same.

Often the planes don't go out and for a day we all relax. We meet at the club for a late breakfast of eggs and toast and go for long bicycle rides or a swim in a nearby pool. For twenty-four hours there are no worries, no fears. We talk of our families and how long it will be before we are home again. We go to see the ground crews at work, getting the big forts ready to fly again. We count the flack holes and laugh because we know that for today anyway they are safe.

Perhaps some day we will not see them land, or not hear that soft knock on our window. We pray that this will not be so and somehow we believe that Warren and Hinkie will come through all right.

CHAPTER 9

The Crusaders

June 4, 1944–September 23, 1944

Fitje was with the 91st Bomb Group less than two weeks before she transferred to the 386th Bomb Group on May 31, 1944. It was her fourth posting in eleven months in Europe and the last until August 1945 when the 386th went home.

The airfield was on the grounds of the Easton Lodge estate, a stately Victorian Gothic home at Little Easton, three miles northwest of Great Dunmow.

The 386th Bomb Group, which flew B-26 Marauders, was activated on December 1, 1942 and moved to England on June 3, 1943. It was initially part of the 8th Air Force, which focused on strategic bombing, primarily in Eastern Europe. In October 1943, in anticipation of D Day, the 386th was one of four medium bombardment groups transferred to the 9th Air Force to focus on tactical bombing, primarily in Western Europe.

From July 30, 1943 when they flew their first mission over Woensdrecht in the Netherlands until the last mission over Stod in Czechoslovakia on May 3, 1945, the 386th flew 409 missions. During the time Fitje was with the 386th, the group flew 220 missions. She "sweated out" every mission writing, "When boys like that don't get back from the mission you feel like you have lost a very good friend." While it is unknown how many of the "boys" died while Fitje was with the group, 182 of them died in action during the war. She must have known many of them.

By the time she transferred to the 386th Fitje had been the assistant manager of one club, and manager of another two. Experience was a great teacher; she was by now a professional, confident in her own abilities. On September 23, 1944 she wrote she had visited a Red Cross club in a nearby town to attend the wedding reception of one of the boys on the base who had married an English girl. She met an American Red Cross girl from Boston who had been in England for two weeks and was struggling to adjust. She later wrote that the girl ". . . was terribly worried about a lot of things and it was amazing to talk to her because it took me right back to the first couple of months that I was here and how amazed I was by it all. I guess I have completely lost my sense of perspective or something. It certainly is going to be strange to get back to some sort of normal life."

June 4, 1944

Dear Mother & Dad,

By this time you have probably heard the good news from Ibby, as Roger said he wrote her last night. Anyway in case you haven't, I have been transferred again and am now on the same base that he is on. Isn't that wonderful? I am so happy about it because I know more people here than I knew in Providence I think. Lots of them were at bomber command when I was there before they were transferred out to this group. The C.O., Col. Kelly, was there and a good friend of ours. I have been here

Colonel Joe W. Kelly

for two days now and people that I knew a bomber command keep coming in or calling. Lots of the boys have already been over to see me as I am very near where I was. Everyone is so nice and the club is swell. I know you will wonder why I was transferred again so soon. I promise you that it wasn't because I did anything bad. Anyway I'm glad to be back with the 9th Air Force.

The most exciting of all was getting here as they flew up to get me in a B-26. It was all quite sudden and I packed up while the plane was circling the field. I could hardly wait to call Roger but the news had already reached him so he wasn't surprised. He looks very well and his damaged eye doesn't show at all.* We meet all the missions here with coffee and sandwiches so I will be able to keep close track of him. Last night there was an officer's dance on the base and I went with him. Tell Ibby that everyone kept kidding him and saying "I thought you were married Roger."

This is another place, which was formerly someone's estate. It is lovely. There is a lovely castle, with beautiful gardens where we went to pick flowers yesterday. The accountant here, Pat Dean, is very nice. She was born in South Africa and lived in Singapore until a few days before the Japs got there. On her way home her ship was torpedoed and she was literally lifted out of the water by her hair. The club is Nissen and large and very nice. Our quarters are also in a Nissen hut and are just being completed so we present I am living with three of the staff right near the club. The Field Director, Dick Moncure, is terribly nice. In fact the whole setup is perfect and I feel very fortunate. The night I got here I went to Col. Kelly's for a drink

---

* Roger was slightly injured when his plane was hit and a small piece of plexi-glass hit him in the eye.

late in the evening. He and Col. Beatty live in the cutest house that used to be the gardeners cottage, with roses climbing all over.

I will write more details later but I didn't want you to hear the good news as soon as possible. I will also write Ibby. Right now I have to go up to the castle to have a drink with Dick, and Mr. Buford from the ARC who is here. It is always very confusing the day after a dance.

Much love
Fitje

June 8, 1944

Dear Mother & Dad,

As you can imagine my birthday* was just about the most exciting thing around here that you can possibly imagine. The day before I heard from Roger that I was an aunt, and I was very pleased. Your letters caught up with me yesterday having been forwarded twice. I loved the letter from my nephew.

We went to bed Monday night fully expecting that the great day was approaching so I wasn't a bit surprised to wake up about 6:00 hearing the radio blaring in the next hut blaring forth the news. The planes going over all night didn't even wake me up as I am so used to the sound. Even air raids don't wake me up anymore. We have been so busy serving coffee and sandwiches to missions ever since that we have hardly had time for another thing. Now we have arranged to keep the fires going all night so we can make coffee at any time. The staff is wonderful, and drops everything when we get word to make sandwiches. Roger is doing fine. We have been very lucky so far.

My birthday was not forgotten in the excitement. In the evening Col. Kelley, the C.O., asked me up to his quarters for a drink and gave me two roses and eight oranges for a birthday present. When I got back to my quarters there were a lot of little packages from Roger, Pat and some of the other officers containing, safety pins, airmail envelopes, etc.

Serving the missions and hearing all about what is going on and what the boys see is very exciting as you can imagine.

I got a letter from Tim, Mother, saying that you spelled two years "too" so you see you better not criticize my spelling anymore.

Sorry this is such a short letter. I will write more when the excitement dies down and I have a little more time. I want to write Jane and tell her how she can get in touch with me. I wish you would send me pictures of the baby and of Bill so I can see what they look like.

Did you get the pictures of myself and Major Russell and myself and Martha that I sent recently?

The Catholic chaplain, Father Calner, is from Providence, and is terribly nice.

Our quarters are finished and we have moved in. We have our own hot water boiler and nice hot water all the time. We each have our own room too, which is very nice. A nearby plane explosion blew

---

* Fitje's twenty-seventh birthday was on D Day, June 6, 1944.

the sections of the ceiling half way out right over my bed the other night and I am wondering how long it's going to be before they fall down on my head.

I didn't ever send the money home as I have started a bank account over here and now have fifty-six pounds in it. I also got a raise so am going to be able to save a lot. In case you ever need to know for any reason it is in the Barclay's Bank, the main branch, which is in London.

Much love,
Fitje

June 11, 1944

Dear Mother & Dad,

Roger and I are anxious to hear your reaction when you find out that we are here together. I wonder if you have heard the news yet. Tonight Pat and I met Roger and Frank, one of the pilots, at the bar and had a drink before dinner with them. Roger was running true to form. First he picked up a chair and both of the arms fell off, then he introduced me to the only other man on the base with less hair than he has. All his friends call him flat top and he is most insulted. They also call him Freedman and accuse him of going to church on Saturday all of which makes him very mad. It's all in fun of course. On the way home from mess we met five little boys not more than eight years old with huge pieces of plexi glass, which they had picked up. Roger wanted a piece so he told us he had a way with children and to hear him bargaining with them so funny that I could hardly stand up I was laughing so hard. He didn't get the plexi glass. He has some lobster that was sent from home so he is going to bring it over and we are going to have lobster salad over in my quarters after the club closes.

Last night I went to Col. Kelley's quarters and had the best dinner; chicken, French-fried potatoes, carrots, tomato salad, chocolate pie, coffee, etc. It was delicious. I rushed back to the club for the evening, and after it closed, went with him to help a new general celebrate his promotion. It was fun but I have to stop keeping these late hours. Nobody ever seems to sleep, but I still need a certain amount. We are now meeting early morning missions so I have a telephone in my room so I can be waked up and see that the staff is up to make the coffee, etc. Three of the staff live here and don't seem to mind when they have to get up. Our quarters are terribly nice. Separate from the others and all to our selves. We each have a room of our own in a Nissen hut. I guess I have told you all that before, though.

Martha is coming tomorrow to visit me for a few days, as she has a weeks leave. This is a terrible time to have anyone visiting me as they are putting a new floor in the snack bar and everything will be very hectic for a day or two. We have to get in our office by climbing in the window literally. I don't know how we will ever serve any food for the next three nights but I will not worry about it until tomorrow.

Tell Ann that I got a letter from Warren[*] that took five weeks to get here. I can't imagine where he

---

[*] Ann Pitts, Herman's wife was originally from Canada. Her brother Warren he was in the Canadian Army.

is. He says that it is very warm and he is getting a lovely sunburn. I wrote him about the baby thinking maybe he would hear sooner from me than from home.

Roger is here now and I have just made some delicious salad. He says that Ibby sent him the lobster. He hardboiled two eggs but when we cut them up they weren't nearly hard enough and anyway he had had them for two weeks and they aren't very good. He says to give you his love. He says that Terry can walk but I don't believe it.

What are Ann and Hermie going to call the baby for short?

Well, I must go over or all the salad will be gone.

Much love to you all.

Fitje

June 13, 1944

Dear Mother & Dad,

Today is a rainy day so I imagine it will be a very quiet one. We usually serve coffee and toast in the little snack bar in the mornings from 9:00 to 10:00 but this morning we are not doing it because the servery is having the new floor put on it and because this is the day allotted to spring cleaning in the kitchen. This club is very dirty but is being slowly cleaned up. Because of the weather, everyone is relaxing. I think I am about the only person in the club. Dick Moncure, the field director here, is nifty. He was a lawyer from Richmond before the war and he is more fun. He is also wonderful at his job. He is always around and the boys think that he is wonderful. This floor that is being laid is his pride and joy and he spent all day yesterday walking up and down the edge of it as they laid the strips telling everyone that would listen all about it. He even invited Col. Kelly down to see it.

Red Cross field director
Dick Moncure

I don't think that I have described the club to you. It has a huge big snack bar. Off to one side of it there is a separate entrance to the snack bar and into the games room, which is a huge room with three snooker tables, three Ping-Pong tables, dartboards etc. At the other end of the snack bar you go into the lounge with the radiogram and comfortable chairs, etc., then into the library with a lovely big stone fireplace, then the front entrance and then the little snack bar where we serve in the morning and is used for special things like bingo and dancing lessons and a dressing room for the girls on dance night, which is Friday. Our office is right off the snack bar. It is a nice big office and we have the niftiest little lockers made from an old flying locker that got broken up, or that's our story. It has seventy-two different compartments all fixed in a tricky design against the wall and painted pink. Each locker is filled with something and every time you look for something you always start at the wrong end and go through all of them and find it in the last one. We have pink geraniums at the windows and one of the staff keeps a vase of peonies from her garden on the filing cabinets and you know how much I love them. I forgot to say that in the very center the club (it is built in sort of a circle) there is an outdoor flagstone courtyard with tables and chairs.

This is a nifty base. For some reason moral is excellent. The officers are proud of the fact that the officer's mess here is without a doubt the worst in the ETO. The mess officer is a flying officer, grounded because of ear trouble and naturally is not too interested in mess but is a nifty guy. He is always down on the line watching the planes. Right beside the servery, pasted up on the wall, there is a huge big menu from a restaurant in New York just to remind you that you may be eating better someday. There are millions of dogs round and they crawl around under your feet all the time you're eating. You never hear anyone complain and I heard plenty of complaints the last two places I was where the food was excellent in comparison. It is hard to know what makes some groups so much cheerier than others. They are so nice to us. Everything that we want for the club or for us is ours for the asking. I am used to struggling for things.

Next Sunday we are having a lawn dance on the castle lawn, or rather Special Services is having it as beer is being served. We have been making invitations and helping with the arrangements and I think it will be fun. I am trying to get away this week for a few days vacation as I haven't had any for so long, and Lord knows what might happen next to keep me from getting any. Martha is coming today so I am hoping that she will go somewhere with me. Eleanor, my staff assistant, is going to be bridesmaid tomorrow for a friend of hers who is marrying a soldier on leave from Iceland, or somewhere. They are going to fly down to get her today in a Liberator.

Two of the flying officers brought in a little baby chaffinch which has fallen out of its nest for me to take care of until can fly, It is the cutest thing and very tame. It reminds me of the little sparrow that I had. Jake, one of the gunners, and I fixed up the cage for it out a wicker scrap basket turned upside down, with a poker for perch and newspaper under it. It is sitting on the poker at the moment chirping happily. An egg is being cooked for it in the kitchen. Martha and I are going to decide what to do about Milo when she comes. All day long people keep calling me from bomber command to say that Milo is sitting on their desk. She spends a lot of time up in the orderly room and I don't know what they do to her but Sgt. Dutton calls up and says talk to your mother Milo and then I hear this horrible meow on the other end of the phone. Apparently she even goes up to see the general. The two girls who are there now don't like cats so Mrs. Thompson has to keep her out of sight. I guess Martha will probably take her, as her position is slightly more secure then mine at the present time. She is now in the Rest and Convalescent Home Department.

I wish Jane would hurry and get here if she is coming. Be sure and keep me informed about her, as I want her to be able to get in touch with me. Tell her to go to the Red Cross Headquarters at 12 Grosvenor Square immediately if she has any trouble finding me. I guess she has my latest address.

Love,
Fitje

June 17, 1944

Dear Mother & Dad,

Martha and I are having the most wonderful vacation. We came to London Thursday afternoon and we are staying in the cutest 4th floor apartment with Judy and Ilsa, two friends of Martha's. There are two beds, me in one, Judy and Ilsa in the big bed, and Martha on the floor where she swears she sleeps very well. The apartment is at 2 Baker Street (street famous for Sherlock Holmes) over an antique china store. Judy and Ilsa, one an artist and one a pianist, are out most of the time and Martha and I have been buying radishes, lettuce, asparagus, tec., and messing around in the kitchen cooking the best meals. We have hardly been out of the apartment except to go to the hairdresser yesterday and have permanents.

E. May came up for a drink yesterday and I gave her all sorts of instructions as to how to reach me the minute Jane arrives.* She is living in a house in Chelsea and is planning to have Jane live with her. The maid who cleans the apartment in the afternoons is a scream. She has her own idea about the new German secret weapon† and thinks they are piloted by <u>small,</u> ten-year old boys who don't do anything but keep the engines running. She says she would feel a lot safer if they were grown up men, even though German, as "A ten-year old boy can't be expected to know what he's doing can he?" The guns are noisy at night but we sleep in the daytime to make up for it. I find I can sleep whenever I get a chance now, night or day and if I can get to sleep before they start I don't wake up unless someone wakes me. I was really tired when I came but feel much better now.

Martha arrived at the base Tuesday night supposedly at 11:00 but the train was an hour and a half late. Col. Kelly who was at Bomber Command when we were first there and is now C.O. at the 386th had asked us up for a drink when she got here and the poor guy had to wait until about 1:30 for us.

Wednesday afternoon we put on old cotton dresses and sneakers and went back to Bomber Command and what a reception we got. We went to the club first and Mrs. Thompson greeted us with tears streaming down her cheeks saying "My little kids, my two children." Then Mac, Mike, Snuffy, Dutton and us went to so see Doc Jones (also Milo who wasn't a bit glad to see us and finally ran away). The dispensary was closed for reconditioning but Doc was there and we had the best time. He called all the boys we wanted to see saying something like "Sgt. Cassidy, according to my records you haven't had your Thyroid shot. You get right down here and get it," and the poor boy would come down knowing darn well he'd already had it and completely baffled. We went to the G.I. mess for dinner with all our friends and Mrs. Thompson came too. Then we went down to the officer's bar and saw the general and

---

* Fitje's sister Jane never made it to Europe during the war.

† The V1, and later V2 Rockets were *Vergeltungswaffen*, Retaliatory Weapons, developed by the Germans in the early '40s. Launched from the northeastern French coast the V1 Rockets were first used in June 1944. They killed 6,184 and wounded another 17, 981. The V2 Rockets were introduced in September. They took five minutes to travel 200 miles, killed a total of 2,754 and wounded 6,523. The last rockets were fired in March 1945.

Dance on the Easton Lodge lawn,
June 18, 1944

everyone else. Apparently the girls here now don't like it so well and things aren't running too smoothly. I'm sure it will work out all right though. I hate to see anything go wrong there. Everyone was so nice and so flattering that we both thought we were wonderful when we left.

I told you about the little bird two of the boys gave me. I found it dead in it's cage a couple of mornings later, Poor little thing. It was so cute and didn't seem at all sick the night before.

The picture of Lucy and Bill came and I was so glad to see it. Bill looks very, very nice just as I knew he would. I wish he would come over here so I could see him. Now I am sweating out a picture of my nephews. I also got a long, very nice letter enclosing some bobby pins, which I was very glad to get. Will you thank her? It seems hopeless for me to write her, as she is moving around faster than I am.

I wonder if you have caught up with me yet. This assignment is much more permanent I think. I wish Jane would hurry. Let me know what I going on.

Much love,
Fitje

June 19, 1944

Yesterday was the day of our big lawn dance and I wish you could have seen it. Instead of the usual Friday night dance at the club we had it on the lawn in front of the castle. Crowds came, the weather was perfect. The Clubmobile came and served coffee and doughnuts, and we had sandwiches made at the club and cake made in the mess halls. The orchestra as wonderful and dancing on the lawn was much more successful than I thought it would be. People could even jitterbug. Fifteen of the WACs from Bomber Command came and I felt very triumphant, as they never would come before. Everyone had a wonderful time. Martha was here for it, and some of the boys from Bomber Command came over. They say I'm never happy unless I have something to worry about and kept saying "Fitje is happy, she's worried about losing the cups, or not being able to round up the girls when the dance is over." Of course we couldn't find all of the cups and for all I know some of the girls are still on the base. Even Major Lindsay, the Command Special Services officer, came and thought it was wonderful. The castle really is lovely. There is a pool with water lilies in it and lots of woods and lovely gardens. The rose gardens are particularly beautiful. The ministry of something or other supplies three gardeners to take care of it so in spite of all the soldiers around it is still lovely. Eleanor and I wore our new summer uniforms, which are light blue jersey and very nice.

Father Calner, the Catholic chaplain from East Providence, brought some Providence papers dated around May 14th, and I have been reading them this morning. Nothing about our planes in them and I am disappointed. I will give them to Roger when I finish. Lucy keeps asking about his eye so tell her that the damage is not noticeable. It was the pupil of his right eye that got hurt. It bothers him a little but not much and can't be bad or he wouldn't still be flying. He is fine, by the way. He brought down a whole book full of pictures of the baby for me to see and I can hardly wait to get pictures of my nephew as I told him that my nephew was cuter.

Now my shoes are wearing out and I have got to get Jane to get me some new ones in New York. I will write her but will you pay her out of my bank account? I really am getting pretty shabby and don't know what I will do in another year.

I thought it was hard to sleep on the base with all the noise and planes, etc., but after the noise in London the last three days I really slept soundly last night and would still be asleep if the telephone ringing at 9:00 hadn't waked me up. You haven't changed the mattress on my bed I hope. I would like a chance to spend three quiet nights in it with nothing to wake me up all night long. The other night one of the volunteers told me that one of our night cashiers was going to leave us in September and could she have the job. I was so surprised at someone thinking that far ahead and I said, "Good Lord, you don't think we'll still be here in September, do you?" She was terribly surprised and said it had never occurred to her that we wouldn't.

Much love,
Fitje

June 24, 1944

Dear Mother & Dad,

No word from home for a long time but I guess the mail has been very slow lately. I am anxious to hear about Freddy and how my nephew is faring, also about Jane.

Yesterday I went to London in a two and a half ton truck to pick up stuff for the club and what time we had. Pat Breezie, the driver, knew less about London than I did and we had to go to three different warehouses on the outskirts. Once I get out of the center of London around Grosvenor Square I'm lost. We had a very nice time though. I went to the Charles Street Club for lunch and got them to let me take Pat some lunch on a tray as he wouldn't leave the truck. Then we went out to the ministry of works at Merton and they insisted that we have tea while they were loading the truck for us. On our way out of London going home we decided to depend strictly on our sense of direction and literally spent about half an hour going around in a complete circle. We were terribly surprised when we came out beside a church that we had passed half an hour before. As we were leaving we saw one of the robot planes and a couple of minutes later passed the spot where it landed. I was very glad to see one. When Martha and I were in London we heard a lot but I could hardly believe it. It seems so strange.

Late in the evening after I got back to the base Col. Kelly and Gen. Thatcher* came and picked me up and I went with them to Col. Kelly's for a drink. They are so funny. I told Gen. T. about seeing the robot plane and he said "Fitje, just don't be silly, don't you know that's all a figment of peoples imagination. There is no such thing." He tried to tell me it was a B-26 or an A-20. Pretty soon I began to think, well maybe I'm getting sort of queer over here after all these months and maybe I didn't see anything at all. We hear over here that the robot planes have pushed the invasion and the bombing of Tokyo right off the front pages of the papers at home. The English people are so different and so calm about everything. Maybe it's because they put up with so much already.

I wish you could see Col. Kelly's menagerie. He and Col. Beatty live in the cutest little house that used to be the gardeners cottage with roses all over it. They have two dogs and a cat. The dogs, just puppies, a Labrador retriever and a cocker, are Joe and Gus, and the cat, a little yellow Angora, is Lucy. They are terribly funny together. Joe walks around with Lucy's head in his mouth most of the time and it doesn't seem to bother her a bit. For some reason they all like me, and when I go up there they all end up by going to sleep in my lap. Col. Kelly says it's just the feminine touch as I'm the only woman they've ever seen.

Roger came down the other night after the club was closed, and he, and Pat, and Frank Mullen, one of the pilots, and I had fried eggs and toast to eat. They were good and Roger said he'd like to meet the chickens. He agrees that Bill looks awfully nice in the picture of him and Lucy. He is so funny especially about his baldhead. Right now he is in London on pass and I was supposed to call him up yesterday but I had so little time that I never did. The other boys kid him while I'm around so I will write home to Ibby. Things like "Hey flattop are you going to see that blond of yours when you're in London." Roger is trying to get something on me so he can threaten me if I do write to Ibby.

I wish you could see the hut full officers that live right next to us. They have two pup tents out in the back of our hut and two of them sleep out there every night. Every sunny day they are lying out in the sun with beer, radio, and everything. In fact when I got up this morning one of them was already out there. When we moved in they dug their slit trench bigger so we would fit it to.

Eleanor, the staff assistant, is really awfully nice. She plays the piano beautifully and the boys like her, an awful lot. She also teaches dancing lessons. Pat has been telling me more and more about her life in Singapore and it is fascinating. I guess I told you that she is the accountant here and that she got out of Singapore when the Japs were three miles away. Her father and mother had been out there for thirty years. The staff here are awfully nice and very good, especially Elsie, one of the cooks, who is fat and cheery and wonderful.

Well here comes the tea. We have it at 3:30 now because by that time I am starved. More people stop in here. There is a boy from Providence here now, Chuck McCauley. He is a gunner and I first met him down in the briefing room while we were serving coffee on one side of the room and the medi-

---

* Herbert B. Thatcher. In 1943 Thatcher was wing commander of the 8th and 9th Bomber Commands, leading or participating in numerous successful bombing raids over Germany. In early 1944 he became one of the youngest brigadier generals in the Army Air Corps. His numerous decorations included the Silver Star, two Distinguished Flying Crosses, nine Air Medals, and two Purple hearts. He was given a Distinguished Flying Cross by King George VI in 1944.

cal department was serving rye on the other. Chuck had had more than his share of rye and when he heard that I was from Providence he spilled what was left right on the floor and said what do I want with this when there's a girl from Providence around. Now we are very good friends. There are so many Providence people on the base that I am going to invite them all down to tea soon.

Being here is so exciting now that all this has started. You have no idea how interesting it is. When do you think Jane will come? I am so afraid that I will miss her somehow.

You should see all the lovely flowers that we have around. The gardens at the castle are full of roses etc., and we just go up and pick all we want for the club. Our new floor is lovely and so shiny that we really should have a new building to go with it.

Hope to hear from you all soon.

Much love,
Fitje

July 3, 1944

Dear Family,

A dreary, rainy day made worse by the fact that there was an officer dance on the base Saturday night and judging from the telephone conversations I have had all morning it is still going on. I went with Roger and had a wonderful time. Roger is so nice and so funny. We spent rather a weird night after we finally got to bed. We had a woman newspaper reporter from New Zealand staying in my room, and various people wondering in and out all night looking for beds for their girls, and the telephone ringing continuously. I would like to write a book just about the dances on these bases.

In answer to your questions about what I'm doing, what you do in these clubs is about the same. At the 91st the staff was wonderful and the club more or less ran itself. Here the staff are country people and very nice but there is much more to do around here, just checking up on the cleaners etc. It's just like running a big house. I am the director and Eleanor Roth is the staff assistant. She is terribly nice and has a wonderful sense of humor. The reason why my address is Headquarters 386th Bomb Group is because I am attached to the headquarters squadron of that group. The only place I have been that wasn't operational was IX Bomber Command.

How are Jane's plans progressing? Now I hope she won't come for a month or so until things settle down. I am dying to get pictures of the baby.

We didn't go up to the mass today because of the rain and Mrs. Mason just brought us a lovely sardine and tomato salad. Everyone is so nice to us over here and I am going to be spoiled for the rest of my life as a result of it.

Much love,
Fitje

July 11, 1944

Dear Mother & Dad,

Haven't heard from you in ages but I guess the mail is still slow. Today I got a letter from Mike Villard saying he was in London. I was surprised to hear from him, as I didn't know he was coming over. Where is Bobby now?

Eleanor and I are waiting until we hear the planes fly over. Then we jump in our little truck, which is already loaded and go down to the briefing room to hand out coffee and sandwiches. There is one boy fixing the billiard cues and another boy sitting drawing and singing. The conversation is going something like this: Jerry, fixing cues, says to Pat, singing: "Did you ever sing in sewers Pat?" "No, but I once worked on a garbage truck for $12 a week and all I could eat!" Jerry works on the Link Trainer* and we go up there a lot get our flying time in. We're getting so good we're afraid they'll ask us to fly on missions!

A few minutes ago I was combing my hair and one of them said, "Why don't you get a wire brush Fitje? Maybe you could get the kinks straightened out." Pat said "Hey Jerry doesn't she look like the wreck of the Hesperus?" And Jerry said, "More like Dracula's daughter to me." Then they decided I would look better with my hair six inches longer, especially over my face so they wouldn't have to worry about my face. The last remark, "Well Fitje is a good kid, but who likes kids?" And I thought I used to take a beating from Johnny.

July 12, 1944

We took so long in the briefing room last night that I never got back to finish this. For some reason it is often very gay in the briefing room especially when a mission comes back in the evening and everything has gone well. Maybe it is the shot of scotch they get, or just the fact that the day is over and there won't be anything else until the next day. Eleanor and I often spend most of the evening down there.

We had more fun the other night. About 10:30 we took coffee and sandwiches and went out on the line. We fed all the guards and all the Ack-Ack gunners and all the ground crews we could find and had a hysterical time. Soon it got to be after 12:00 and we have found ourselves handing out black coffee to the drunks trying to navigate home from pubbing. They thought it was a scream to be met by the Red Cross on the way back from the pubs. Eleanor is more fun to be with. I certainly have hit the jackpot every time as far as my coworker is concerned.

The other night Gen. Thatcher called me up and asked me down to sample a bottle of Sauterne someone had given him. I had the most interesting time. He is C.O. of the wing and a nifty guy. He lives in another old, old house with a nice big fireplace. I had already eaten dinner in the mess but ended up eating another with him and staying until 1 o'clock while all sorts of interesting people kept dropping in. Remind me to tell you about it when I get home.

---

* Developed by Edward Link in the 1930's. Link trainers were flight simulators designed to train pilots to fly in low visibility.

You would die laughing at the group in the ration breakdown hut next door to us. I have told you about them in detail I guess. The funniest by far is Herman (Capt. Reffe)* who sleeps in the pup tent right outside my window and no further than four feet from my bed. We lying in bed and talk at night. The other night when we came home there was an alert and they were all standing in back of our hut with their helmets on drinking brandy, which they had bought at the auction of an old estate. They gave us a drink and we all decided we would build the fireplace out there and have dinner cooked outside at night. One of them Capt. McDevitt from New Bedford is a good friend of Adamon Jenks.

Am so glad you got to Maine for a while. I imagine that's where you are now and that's why I haven't heard from you. Your last letter was dated June 20th. We are anxious to hear about Franny. Roger is fine.

Much love,
Fitje

July 15, 1944

Dear Family,

Have just eaten a delicious breakfast of eggs, bacon, fried tomato, toast, and coffee, larger than usual but for some reason I was hungry. The commissary is right across from our quarters, and on the way to the club every morning we are stopped by the commissary officer demanding that we bring breakfast for him and his sergeant. He is very funny, Lt. Fink by name, and since we depend on the commissary for lots of things we take him down toast and coffee every morning. Lt. Fink says things like, "You remind me of something—the terrible days of the blitz or the horrible crossing over here." He also says, "Well if a doodlebug hits you try not to go to pieces." I used to be able to get an egg for breakfast every morning just by telling him the story of my name (Fitje, Ditje and Miritje) and now when he sees us he says 'Good morning Fitje, Ditje, Miritje and Eleanor. Did I tell you that I have Milo over here now and she is definitely going to have kittens very soon? Lt. Fink says I suppose you're going to name them Milo, Lilo, Silo, and Dilo. Her real name as I guess you know is CC Milo Vega and now we call her Mrs. Vega.

The ration breakdown hut has just gotten a dog as big as a pony, and they never go to work anymore. They just sit and play with the dog, George by name. It is really a beautiful dog, a Bull Mastiff, and much too good to be on an army base. I am afraid that it is going to eat Mrs. Vega.

Last night we had a dance at the club and it was a lot of fun. There were about seven boys from Providence here. One, a very nice looking gunner who was brought up in the State Home and School named Jacobs; another really tough and very scared gunner named McNally; and an older gunner, more like they were when I first came over here, Howie Scholtz. They are very nice and I watch especially for them when we meet the missions. Last night I introduced them all to each other, as they have never met before.

---

* Fitje's letters often refer to Capt. Reffe as Boo-Boo.

I guess that by now you know the good news, although I'm scared that you don't so I hesitate to give it away. Anyway I guess you were all surprised weren't you. I knew it even before Roger did and after he disappeared that Sunday and didn't come back I was afraid that he had just been transferred and wasn't going home after all. I pestered Col. Kelly about it until he finally checked up and said he was definitely going. Then Lt. Mullen who is also on his way called up and told me that he had left. Tell Roger that his pilot, Peter B Greene, is now back, an operations officer, and a captain. I talked to him for a long time the other night and he finds it very sad to be back with the rest of his group gone. Also, tell him that poor old Jesse Moore is the unhappiest person, although the fact that he was made a captain a few days ago cheered him up considerably. He says that someday fifty years from now some Englishmen in a pub will point in a corner and say "what's that" and the pub owner will say, "Why that's something the Yankees left behind when they went and it will be poor old Jesse." Tell Roger I will send him the letter from Terry, which I forgot to give back to him. Boy, am I ever glad he's gone home. I didn't like worrying about anyone I knew that well at all, except that it really was wonderful to have him here.

July 16, 1944

Got up early this morning to drive Martha to the station. It is a lovely Sunday morning and not a soul on the road. Martha has been visiting me.

Got your letter written in Maine yesterday mother, and enclosing the pine for Roger. Maybe he is in Maine right this moment. I have a feeling that he flew. Tell Roger that Pat just talked to Frank over the telephone and he is disgusted because he is still waiting.

Yesterday we discovered rather an upsetting thing. Apparently Friday night after the club was closed the safe in my office was broken into and almost 100 pounds stolen, in fact all the paper money in it. I feel terribly because the facts seem to prove that it must've been someone that is around a lot; also I was the one that left the window open in the office because I remember pulling the blackouts and noticing that it was open then; also I left my key to the safe in my desk drawer all night and that is how he opened the safe. You do get careless after a while and this is the first time anything has ever been stolen to my knowledge from us in all the time I've been here. We had detectives around all day yesterday, but of course they will never find anyone.

July 18, 1944

Have gotten your letters from Maine enclosing the four-leaf clover and the Indian paintbrush. I bet it is lovely up there right now.

I am going to have a vacation too after talking about it for so long. I really am tired now. Mrs. Worthington, the wife of Cannon Worthington has asked me to visit her for as long as I want to get rested up. She is rather elderly and one of our volunteers. She is very, very nice, and lives about a mile and a half away in a lovely old house in the country. Nothing to do all day but sleep and read and I can be back here in fifteen minutes if I have to. I hope to stay about a week. I really don't want to go anywhere but I know I need it and I'm afraid to put it off any longer for fear I'll never get it.

July 20, 1944

I have just gotten back from paying the bills in town and I guess I had better finish this letter and get it in the mail.

A boy named Pete Silopine who I knew over here may call you or go to see you. He is from Providence. Also be on the lookout for Howie Schultz and Chuck McNally as both are from Providence and promised they would go see you. I know those two the best. They are awfully nice and I am sure they will look you up.

Today is a lovely warm day and we are feeling very lazy. I would like to go swimming.

Have Jane's plans changed at all? How is Jones? We are still waiting for Milo's kittens.

Love,
Fitje

July 26, 1944

Dear Mother & Dad,

I wish you could be here with me now. I am staying in the nicest place with the nicest people. It is about a mile from the base and I have been here since Saturday and am going back tomorrow morning. I am staying at the Rectory with Canon and Mrs. Woodrington (Mrs. W. is one of the volunteers who does sewing for the boys in the evenings at the club). Also here is Felicity, their Australian daughter-in-law whose husband is in France, and Peter their four-year old grandson whose mother, the wife of a Rector in Ipswich is quite sick. They have another daughter, Zeta, who is married to an American. Zeta and Felicity were in a dancing troupe in Italy when Italy declared war and were in jail there for ten days before they got permission to return to England.

The house is a lot like the Powell's house in the country in every way and Mrs. W. is a lot like Mrs. Powell. At one point they had thirty-two refugees here. A family in each room, Mrs. W. says. Canon Woodrington is wonderful. The kind of a guy who when we talked about the English Medical System could trace it way back to the Greeks. He took me through the lovely little church today. It is 960 years old.

There is a fat pig in the barn and three very mean geese and two ducks wandering around the yard. The front door has wire in front of it to keep them from coming in and you must climb over it every time you go in the house.

I have done nothing but sleep, lie in the sun, and play with Peter. He is very cute and we sail boats, made of sticks with geese feathers for sails, in the duck pond and go climb on a big tree, which has fallen down over the moat. Every afternoon we go to some house in the village to get Mrs. W. who is always at some sewing thing or something. I feel as if I have met everyone in the village now. It is very small and to drive through it you must drive right through a ford across a stream. The funny thing is that the Woodrington's know Gordon and Ruth Washburn in Providence. Mr. Washburn is the new head of the Rhode Island School of Design Museum, as you probably know. I think they knew them in France where they used to live in the summer.

They have been so nice to me. They bring me breakfast in bed in the morning in spite of the fact that they have no maid now. I try to wake up before they get up there but I seem to sleep indefinitely until someone wakes me. They have a lovely vegetable garden and Peter and I picked spinach for dinner this afternoon. They also have an enormous raspberry patch, which is very hard to get to because of the nettles. English kids seem to be brought up just the same way we were. Peter knows the same stories and songs and uses the same expressions. This afternoon he has a hose bath just the way we used to.

Now we are all sitting in the living room listening to the news. I am practically ready to go to bed.

Jane sent me the pictures of the baby and I think he is lovely, not at all edgy. Have you seen Roger yet? I miss him a lot. Tell him everyone has been very busy so he should be glad he isn't here. Tell him that Frank finally left after waiting ages.

Jane said you both looked well after your stay in Maine. I hope you had a good time. If by any chance Roger isn't home yet (but I'm sure he must be) don't say anything to Ibby.

Mother, would you get me a nice slip in size thirty-four to give to one of the staff at Bomber Command who is marrying one of the soldiers. It is for Joanie who I have probably written about. Maybe a nightgown would be better. Whichever you think. I feel very responsible for the wedding since I hired Joanie to work at the club. Maybe you'd better send a couple as I am always wishing I had presents to give wives of the boys who get married. No rush, anytime you get a chance. You might stick in a couple of bars of Roger and Gallet soap and some Lifesavers.

Is Lucy still in Florida? I love the picture of Lucy and Bill leaving the house. Have you seen Franny's baby?

Just got a telephone call from Francey Beaker who is at the base sleeping in my bed tonight, as she knows some officers on the base. I will see her tomorrow morning when I go back.

I went back to the base on Sunday to a party given by the Ration Breakdown Group. We had hotdogs cooked on an outside grill right behind our hut and potato salad from the club. It was lots of fun.

Well, I must go to bed.

Much Love to all,
Fitje

August 6, 1944

Dear Jane,

I'm glad you're coming anyway. I knew you would so I wasn't very worried. I was sort of sorry about what I had said to Roger later, but I didn't see him again to rectify the matter. You see it was at a party and I was pretty disgusted at the moment. The reason shouldn't make you hesitate for one minute, as when you're there it isn't as bad as it sounds. The main reason Roger couldn't tell you and I will tell you when I see you. I know you will love it. It really is wonderful over here and I love it.

Thanks an awful lot for getting the shoes and the blouses for me. Did you have any luck with the girdles? Be sure to bring plenty for yourself.

Today is a lovely warm day I am about to go over to the hospital to see Eleanor and Pinky so must go.

Hope to see you soon.

Fitje

✍

August 7, 1944

Dear Mother and Dad,

This is a cloudy day and very quiet around here so far. I got up early this morning to get some eggs from the commissary, as we had Bingo last night and I gave out about twenty-four slips of paper promising twenty-four boys eggs. Luckily I got them or I probably would have been lynched. They bring the slips in the snack bar in the morning and have a fried egg for breakfast.

This has been a bad week for some reason. I had to come back early from my leave as Eleanor got sick and last Thursday morning she went over to the hospital. Thursday night she was operated on for a perforated stomach ulcer. She was very sick for a few days but is much better now and feels a lot better than she has for a while so she says. The doctor is planning to send her home where she can get the right food, but Eleanor doesn't want to go and we don't know yet what is going to happen. In any case I am sure that she won't be able to come back here. She is really having a good time, as a girl is such an oddity in an army hospital that she has a steady stream of company all day long. I miss her a lot here as she was so nice and everyone liked her so much. I don't know how long it will be before I get another staff-assistant.

The worst thing though—I am sure that I have written you about Pinkie, my favorite WAC and Chic, the Sgt. she was engaged to. They almost got married and had the reception in the Club at Bomber Command, and then decided not to, as, if they got married, they would be separated. A couple of days ago they were in an auto accident and Chic was killed; also little Dick, one of the boys we also knew well. Pinkie is in the hospital right down the hall from Eleanor, so I went to see her yesterday while I was over there. She got a big cut on her head, but I guess she is OK aside from that. Well, that's the way it goes but it seems so awful when it happens that way. Chic was a gunner with twenty-four missions over enemy territory and then he was killed in an automobile accident.

Well one bright spot in the week—Milo had four lovely black kittens last Sunday morning early and they are awfully cute. I guess I have brought about a thousand boys over to see them since then and I never know who I will find over there when I go over. Milo is a wonderful mother and hardly leaves them for a minute. I don't know what I'm ever going to do with them all, but I guess I will be able to give them away when they are a little older. Tell Roger if you see him that Mable had three puppies

153

finally, but one of them died. Poor George, the mastiff belonging to the ration breakdown boys got St. Vitus Dance* and had to be killed as it just got worse and worse.

Father Calner sent me down the picture of "Flat-top", Ibby and Terry yesterday. It is very cute isn't it? I am so glad he is home. He must have gotten there very quickly.

This is a short letter but I can't seem to think of much to say.

Much Love,
Fitje

ℒ

August 13, 1944
386th Bomb Group

Dear Mother & Dad,

Just a note so you won't wonder what happened to me as I am going to Scotland for a week with Pinkie. We are flying up to Edinburgh and will probably stay a couple of days and then go somewhere on Loch Lomond for the rest of the week. Pinky just got out of the hospital yesterday. Have fried ten eggs so far this morning as we are short of staff and everyone seems to want them.

Roger apparently got a little confused about what I said about Jane. London is so wonderful because it is emptier than usual. Everyone still goes there on pass. I was there one day last week. I am looking forward to Jane's coming a lot. I don't know what life is like in London, but boy I sure know what it's like on a base. Roger and I only discussed it once and that was the night before he left here. I guess I was so glad to have him go home that at the time I didn't feel like I wanted to worry about anyone else closely connected with me. I know Jane will love it. It is fascinating and it will be wonderful for me to have her in London.

Poor Eleanor is terribly upset because she doesn't want to go home. No decision has been arrived on that yet and I feel mean to go off and leave her right now.

The kittens are terribly cute. I brought so many people in to see them that Milo has moved them under the bathtub.

Will write when I get back.

Love,
Fitje

ℒ

August 22, 1944

Dear Mother & Dad,

Got back yesterday morning early from Scotland and we had a very good time. Lots of funny things

---

* Sydenham's Chorea, a canine nervous system disorder

happened. Last Monday I got driven over to bomber command and Pinky and I sat around all day waiting for a plane ride. Finally about dinnertime we took off and flew up as far as right near Liverpool. Don Sorenson and the Greek, who also went along, left us at a bus stop, as they had to go back. On the way into Liverpool on the bus we got talking to a very nice English officer who took us to the station and looked up trains for us. We had dinner and started queuing up at 10:00 for a train to Edinburgh that didn't leave until after 12:00. Traveling is really rugged over here these days. There we met a very nice Scots officer who helped us smuggle our bags through the barrier, as you cannot go on the platform without a ticket and the ticket office wasn't open so we couldn't get one. We finally bought penny platform tickets and managed to get on the train. Once on we were not thrown off. The Scots officer told us to just act like dumb Americans if anyone asked any questions. We got to Glasgow early in the morning after sitting up all night, and took various buses to Luss on Loch Lomond. There we stayed in a little inn called call Colququin Arms. It was lovely there although the weather wasn't too good. There were three very nice Australian gunners up there and we had a lot of fun with them. We climbed half of Loch Lomond one day with two ATC* men that we met, and another day took the boat to Adlui at the other end of the Loch. In the evenings we went for walks near the inn. There was lots of Heather around and I am enclosing some. The village of Luss is the cutest little place and so clean. All the little stone houses have lovely gardens all around them. On Friday we went to Edinburgh and saw the castle and went shopping, although there is nothing to buy without coupons. Pinkie bought some silver to send home to her mother. I met soldiers up there that I've known on every base I have been on. It was amazing to see so many. Think how many people I know having been over here for fifteen months. We were hoping for a ride home, but the weather was bad so we took the train Sunday night and got to London early Monday morning. Now Dick has gone fishing in Scotland for ten days, and Martha is down in Bournemouth for a couple of days. Martha is here visiting me.

The kittens are getting so cute. One of them is very strange and we call it the idiot cat. I think eventually it will have to be killed. Martha has picked out one but they are too young to leave their mother yet. Mary† loves them and doesn't want me to give any of them away, but we will probably have more before we can turn around. The kittens' names are:

1. Wright the idiot cat
2. Handsome Harry Hankie
3. Peter Pan
4. John

John belongs to Martha and she named him after S/Sgt. Kruchak. Martha says Milo is a better mother than she is a cat. She climbs in an out of the windows all night and wakes me up about twice

---

* Air Transport Command

† Mary Haynesworth. Mary was Fitje's assistant and arrived at the 386th after Eleanor, the previous assistant returned to the US. She stayed with the group until late summer 1945. Mary was an actress before the war. Fitje and Mary stayed in contact in the years after the war ended, visiting each other on several occasions.

an hour. She forgets and climbs in my window and the kittens are in the bathroom and so she has to climb out and in the other window. It makes her awfully mad, as the windows are very high and hard to climb in and out.

Mrs. Widdrington was here last night with Felicity to do some sewing for the boys. They are very upset, as Felicity's husband has been very seriously wounded. Mrs. W. was anxious to hear news of the Washburns so write anything you know.

Mother, do not worry about what Roger told you. I don't know why he did. I wasn't complaining to him about life in London because I don't know anything about it. I was talking about life on the base, and that can get pretty rugged at times as you can imagine. London is a nifty place to be even now and boys on the base go as usual. We were at a party the only time we ever talked about Jane coming over here very seriously, and things were a little confused I guess. I will be very disappointed if she doesn't come as I have look forward to it for so long.

One of the boys (the office is full of them as usual) is writing a letter and just showed me what he said about me. "And last I will tell you about the personality that is the guiding light of this little shelter for G.I. Joes. . . She also is our guardian angel, who else brings us breakfast, eggs (which she gets from us) and coffee with buttered toast around 10 o'clock in the morning? Why the other day she came in, and sitting down, proceeded to talk me into letting her have the eggs we had saved for the Colonel who is the base commander. But she wanted the eggs as prizes for the weekly bingo game so after about a half hour of intense browbeating I had to let her have the eggs. Hope the Colonel is too busy to eat this week; no eggs no nothing." Needless to say the boy is a Sgt. in the commissary. I bring their breakfast down every morning strictly for diplomatic reasons. The other boys in the office are having tea with Rudner, one of the drivers, who is pouring. In the afternoon at 4:00 my tea comes in on a huge trolley with about ten extra cups on it, as there are always so many extra people around. One gunner just came in with a picture of his sister who is Hilary Dawn, a dancer. Just before that another gunner came in with a picture of his wife, who, he swears, is only fifteen. I can believe it, as he is not much older. Now everyone is boasting about who has the best-looking sister. Naturally I say I have. I wish you could see this office. Two gunners just came in with egg sandwiches that they had cooked in the kitchen, for a cup of tea, and another gunner (Roy, the one who married the fifteen year old girl) just came back complaining that Miss Paige and Mrs. Sanders, the cooks, just grabbed him and put flour down his neck. The kitchen is as bad as the office and I don't see how anyone does any work in it.

Just got your letter. I hope Lucy is better. What's the matter with her? Where are you going to stay while Dad is in Maine, Mother?

Major Christian was here on this base that I am on now. The castle is lovely and I will bring home some pictures of it to show you when I come. I wish you could see the rose gardens. Naturally that is just a small part of the base though, and the rest is mud, and Nissen huts like any other base. I have lived in the country for so long now that I will never want to live in the city again. We are near a tiny town where we do our shopping and only get to larger towns once in a while to meet trains or get things that we can't get near here. Hermie will probably see a lot of people I know.

Watch for a boy named Howie Schultz who is coming to see you. Maybe we'll be home for Christmas, but I doubt it. I have to see Paris and Berlin first.

Much love.
Fitje

September 2, 1944

Dear Jane,

Thanks an awful lot for sending me the shoes and blouses. They are fine. Exactly what I wanted and they fit perfectly. I will not need another pair of shoes as someone who is going home gave me a couple of half worn ones, which still have some wear in them. I badly need the girdles so if you can get them soon I would appreciate it.

I was in London on Thursday and tried to see E. May to find out the latest dope on you. She wasn't in, so I couldn't see her but I did see Ruth Wehle, another friend of mine in the OWI, and she thought the situation still hadn't changed. I am keeping my fingers crossed though and hoping you will be here soon. That doctor must be an awful jerk.

Things are as usual here. We have just had a few of the officers down for tea and it is Pat's birthday. Haven't heard from the family for ages but expect I will soon.

Love,
Fitje

September 6, 1944

Dear Mother and Dad,

My last letter from home was dated August 14th, so I don't feel very up-to-date on the news. How are Jane's plans progressing? I hope Lucy is all well by now. Have you any new pictures of the baby now that it is a little older.

The latest thing of excitement around here is that Capt. Wertz, one of the doctors from Bomber Command came over yesterday and brought me a little black cocker puppy, only three weeks old. Of course it is too young to leave its mother although he said it would be all right. I took it over in the quarters and Milo took one look and tried to kill it. She was simply furious that I would bring such a creature near her babies. Peter B. Green (Major Green, who was Roger's pilot) and is now Squadron C.O. has a dog, Mable, who I guess I told you about who had two puppies about the same time Milo had her kittens. Well we got the clever idea of asking Peter if we could give Mable the puppy for a week or so until it is a little older. Peter was very leery of the whole thing and finally said, "Well, I don't care if Mable does chew its head off because then we could have a puppy funeral and I've never been to a puppy funeral." Really he is so kind hearted, that there is a story about him that once he made a very poor landing even damaging the plane quite a bit. When asked what happened he said there was a rabbit in the middle of the runway and he swerved to avoid it. Last night we presented Mable with the puppy and so far so good. Actually we don't know whether Mable is taking care of it or whether Peter is, as we hear that Peter had it up at operations last night under his flying jacket. I don't know what I will ever do with it as I'm afraid Milo will really hurt it.

The kittens are so funny now. They all lived under my bed on top of my bedding roll and other junk. Milo thinks that they are so wonderful that she will hardly leave them for a moment. I forget if I told you about finally getting the idiot cat killed. It was awfully funny; I guess I did tell you.

Can't think of much that happened lately that I can tell you about. Mary and I went to London the other day to pick up some stuff. I tried to see E. May while I was there but she was away. Bobby's husband, Mike Villard came out to this field the other day to look at a plane we have. I had dinner with him at the mess, and went out with him while they looked at the plane. He is awfully nice I think. I never really talked to him before.

It is pouring rain today. Mary is in London for couple of days' vacation. I was so tired last night that I went to bed at 11:30 and didn't even wake up until the telephone rang at 10:00. The night before last, after the club closed, Mary and I went over to the ration breakdown hut and cooked some sweet corn, which I had happened to see in town. The first I have ever seen over here. It was awfully good. The officers in that hut are so nice. The Adjutant of the group, the Quarter Master Officer and the Photo Officer are all there and very good people to know. We feel that we are very fortunate to have them for neighbors.

We have a new CO present as Col. Kelly has gone home on leave. It is Col. Tom Corbin, who I am sure I have mentioned in my letters before, as he was a Major and Lt. Col. while I was at Bomber Command, and a very good friend of Martha's and mine while we were there. Naturally it is nice having him here. I went to an officers' dance at another base with him the other night and had a wonderful time. His wife was at Smith when I was there.

The war news is wonderful, isn't it? I have a huge war map beside my desk and it is fascinating to follow it with the firsthand information we get from the flyers.

Hope to hear from you all soon. Give my love to Ann and Hermie.

Love,
Fitje

Colonel Thomas G. Corbin

September 11, 1944

Dear Family,

Am still waiting for a letter from you and can't imagine why I don't hear. Since my correspondence is now entirely limited to only you all, if I don't hear from you I get no mail at all. Isn't that pathetic!

The weather has been lovely lately. Cool and sunny. Just like fall days at home. Mary and I got very ambitious today and started to paint the coffee urns red and grey. We took them out in the sun in front of the club, dressed in our oldest slacks and dirtiest sneakers. Pretty soon we had about fifty helpers and ended by spending the afternoon lying in the sun and even having tea out there. We brought the kittens out for a while to entertain everyone. They're so cute now and I don't know how we will ever part with them. Mary wants to keep all three. One of them, Mike, has double paws and is quite a rarity according to the boys. The puppy is doing very well with his foster mother. We have named him Peter B. Lea, after Peter B. Green (Roger's pilot who owns his foster mother) and Lt. Lea who took him to his foster mother. Peter took Pat and me over to see him the other night. The other two puppies are much bigger and poor Peter B. leads a hectic life. These English people are so wonderful. I never even think about feeding my cats because one of them goes over to the quarters two or three times a day and takes them something. They never forget and I never asked them to do it. They are very fond of Milo. The other day I was in the kitchen and Mrs. Mead was washing the floor. When she got to the spot where Milo was eating her lunch, she stood and waited until Milo had finished rather than disturb her to wash that particular spot.

Martha has been down visiting me again for a couple of days. She is spending the day with a couple of boys from another base but is coming back later tonight. Of course, we had to have a party last night with some of the boys, The Greek, John, Mike and the WAC, Pinkie, who came over from Bomber Command. Eleanor is on her way home and has also been here getting her stuff together. She really hates to leave but I guess she figures that she would be much better off where she can get the right food, as she really is on a very strict diet. I hate to see her go, as she was really wonderful at her job. Mary is terribly nice too. She is from Greenville, South Carolina and was on the stage for a while with a troupe over here in England and France before the war. I have been so darn lucky as far as the people I have been with are concerned, about everything in fact, so far.

Today one of the officers who is tired of seeing us with wet, muddy shoes had wonderful rubber, fleece lined boots issued to us. Mine are medium men's sized and so big that the Officer insisted on taking a picture of me, which I will send you when it is developed. I feel as if I had diving boots on.

9/13/44

Another lovely day. Mary and Martha left for London early this morning. Although it is not yet really cold we have a fire in our office every morning. As yet I have no stove in my room and will have to start asking for one before it gets too bad. Mary sleeps in her sleeping bag already so I imagine she will freeze before the winter is over. Did I tell you that the Scotchman Pinkie and I met while we were in Edinburgh sent us each a lovely tartan scarf. They are beautiful.

The other day was Mary's birthday and Pat and I gave her a huge bunch of roses, which we picked in the rose garden. Enclosed is the card Pat made to go with them and I thought it was so cute that I got her to make a duplicate for me. Notice Dewey with the halo and wings. He was the idiot cat.

I hope Lucy is all right. Am dying to know what Jane is doing.

Love,
Fitje

∽

September 15, 1944

Dear Jane,

I forgot your birthday until it was too late to write but happy birthday anyway. How goes everything? Mother wrote something about you doing something new but of course it didn't say what it was so I am wondering. Was in London the other day and tried to see E. May but had no luck. What are your plans? Do you think you're going to get here or not? I am going to London for two days next week so I will look E. May up again then and see if she knows anything about you.

Things are as usual here except the weather is better than usual. It is so nice that it makes the thought of another winter in the mud and cold seem rather dismal but I guess it will be another winter and there's nothing we can do about it. How is Lucy? Mother wrote that she had been sick but didn't say what was wrong with her. I guess nothing much.

I can't think of anything special to say. The latest bit of excitement has been a peeping Tom or something that stirs us every night. We have gotten so used to it now that we are rather fond of him. Last night Mary and I were sitting in my room after the day talking and we heard him fall off this sort of horse outside our window that he sits on. We felt awfully sorry for him. The officers in the hut next-door are simply furious and set all sorts of traps to catch him but so far he has escaped.

Am still hoping to see you. Don't forget the girdles.

Love,
Fitje

∽

September 23, 1944

Dear Mother & Dad,

Well things are going as usual except I have just gotten back from a very nice two-day leave in London. I met Joyce up there (the girl that was our accountant while I was with the 95th), and we stayed at the Brown's Hotel and had a good time. Joyce was up to do what winter shopping her coupons would allow her, so I shopped with her. Clothes are so darned expensive. She bought a hat for 4£ and a blouse for 5£ and neither would have cost over $4 at home. We saw *Sweeter and Lower*, a wonderful musical review, and went to bed early tonight, although no one on the base will believe it for a minute.

When I went away I was dead tired, mostly from struggling with the cats every night. It seems as if they like to play at night and no sooner than I get to bed about 1:00, then they wake up and spend the night walking back and forth over me while Milo climbs in and out the window all night long. All the boys started saying, "What's the matter with Fitje?" and when Mary told them the cats were keeping me awake, they threatened to take them all away unless I got rid of them by Wednesday night. The funny thing is, they are not kidding when they say something like that and rather than have them just removed from our quarters when we weren't around and dumped somewhere, I gave all three away to one of the women who works for us. It is such a relief to be without them. I am going to have to give Milo away too, as I am sick of cats and can't have my puppy until I get rid of Milo, as she hates dogs. The puppy by the way is fine and very cute.

The other day Mary and I went to a Red Cross club in a nearby town, to the wedding reception of one of the boys on the base who married an English girl. While there I talked to an American Red Cross girl who had just been over for two weeks. She was from Boston and was so amazed at our life over here. She was terribly worried about a lot of things and it was amazing to talk to her because it took me right back to the first couple of months that I was here and how amazed I was by it all. I guess I have completely lost my sense of perspective or something. It certainly is going to be strange to get back to some sort of normal life. By the way, I consider that I will be lucky if I am home by a year from this Christmas, Mother.

Well this is a short letter but I will write soon again.

Love,

Fitje

September 28, 1944

Dear Mother & Dad,

I did not forget your birthday, Dad, but never seemed to get around to writing you. Anyway, Happy Birthday a little late.

Mother, I will straighten you out about the people who are here with me immediately. <u>Eleanor</u> was my assistant who got stomach ulcers. She is now home or on her way. By the way, she used to teach at Wheaton and will drop in and see you if she is around that vicinity. She is very nice. <u>Mary</u> is my new assistant. She is older than I am, from Greenville, S.C. and has great big brown eyes. All she has to do is look at someone and he follows her around from then on. She used to be on the stage and toured all over Europe playing Shakespeare. She is very lazy, but has a wonderful sense of humor and is a lot of fun to be with. She is good at her job and runs picnics and parties by the thousands.

Martha has now moved again and is quite a way off now so I doubt if I will see her again. She liked to come to this base because she knew so many people here. Dick is Richard Moncure, the Field Director on the base. He is from Richmond, Virginia and is terribly nice. Pat is the accountant, I am sure I have told you about, who lived in Singapore until the Japs were three miles away. Does that straighten you out?

The people I wish you knew though are the five officers that live next door to us in the ration breakdown hut. They are wonderful and do everything for us, from protecting us from anyone who might be hanging around, to bringing us midnight snacks. The photo officer, the queue officer, the base adjutant, the statistical officer and the S-4 officer constitute the group. Last night every single one of them came over and took a bath in our tub.

The weather is beautiful today. Mary is going to meet a stage friend of hers in London and I have on civilian clothes for change, as I am tired of my uniform. This job has had long hours and I have been busy, but I will write a long letter soon. It is terribly exciting here, but I don't think we could feel as optimistic as the people at home seem too.

Mary Haynesworth

Thanks for the sweaters and slips which I just received. I have wrapped one of the slips up for the wife of one of the queue boys. I have sent a box of summer things home, but you will probably have to send them back if I am still here next summer.

Much love,
Fitje

CHAPTER 10

In the Mud

October 3, 1944–March 26, 1945

The 386th Bomb Group moved to an airfield at Beaumont sur Oise France, about forty kilometers northwest of Paris, on October 2, 1944. With a population of fewer than five thousand, Beaumont was small. By 1944 deportations, executions and allied bombing had further reduced its numbers.

In the months leading up to D Day the U. S. 9th Air Force, including the 386th, bombed the airfield which was being used by the Germans, as well as several bridges in and around the town. As a result when Fitje reached Beaumont she found that what the 386th would use as a base was Spartan compared to the relative luxury they enjoyed in England. Fitje and Mary were given the only building still standing to use for the club. It was just barely standing. According to her letters, the second floor was unusable and there were no windows, heat, running water, or even a latrine. Rain and mud, which came over the tops of their boots added to the discomfort.

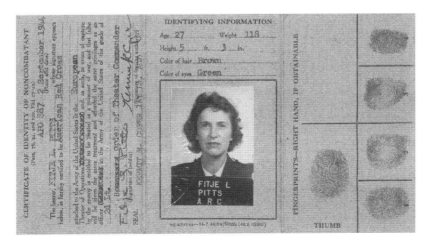

Fitje's Noncombatant Card, issued in
September, 1944 before the 386th moved to France

163

Despite the discomfort she seemed to love it. Fitje and Mary had to scrounge, beg, borrow and steal to get basic furnishing for the club. One of the first things they needed to do was hire a staff. They interviewed several locals and anyone they wanted to hire had to be approved by intelligence as some had been collaborators.

At first the locals seemed confused about their actual roles with the 386th. They couldn't understand why there were two women for all the men while the Germans seemed to have one for every officer.

It is in France that Fitje develops a serious relationship with Captain Jack Zeltner, the S-4 officer in charge of logistics and supply for the 386th. It is a relationship that continued until Captain Zeltner left Europe with the bomb group in August 1945.

October 3, 1944

Dear Mother & Dad,

Well here we are in France. I can't believe it. After much planning, and also plotting on my part so I wouldn't get left out, we finally arrived yesterday. As you can see from my address Mary and I moved right along with the bomb group, so for weeks we have been sorting and packing and throwing away stuff as the whole club had to be closed and everything in it disposed of. We were allowed a certain amount of weight and cubic feet of club stuff to take with us, and all that had to be packed in boxes and labeled. We really got a wonderful deal and everyone was so nice to us. Capt. Zeltner, the S-4 officer responsible for moving the group, lived in the ration breakdown hut next-door and he saw that we were well taken care of. He asked me things in the beginning like, "Well Fitje you can take so many pounds so make up your packing list." It didn't take him long to find out that I didn't know whether a piano weighed ten pounds or a ton so he assigned Joe Engler to us. Joe is forty-three, a S/Sgt. who was a lawyer in Washington before the war, and simply wonderful. Consequently we got moved with no major mishaps. It was awfully funny though and everyone, from Col. Corbin down, teased us, mostly about our latrine, which we still haven't got although we have been here for a day so far. We just have to forage for ourselves but you learn to meet all sorts of crises in the army I guess.

Getting here was a scream. The last night the telephone in my room was the only one on our end of the base in action so all night officers walked in and out, using it and trying to ignore me asleep in the bed. We arose at dawn and then waited all day sitting on the grass watching them load up. If a dog wandered

Captain Jack Zeltner

along he went in too so I guess all the dogs that we had in England are here. One of the crews flew my puppy and at this minute he is sitting in my lap chewing the arm of the chair.

Finally we arrived and what a desolate sight. The base is in a sad state of repair mostly due to the excellent bombing of our own group earlier in the war. We are fortunate to have part of the only building left standing; a two-story job around a courtyard, but the second story is all beat up and not usable. This building will also house the general manager and commissary. It used to be a house and farm I guess. No windows, they are all blown out and so far no stoves and no water. We have done lots of dirty work and haven't washed since we got here. We picked the least beat up room to live in and have two MPs posted at the gate right outside our window with no glass in it so we don't have to worry about a thing except the MPs. We have regular army cots and wonderful bedrolls meant for the Arctic so they really keep us warm. Last night we went to bed at eight—no lights so nothing else to do—and got up at six this morning. We use our mess kits and stand in line for chow. Everyone looks dirty and bedraggled, but happy. The French kids are hanging in our windows all day and we can really make them understand us. We have already made arrangements to have our laundry done through one of them. They all have to shake hands with us and you can get anything for candy or cigarettes or food. Money doesn't seem to mean a thing.

We spent the morning fixing our place up a bit, and it is going to be wonderful even though a little rough. There was some overstuffed furniture on the base, and they gave us that. I wish you could see the place; I could never describe it. When I moved from the 91st way back in June, it was for the purpose of being permanently assigned to this group so I could move with it. That is why I didn't want Jane to be swayed in her decision to come to England, because she thought I would be here. But of course I couldn't tell you that. My footlocker is stored in London as we brought a minimum of stuff with us. I hope to get back to get it someday.

Well we're really in the army now. No more soft living and most of the officers don't think we will be able to take it. They don't know how much the GIs do for us though. We're living just like they do, but they sure do all they can to help us.

It's raining today and my hair is straight as a string. It is funny to hear all the GIs trying to speak French instead of "cheerio" and "ta-ta" as we did in England.

If you know anyone in Paris let me know as I hope to go soon.

Mary just said, "I wonder which we'll get first, dysentery or lice."

My address is still the same as you can see.

Much love to all,
Fitje

October 6, 1944

Dear Mother & Dad,

Really, I think of you all the time and wish you could see us. I'm sure you would die laughing. My hair hasn't had a bit of curls in it since I got here. We have only washed our hands and just barely them.

Il n'y a pas d'eau.[*] I have worn the rubber boots Eleanor left behind constantly because the mud is terrific, and still no stove, no light, and no latrine, but believe it or not we are having a wonderful time. Living outdoors makes everyone hungry all the time. We stand in line for hours for mess and eat in the open air sitting on packing boxes, as only the kitchen is undercover in an old barn. While exploring, we met a French family down the road with thirteen kids from one to seventeen, and we have called on them with a couple of the boys twice in the evening. With much sign language on all parts we managed to make ourselves understood. Mary is good at that as she was on the stage before joining the Red Cross. They told us a lot about when the Germans were here, and it's fascinating.

Mary and I spent the day time prowling through the ruins and getting all sorts of things from old cognac bottles for candles to a wonderful German foot locker with some German's name and address on it in which I now keep my stuff. The club is full of statues from the ruined Church across the road. Yesterday we went to Paris. It took me months to get used to saying London instead of New York and now I am continually saying London instead of Paris. We spent the whole day doing business like collecting some field ranges and finding out where we could pick up food supplies so didn't have much time to look around. Saw the Eiffel Tower, the Etoile, etc. though. Paris is so wonderful and amazing. The people are wonderfully dressed, and you see lots of things in stores that we never saw in England; very little food though. I guess it's just the difference between the French and English. The Parisians seem to look so well in anything. Shoes mostly have thick wooden soles and are nifty. There is no place to eat but the Red Cross Club, which is huge and very nice, and no place to stay.

There is no transportation here as yet, so today we walked to the nearest town and had a wonderful time. We take turns talking when we come into a shop and succeeded in getting some worm medicine for the dog, (all credit goes to Mary) and some thumbtacks. There is absolutely no food in the stores that we could see, except macaroni, apples, onions, potatoes, and cabbage. We went to a coiffeur and Mary had her hair washed. While that was going on, we managed to tell the hairdresser that we had no water, so she and the other customers talked it over for a while and then she put on her coat and took us to the house of a friend where we arranged to take a bath every week beginning *demain a trois heures.*[†] Then we went to see an English lady who runs a shop to see about hiring staff for the club, then bought some white wash for our walls and went home. Practically as soon as we got there the women started coming up to be interviewed and we almost died because we had planned to have a translator. Together we do all right because I understand more than Mary does, and she can speak more than I can. We struggled through it though, and also an interview with the police who have to pass on everyone for security reasons. *Ami de Boche*[‡] is a familiar phrase around here. Can you imagine me directing the French staff? We will only have six or eight here. We only serve coffee and donuts and use prepared donut flour.

Of course we laugh all the time, so many funny things have happened. The latest: we just heard about was Major Carruth who, when he opened one of his packing boxes, found a rat that had traveled in it all the way from England and had eaten all Major Cs chocolate and even build himself a nest. Also

[*] There isn't any water.

[†] Tomorrow at three o'clock.

[‡] Friend of the Germans

the puppy makes such big puddles that Mary woke up last night and thought we had a horse in the room. She was terrified and I woke up to see her shining her flashlight all around.

Tell Roger if you see him that the group has just gotten a citation from the President. Isn't that wonderful? We can now wear a blue ribbon, as we are part of the group I should think he wished he were still here, but I don't guess he does.

Mary and I are now sitting at our dressing table with a huge mirror, 4'x4', which we salvaged among the ruins and our two candles in cognac bottles, both writing our parents. We have had callers all evening including two flying officers who succeeded in scaring us to death because we are living here alone. They promised to come back tomorrow and put a lock on the door. Our room is all beat up. The windows are all broken but we close the shutters, which are intact. We even have bullet holes in the walls! Mary has put pin up girls all over the room, and we have a Madonna from the church on our table. We feel like two gun molls in a deserted house hiding out from the police.

Tell Johnny happy birthday for me.

I am dying to hear your reaction to my latest move. I guess I told you I have sent some clothes home. I guess I won't send any Christmas presents this year either unless I find something I think you'd really like. I don't know if I'll ever get to Paris after things start to function at the club. There certainly isn't anything to buy around here.

Much love to you all.

Fitje

October 10, 1944

Dear Mother & Dad,

You will probably hear from me a little more often because there is so much more to write about. Mary is busy making a curtain for our dressing table. It sounds very fancy but actually it is just an old table that was once a workbench. Just now our two little friends Francine and Monique stopped at our window to collect our laundry *pour Mama*, who does it for cigarettes and candy, which she would much rather have than money. While they were there, Mme. Dabiquy, the mother of the thirteen children I wrote you about, stopped by to give us four eggs for breakfast. Mary and I went to see them last night and we all sang La Marseillaise and Lily Marlene while their son George played the accordion. We are opening Saturday, and he is going to play Sunday night in the snack bar, an old shed.

Nothing is holding us up now but water for the kitchen. No one seems to have any solution for that, but I hope we will get a water trailer before Sunday. Did I tell you about our staff? I don't think I did. We have hired six women. Five have husbands who are prisoners in Germany. The Germans shot the husband of one when he was caught trying to smuggle a message to the English when they were nearby. We hired them through M. and Mme. Dabiquy. Mr. D. is the head of the FFI* here and what

---

* FFI, French Forces of the Interior, was the formal name Charles DeGaule gave the French resistance fighters after D Day.

characters. We met them by chance and went to call on them and they told us the most interesting stories. They showed us a hole in their garden where they had hidden an English aviator for twelve days and took us to the cemetery and showed us the graves of two American flyers who crashed nearby in July. The French people had put up the tombstone with all the information from their dog tags on them, even tetanus '43-'44, and had planted red, white and blue flowers. The Nazi plot was right next it with crosses and Swastika drawn on them.

We are terribly popular over here because American girls are such an oddity, and isolated units have traveled miles to see us. It must be a terrible disappointment because we look so awful in our slacks and high G.I shoes. It is wonderful for us though because we have become such 'old shoes' with our group, and they are inspired to do all sorts of things if they think anyone else is interested.

Col. Corbin came over yesterday to see us, and he laughed and laughed and said we were the two saddest looking creatures he ever saw. We persuaded him to stay for a drink and he said he knew where to come when things got rough, because one look at us and he could at least be glad he didn't look as bad as we did. He felt so sorry for us he had a French workman come down and put windows in our room and in front of the club today. The men urge us to come down to breakfast because they say they feel awful when they get up, but one look at us and they know there is someone worse off.

At last we got a latrine in an old shed and we were very happy for about an hour. Then when we weren't looking, someone stole the door and the window. We were simply furious and demanded its return but of course nothing happened, and Mary made a lovely bed curtain to put where the door should be.

We went over to wing the other day and had a wonderful time. Some Captain took us all around. It is in an old chateau with a champagne tower and cellar and lots of underground tunnels which the Germans dug for air raid shelters. We have really have had fun and very little work as there is so little we can do. Most of the time we wait on someone to help us. Our bedroom is right in the middle of the club and even at this moment G.I.s are calling *Madame Nulle*, which I guess means they want something. Luckily our door sticks, which gives us a chance to say, "Stay out" or everyone would walk right in.

Did I tell you I had a physical examination before I left England and was pronounced in perfect health not even a tooth that needed filling? The doctor said we were an excellent pair because I was hyperactive and Mary was just the opposite. The fresh air and sleep I have had since I have been here have done me more good, and I feel terribly healthy. It is getting quite cold, but now that we have windows we don't care at all.

I am sending a money order home either in this letter or the next as I have a lot of money on hand. Will you see that $100 of it is deposited in the bank for Warren Canfield Pitts. I have never given him a present and want to give him something very much. Someone must have started him a bank account by this time.

October 11, 1944

Just at that moment a jeep stopped at our window and there was Col. Corbin and Col. Maxell about to collect Major Reeve to take him on a Snipe hunt. Do you know what that is? They came in and had a drink with us before starting. Then we went and had dinner with two of the boys who cooked potatoes and onions (there is a whole lot of them in the barn) on the stove in the office. This morning Major Reeve came to wake us up and give us some flowers a French workman had sent us. He was simply furious about the snipe hunt.* Apparently he walked home from miles away.

Much love to you all,

Fitje

✍

October 14, 1944

Dear Mother & Dad,

What a day! We are opening the club tonight and all day we have been struggling in the kitchen to talk to our staff, four in the daytime and two in the evening. Somehow we have succeeded in getting 1000 donuts made (pretty good for the first day although we hope to have 2000 or 3000 later). Now we are waiting for them to finish the doughnuts so we can show them how to make the coffee. I hope they are done in fifteen minutes or the coffee won't be ready for the grand opening at 6:30. It is very difficult as even their weights are different than ours, and we have to weigh everything.

You should see the way we dress, pants, sweater, and high G.I. shoes. I never thought I would ever wear high shoes, but they are mighty convenient. You should also see our kitchen, no drainage so far, we have been throwing dirty water out the window. In fact, we had no water until today. Mary and I carried 100 gallons ourselves yesterday from the nearest square. Today we have a sixty-gallon German boiler outside the door which is filled twice a day and from which we dipped the water we need. The gasoline ranges give us the most trouble, and I am about to begin agitating for a man to take care of them. It really is rough, but we love it.

We discovered a German officers barracks a few miles away fully furnished, so we got a truck and got chairs, and tables, vases, etc. They certainly lived in luxury. The staff insisted on washing it with soap and hot water. There is a searchlight unit near us and, we have had dinner with them twice, and then taken a bath at their place after dinner. They are wonderful to us. They have been over here for quite a while and haven't seen American girls for a long time. They think we are abused, because we are not waited on hand and foot as they think we should be. As a matter fact they have become quite a nuisance. They want to do so much for us. As Mary says, they don't understand that we are here to do, not to have things done for us. They come for us in an enclosed jeep, our group takes us in an open jeep in January if we get anything; they slow down going over bumps, while our group delights in giving us the worst possible ride. They flatter us, help us up and down stairs, and bore us considerably, but we do get a bath. *Maintement a la cuisine!*†

---

* A type of practical joke in which an unsuspecting newcomer is tricked into trying to catch a non-existent animal called a Snipe. The target of the prank is led to an outdoor spot and told to wait in the dark, holding an empty bag and making noises to attract the prey.

† We have a kitchen!

October 21, 1944

What a week. Everything possible has happened, but I guess we weathered the worst of it. Now we even have electricity: Lt. Patterson (Pat), a flying officer, took pity on us and wired the whole place with quite fancy fixtures, which Mary got from the German place. We even have indirect lighting in one room. We got hooked up to a squadron generator so we have lights until 11:00 at night. We got our floor painted and today we even got a lock on the door of our room and bars on windows as Col. C got perturbed about the peeping Tom.

Our worst trouble are the stoves: If they go all day, they go out at night, and we have donuts but no coffee; If they won't go all day but work at night, we have coffee but don't have doughnuts. One day we got mad and disgusted because they wouldn't give us a man to take care of them, so we just closed the club and went off to the hospital and took a bath and washed our hair. It caused no end of excitement because no one could find us, but the next day we got a soldier assigned here to take care of the stoves.

Mary is a scream: She discourages business like everything by telling everyone about the septic tank right outside the kitchen door with no cover on it, and the flies on the donuts. I will never eat another as long as I live.

Am sending you three pictures, which were taken our opening night. Notice the German on the door and the candle in the bottle (before we had electricity). The person pouring the coffee is Mary but you can't see much of her. Our staff is wonderful. You can get a little idea of how to beat up the place is from the pictures of Mary.

We got report from the boys about what the French workmen think we are. They say things like, "The Germans had a girl for practically every soldier, and you only have two for the whole group." Every one teases us about it.

I am also enclosing two money orders, one to be deposited to my account, and one for Warren. I don't know Anne and Herman's address or I would send it to them. I will probably send more money home in the future, as there are no banking facilities over here. How does my bank account stand now? Maybe it would be a good idea to buy me some stock with any money I send home in the form of a money order from here. I will try to send another $80 in a couple of weeks, and then there will be $160 to buy some Providence gas or something with.

Mother, if I haven't said much about myself lately it is because since June we have been expecting to move over here, and most of my activities have been along those lines, so I couldn't write about them. I am fine, never been healthier or had more energy. I'm in the Army now you know and I couldn't come home if I wanted to. When the war is over I'll be very happy to come home, but not until.

Much love.

Fitje

October 23, 1944

Dear Mother & Dad,

   5:30 and the only quiet time in the whole day because everyone is eating. Half the time I go without dinner just to have a moment of peace. Mary is away for a couple of days at another base. I have a roaring fire in our little German stove, and our heater that one of the boys fixed for us is red hot. We have no coal of course, and I just hope we can find wood to keep us, and the club, warm. So far we have to hunt for our own. You can't imagine how roughly we live or how much I love it. Our water for the whole base is hauled by truck every day and we have a 65-gallon German boiler to keep it in. It is not nearly enough but they are putting up a 250-gallon tank for us now.

   Yesterday there were some generals around inspecting, etc., so they asked me to bring coffee and doughnuts up to the briefing room tent and serve them. We were ready at 12:00 but the generals didn't arrive until 4:00. I spent the hours in between running up to Capt. Zeltner's tent drinking cognac to keep warm. When they finally arrived, however, everything was a great success. I wish you could meet some of these people. I know I have spoken of Capt. Zeltner before, as he was one of the ration breakdown boys in England. He is wonderful but thinks I'm awfully dumb and getting more like Zazu Pitts every day. I guess I am too, because I've decided it's the best way to get along over here where it's so rough that you have to have a lot of help.

   Our building is like this:

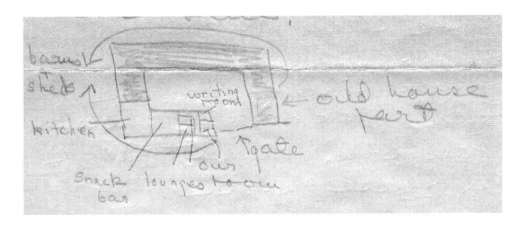

   The black in part is used for motor pool, Link Trainer, etc. In the center is a very muddy courtyard full of trucks most of the time because of the motor pool. It is a very busy little place. Only in our section do the rooms adjoin. Mostly you have to go outside and in again to get from to another. Out lights are wonderful but always going off, which they have just done so we keep a candle handy all the time.

   Out French staff are wonderful. They call Mary "Marie" and me 'Mademoiselle', and are always telling us that the boys love us (I'm sure it's the highest complement the French could pay us), and that we work too hard.

I am dying to hear what you think of where I am now.

I am so sorry about Dr. Mattison. I can't imagine the hill without him. I love the pictures of Warren and Bill and have them up on the wall with Franny and Herb and Joady.

Love to all.
Fitje

October 30, 1044

Dear Mother & Dad,

I really couldn't begin to tell you all we have been doing lately. At the moment the club is closed for two days while the kitchen is being made more usable, and our staff is busy scrubbing everything. It really looks clean for a change. The kitchen was terrible, so they are painting it to make it cleaner and putting up a water tank and a very primitive drainage system.

I am sure you would die laughing at some of our "bath" stories. The other day I went to Paris with Jack Zeltner, and the photo officer, Gill Charters, and the dentist. We went to an Ack-Ack unit near Paris to see the dentist's brother. There were thirty-six officers living in a lovely chateau with hot water and bathtubs all over the place. We had lunch there and after lunch I took a bath. They were wonderful to us and asked us to come back for dinner, which we did. They had French cooks and the food was wonderful. After dinner the Col. invited us up to his room for eggnog and I sat in a huge, soft, pink chair in front of a fire. It was wonderful.

While I was having a bath there, Mary was getting frantic here, so she went to a nearby chateau where some engineers are stationed, walked into the Col's office and said, "I'm Mary Haynesworth and I'd like to take a bath!" The Col. ended up running the water for her.

The other day I went with Col. Corbin and Jack Zeltner while they looked for a heater. We ended up exploring around and found the remains of a huge Buzz Bomb depot, in ruins thanks to the accurate bombing of our group. We also found another chateau with lots of bathtubs and some engineers living in it. Two Majors were living there and they showed us around. It was lovely with a large pond in back of the house with lots of fish. We finally traded a heater they had for a bottle of cognac. Col. Corbin wanted to trade me, but the engineers wouldn't take me.

Last night Col. Corbin, Jack, Mary and I went back with our bathing equipment and the bottle of cognac. No one was there so we all took baths while we were waiting for them to come. Col. Corbin was so dirty he stopped up the tub. When they got back they asked us to stay for dinner, which we did, of course, and Col. Corbin and Jack gave us hell later for eating so much. They admitted though that if we hadn't been there they wouldn't have been asked to stay for dinner. We have more people doing things for us now. Col. Corbin says he thinks we must spend hours in the middle of the night deciding how we can get everyone all confused and in an uproar because we certainly succeed.

Mary went into Paris today for supplies and has just gotten back, bring hundreds of lbs. of lard, doughnuts, flour, sugar, coffee and milk as well as perfume, margarines, etc. By the way you can still buy all the wonderful French perfume here.

Tonight since the club is still closed we are going up to Col. Corbin's trailer (he lives in a regular auto trailer) to help celebrate the fact that he became a full Col. today. I spent most of today up at Hdqrs. trying to get things for the club from another German barracks we have just discovered. I didn't get much, but everyone whispered in my ear that they would bring us something later.

Did you get the pictures I sent? I am taking some of my surroundings too. It looks like pictures you used to see of wrecked French villages after the last war. I guess I told you that this used to be a small village but now there isn't a home left standing. Our building is by far the best repair. The group mess is in the remains of what used to be the school and the PX is in what used to be the local pub. I wish you could see it all. In the steeple of the church, which we see from our window, there apparently was a sniper because the top is all marked with bullet holes.

October 31, 1944

I am sending some Christmas presents home, as I see things I think you all would like. I only hope some of them will get to you by Christmas. You can buy a lot more here than you could in England. As usual it is raining and my hair is hanging in my face. Last night two of the flying officers brought us two bottles of champagne. It's lucky we work every night. I'm sure I'd be in trouble all the time if we didn't. These nights that the club was closed have been awfully difficult.

Much Love,
Fitje

November 7, 1944

Dear Mother & Dad,

Election day and I suppose everyone is terribly excited at home although I haven't heard it mentioned here.

Mary has been in the hospital for a week with some sort of bladder trouble. Although they never could decide what it was, she said she gave the doctor enough specimens to float the Queen Mary, and took enough pills to sink the Queen Mary. She came back last night and Col. Corbin calls her the girl who launched 1000 ships. Now I sure am glad she's back as I was scared something would happen to her like it did to Eleanor, and it was a little lonely being the only girl on the base. Last night Mary and I went off and left the club for the first time and went to dinner with the two CIC men[*] who cover this district. They are the people who investigate things like saboteurs, and tell us whether or not the people

---

[*] Counter Intelligence Corps

Unidentified G.I. in front
of Link Trainer building at
Beaumont Sur Oise

we have hired are collaborators, etc. They live in town and cooked steak and French fries for us for dinner. While Mary and I were waiting for them to get it ready, we ate four cans of anchovies on C-Ration crackers. Consequently we lay awake all night we were so thirsty. We mentioned the other day that we liked anchovies and since then I have been showered with cans of them.

I wish you could see this courtyard we live in on the other side of the gate is the engineering section run by Maj. Carruth (Pappy as everyone calls him), and Sgt. Bradshaw who should be in the comics he is so funny to look at and to talk to. Yesterday I met him walking up the road beaming, with a handful of cigars and he said, "My wife just smoked a cigar, have a baby." He is in the regular Army and is from Texas. He lights our fire before we get up in the morning and then makes us coffee on the stove in his office.

Next to the engineering section are the tech inspectors they consist of four Master Sgts., Charlie, Tom (who we call the Big Barn Smell), Bob who has a nifty cocker spaniel named WAC, and Walker, who I knew very well when I was at Bomber Command, and who was recently transferred here. They were responsible for us having our air mattresses and a rug in our room. On the other side, right next to our kitchen, is the group motor pool office. We gave up half our storeroom so they can have an office and we have never been sorry, as they are wonderful about giving us transportation and other assistance. Next is our storeroom, Dick's office, and the Link Trainer room. There are three sergeants to run the link trainer and who live there, Garrett, Levinson and Brownie.

Garrett is thirty-five and has a cute little daughter eight years old. He is wonderful about helping us and works for us all day long putting in shelves, putting up stoves, taking me to meals while Mary was away, taking the money at night, etc. They have nothing to do as the link trainer was lost in route and still hasn't turned up. Levinson plays the piano beautifully and plays a lot for us in the snack bar in the evenings. Brownie's strictly a family man and thinks and talks about nothing but his wife and baby. Next is our latrine, and then the special service office, and then the group motor pool, and the 554th Squadron Motor pool, with about twenty mechanics and drivers living at one end of the shed.

The best character of a whole bunch is probably Harry Youngstrum, who now works for us taking care of the field ranges during the daytime. He has a daughter my age and was in France during the last war. He is a private and such a drunkard that they couldn't use him anywhere else, which is why we got him. He has been with us for three weeks now has never been drunk on duty and is simply wonderful. He is very fond of Marie Havencourt, the little widow who works for us, whose husband was killed by the Germans the day before liberation day.

I am going to Paris next Monday for supplies and will try to see Dr. Jackson then. Mary went in today to buy perfume for some of the boys to send home for Christmas presents.

During the daytime now we put donuts and coffee in a weapons carrier and take them out to the

Unidentified G.I. taking a bath in Beaumont sur Oise

far away squadrons, the searchlight units, and the Ack-Ack units. It is fun but keeps us awfully busy. We are also making curtains for the four windows that we have in the club.

I really get along fine talking French. I have only had a translator twice, once when we hired six people all at once, and once when the staff had a little argument and I wanted to be sure what it was all about. Yesterday they all bought me pictures of their families, and then I showed them pictures of you all. They bring us presents of apples and flowers and we give them soap and candy when we have any.

Our water here is all hauled from a couple of miles away in water carriers, Dad, and has chlorine in it. We now have a 250-gallon tank, which is filled every day. So far no lice, but we all have lice powder.

Much love.

Fitje

November 11, 1944

Dear Tim,

Haven't heard from you in a long time, but guess our mail is slow because none of us have gotten much since we got over here.

We moved over here about seven weeks ago right along with our group and what an experience that was. Lots of work and worry but also lots of laughs. Our club over here is in about the only livable building on the base, as it was thoroughly wrecked due partly to the accuracy of our own planes when we were in England. The building is an old French farmhouse built in a square with a large courtyard in the center. It really consists of a series of sheds and even now we have few windows, few stoves and part of a roof, which French workmen are in the process of fixing. Our room is right in the same building with low windows opening right on a road so the French kids spend all day just standing, staring in. You can imagine what the French think we are—we're terribly flattered.

Probably the funniest thing is trying to find a place to take a bath. We know a French woman in town and we go over there once a week. Col. Corbin and Capt. Zeltner and I were looking for a heater one day and we located some engineers living in a chateau—steam heat and everything. We took a bath on the spot and been back there several times. We also go to the Ack-Ack group, a searchlight group and a small hospital. We manage to keep fairly clean but we do manual labor all day and I always smell like donuts.

At night we serve donuts and coffee in the club and during the daytime we take them around the line and out to the faraway squadrons. I will never eat another donut if there is nothing else in the whole world to eat. Speaking of eating, the food is wonderful over here and I eat like a pig.

Right now I am visiting my friend Pinkie, the WAC at Bomber Command, for a couple of days. Had more fun last night. I went out with a couple of the WACS and about 10 of the boys to a nightspot in town. A floorshow of naked women and everything. It was amazing!

Must eat now.

Hope to hear from you soon.

Love,
Binnie

November 15, 1944

Dear Mother & Dad,

Well, we are struggling along and things get better every day, or at least no sooner do you get one thing settled than something else happens. Like today—last night Harry, who takes care of the field ranges, fell in a hole and hurt his leg. He is now in the hospital and the fires are only just now being lit at 1:30. When I tried to light one it blew up twice in my face so I am scared to light the things.

The other day, Friday to be exact, Sgt. McKenny (you remember me speaking of Mac from Boston at Bomber Command) stopped in on a tour of picking up supplies and persuaded me without much trouble to go up to Bomber Command with him. In the end I stayed for three nights because I couldn't get back. Finally Col. Corbin flew up Sunday in an L-5[*] and we flew back Monday. We had more fun flying real low and buzzing all the caves to see if there was champagne in them. While up there, I stayed with the WACS and it was the funniest feeling to eat in a mess hall full of WACS for two nights after eating with the Greek, Mac, Hump, Mike, etc. We ate with Col. Styles the last night. They are in a

---

[*] The Stinson L-5 Sentinel resembled a Piper Cub and flew a variety of missions including, photoreconnaissance, resupply, evacuation of wounded, message courier, VIP transport, and artillery spotting.

large town, and there is a lot to do. I came home with practically a complete WAC fatigue uniform that Capt. Von Stein gave me and have worn it ever since because it is so warm. On the way up we stopped at 9th Air Force to see Kremkan the supply Sgt. there. He used to be at Bomber Command while I was there. It is amazing to listen to two supply Sgts together. I watched Kremkan steal McKinney's gloves (which were a kind that only a supply Sgt. would have), and after we left Mac showed me a flashlight he stole from Kremkan.

When I finally got back Lt. Paterson was in the process of painting our bedroom and now it looks wonderful. At this moment he is repairing the walls, which have a few holes in them.

For the last couple of days there have been millions of inspectors here from Bomber Command, and last night we went up to the group officer's mess and had dinner with them and Col. Corbin and Zeltner. Zeltner entertained the whole mess with a long description of Mary and I doing the accounts in the morning on our stomachs on the bedroom floor. Everyone was doubled up laughing including us. We have no desk and no office and Zeltner never fails to come down early in the morning to see what we are doing and get a good laugh.

Yesterday some two star general dropped in with a flat tire, and Col. Corbin brought him down to see us while he was waiting to get it fixed. We made some lovely apple fritters fried in doughnut flour for him, and he left he gave us a carton of cigarettes and two bars of chocolate.

One of our good friends, a gunner, who had completed a tour of mission in Fortresses and was on his second tour with us, and who was in a very bad landing crashing on our field back in England and was one of two survivors, was just killed the other night falling off the back of a truck. What a way to die after all of that.

I got the envelope with the rubbers in it Mother. Thanks a lot. Would appreciate some woolen socks if you get around to it—red, brown or dark blue.

Eleanor Roth, the girl with stomach ulcers who was with me in England, is now at home and I've sure she will be up to see you soon, as she used to teach at Wheaton and will be going up there. Her address is:

Eleanor R. Roth
44 Delafield Avenue
West Brighton
Staten Island, N.Y.

Why don't you write her and ask her to come up for the night. She was with me for the first two months I was with this group and can tell you about all the characters I write about. She is awfully nice and we had a wonderful time together.

Today we get our liquor ration; seven bottles; Champagne, Brandy, Gin, Scotch and assorted wine.

Much Love,
Fitje

November 20, 1944

Dear Dad,

Just a note to tell you what I found out about Dr. Jackson.* Yesterday I went to Paris to pick up our supplies and when I had finished I went around to 7 Rue Foche. There I met a woman who said Dr. Jackson had left and then took me around the corner to where he used to live, and where Louise, the maid that the Jacksons had for a long time, is still living. Now a French colonel is living there and Louise is taking care of him.

Louise said that last May the Germans came and took Mrs. Jackson, Dr. Jackson and their son, and they are all prisoners in Germany. They know where Mrs. Jackson is but have not heard a word about Dr. Jackson or the boy since then. I couldn't understand everything as Louise didn't speak any English, but I think she said that Mrs. Jackson was all mixed up in politics and the resistance and that's how it all happened. She showed me lots of pictures of them all. She tried to get Mrs. Jackson's sister who speaks English to come over but was not able to get her, as she wasn't home. She gave me her address though, and I gave her mine. She's going to ask the sister to write me and tell me about it. The next time I am in Paris I will try to see her.

I am enclosing my license form filled out. I don't know what the fee is so will someone else please fill in that space.

Mary has gone up to Nancy to see some friend of hers for a few days. The weather is wonderful for a change so maybe will have some activity around here.

Much love,
Fitje

* Fitje's father probably met Sumner Jackson in 1917 when they served with the Harvard Surgical Unit in France. Jackson apparently sailed to France in June 1916, arriving in time for the Battle of the Somme. Herman sailed aboard the St. Paul on December 16, 1916. According to Jackson's granddaughter, Loraine Jackson Riemer, the two men remained friendly after the war.

Summer Jackson met Charlotte Sylvie Barrelet de Ricou, who he called Toquette, when she was a nurse in Paris during World War I. They were married in 1917. After the war they moved to Maine, but returned to Paris in 1919. Their son Phillip was born in January 1928.

The Jacksons lived at 11 Avenue Foch, close to the Arc de Triomphe. Jackson continued his medical practice at the American Hospital of Paris. After France surrendered in May 1940, the Germans, including the Gestapo, requisitioned most of the buildings on Avenue Foch. Despite the risks, Sumner and Toquette became important figures in the resistance movement.

On May 26, 1944 the Milice, a Vichy paramilitary group arrested the Jacksons and turned them over to the Gestapo on June 7th. After being held in a series of prisons, Toquette was sent to Ravensbrück, ninety kilometers north of Berlin. The Swedish Red Cross moved her to Malmö on April 28, 1945.

Sumner and Phillip Jackson were sent to Neuengamme, a concentration camp near Hamburg. On April 21, 1945, as the British Army approached Neuengamme, the prisoners were put on freight cars and taken to Lübeck where they were put on ships. On May 3 British aircraft bombed the ships. Seventeen-year-old Phillip Jackson survived. Sumner Jackson's body was never recovered.

Toquette and Phillip were reunited in Paris in September 1945.

November 28, 1944

Dear Mother & Dad,

If only you could be here for just one day to see how we operate I'm sure you would die laughing and be much happier about me being here.

We have a new regimen now. Sgt. Garrett, the older sergeant who we liked so much, gave us hell the other day for staying up so late and looking so beat up. Now we go to bed at 12:00 every night, get up at 9:00, and rest for an hour after lunch. We feel so healthy that it's disgusting. We let nothing interrupt our rest hour. Today we had everyone in utter confusion because decorations were being given out and Gen. Anderson was here from bomber command to officiate. Of course we were asked to serve coffee and donuts, and everyone from Col. Corbin down came over yesterday, and this morning stopped by to be sure we understood everything. We've done it a million times before and naturally there is nothing to it. Capt. Zeltner, who wanted to spend the afternoon with us, finally convinced Col. C that we weren't capable of managing the detail alone so he got himself put in charge of us. When he came to transport us up there, we were resting and he almost went mad worrying outside our door while we made him sweat out our rest hour. After things were all over and everyone has relaxed they always say, "Thank God for Fitje and Mary they are the only calm ones who never mess up." They don't realize that we don't have to worry because we're female and not in the army.

Finally we got up to the squadron area with our donuts and coffee, all dressed up in our best uniforms. We were inspected before we left, because Col. Corbin was afraid we'd wear our pants with holes in them like we threatened. They had a tent for us right behind the ceremonies so we had a good view of the whole thing. About fifty men were decorated for one thing another, and afterwards they got completely messed up when they were searching around trying to get where they should be while

Unidentified G.I.s in front of 554th
Squadron building at Beaumont sur Oise

the honor guard passed in review. Mary said in a loud voice that they looked like a runaway train, and everyone said "shh-shh!" at once very loudly.

Of course it was raining and everyone was freezing, but it was very impressive anyway. Afterwards we served coffee and donuts. Col. Corbin was worrying for fear we would call him "Little Eagle" and ask him what he had done in Paris in front of the General. Maj. Reffe was afraid we'd call him "Boo-Boo," and Capt. Zeltner was afraid we'd steal some of the cups we have borrowed from the group mess. (We did manage to get two.) We could see Col. C turned pale when Gen. A. asked us how the group was treating us, but all we said was that we were much more comfortable than we had been the first two weeks and we didn't even mention the latrine. Before he left there General A. told us he wanted to see the club so we rushed back and told the staff who met the emergency beautifully and had the kitchen and snack bar rearranged in ten minutes. When he arrived Mary and I were sweeping our room and we had a huge pile of dirt, which we quickly swept under the rug. He was full of praise with what we were doing and asked us both to come and visit him. He is awfully nice.

The 554th squadron, where we eat most of the time now, has an officer's mess in a tent. Up to now everyone has been eating in the same barn. Mostly we will continue to eat with our mess kits in the G.I. mess having started that way, but once in a while we hope to be able to eat with the officers without too much criticism from the GIs. Tonight we ate there for the first time, and no sooner had we gotten in than the tent caught fire from the red-hot stovepipe. Everyone said, "Just like a ship. It's bad luck to have a woman around."

Did you get my letter about Dr. Jackson if not let me know and I will write it again.

I really don't need anything over here with the possible exception of some woolen socks. I have told you about our lovely warm arctic bedding rolls and air mattresses, which even on army cots are the most wonderful things in the world, also about the pants and high G.I. shoes that we wear all day and the rubber boots Eleanor gave me before she went home. We are plenty warm enough and very comfortable, much more so than the others on the base because everyone does so much for us. We are so spoiled over here you can't imagine how much attention we get. Our morale never gets low.

At last my Christmas box is mailed. I couldn't find much for Hermie and John and nothing for Bill, but will send things on as I find them. Mail is coming pretty regularly now, but we were three weeks with no cigarettes got Dad's letters and yours, Mother, saying Howie had some had come to see you. I am so glad he did and I hope Eleanor will too.

Every night now one of the squadrons sends for us in the truck and we take coffee and donuts up to that squadron. It is lots of fun and the squadrons are so dispersed that not many of them get down here. It is almost 7:00 and time for the snack bar open.

I guess I forgot to tell you that we were in disgrace here for a few days because we had Thanksgiving dinner off the base with a small group of engineering officers who live in a nearby château. We have assured everyone however that we only did it so we could take a bath, which we did right after lunch much to the amazement of the engineers. I'm sure they'll never ask us again. We had wonderful turkey.

If you watch the papers for news of the 9th Air Force you would have known I was in France a few days after I arrived, because it was announced that the whole 9th Air Force was in France and I already told you I was permanently attached to this group, which is in the 9th Air Force.

Much love,
Binnie

⟡

November 30, 1944

Dear Tim,

Mary and I went over to a nearby station hospital this afternoon and took a bath and washed our hair and now I am lying on the floor in front of the fire trying to dry it. First bath in two weeks and it was wonderful. Our room is even clean because Gen. Anderson came to visit us yesterday and we quickly swept the dirt under the rug. We are also drinking champagne which one of the boys, Sgt. Bradshaw, brought us. He is now here drinking it with us, and what a character. He should certainly be in the funny papers.

Haven't heard from you for ages but mail has been very slow over here so that maybe the reason. What goes on in your life now? I don't know where you are or what you are doing so I will send this to Towson.

Tim isn't it funny, just at that moment someone came to the door and gave me a letter from you dated October 23rd. Well, that was well over a month ago. I guess you are settled somewhere by now. I think your decision is good because it is what you have wanted to do all along isn't it? I just hope it is turning out right. You know, dear, that I always wish you the best of luck in the world. Mostly I am wishing you would come over here.

I have written you once from France, haven't I, so you know I am here. We have been here for two months now and are having a lovely time. We even have a few luxuries now such as a latrine (very non-operational). We have it though in spite of the fact that we go around in pants all day and are getting to be awful old hags.

Lt. Paterson has just come in to help with the champagne drinking. He is an awfully nice pilot who is a very good friend of ours. He is mad at me, because I called him a nasty name so he will only speak to Mary. We are getting very trivial over here I guess.

December 1, 1944

Up for breakfast at 7:00—why, I don't know because we aren't usually so ambitious. Ate powdered eggs and Wheatena in our barn, which we call a mess hall, in the dark. Mary and I eat in the nearest squadron mess and stand for hours with our mess kits. The squadrons are just beginning to set up officer's messes so if we are too lazy to deal with our mess we eat there. But we both have enormous appetites, and get much more to eat in the chow line. We are lucky to be able to eat where we please. Mary dropped her knife and spoon in the garbage pail yesterday and it disappeared in the garbage before she could get it. I don't know where she will ever get another.

We have had some parties over here that you would have loved, Tim. For a while, we were having one every night. The demands on us over here where we are the only girls are terrific, and as long as your health lasts there is always someone around to keep you up all night. I got so beat up I couldn't take it any longer so now I got to bed at 12:00 like a good girl.

Have been to Paris several times, but mostly on business because we have to go every week or two to pick up supplies. It is so packed with American soldiers now that you can hardly move.

Am dying to hear where you are now. Write soon.

Love,
Binni

✍

December 9, 1944

Dear Mother & Dad,

Seems like it's been quite a while since I've written, but I have sent quite a few French Christmas cards which we think are a scream.

This afternoon I made the hideous mistake of giving two little kids each a piece of chocolate, and since then there have been dozens knocking on the window. I am trying to ignore three cute little boys now. They hang in the kitchen windows all day long and yell for beignets, which is French for doughnuts.

This week we had a New York Sun newspaperwomen staying with us, and what a character. She is English aged thirty-two, and very attractive in a beat-up sort of way. (But who am I to critique some-one for being beat up.) She is in love with Stuart Hatch a pilot on the base, who, incidentally, is the brother of Glen Leet's wife. She slept on an army cot in the lounge and luckily had brought her own bedding roll. After three nights of parties and nobody getting any sleep I went back to Paris with her for the night. She lives at the Scribe Hotel where lots of newspaper correspondents are billeted, and I heard some fascinating stories. I also got a permanent.

The next day I stayed in bed reading until 3:30. Then we met up with several flying officers from here who arrived at the bar with a bunch of carnations and two long loaves of French bread, which we ate in no time. It is very hard to eat in Paris, as we are not allowed to eat in the French restaurants because food is scarce. We finally got dinner at the Scribe and then went to a nifty place to dance. The only trouble is nothing starts until 10:00 or 11:00 in Paris and we had to get the truck, which comes in for the people on pass at 11:00. The ride home on a Liberty Run truck is something, all different degrees of drunken-ness and language, etc. When one of us is on it, someone sits on the end and warns everyone that Fitje or Mary is there, and they watch their language. Incidentally, get Jane to buy the Sun and save Judy's articles (Judy Barden). Lots of them will be about the group and she wrote one about us, which will amuse you.

The little son of some French friends of ours just knocked on the window and asked Mary and I to dinner at their house the day after Christmas. They are going to kill their pig for the occasion. It is the family with all the kids that I wrote you about.

Yesterday Col. Corbin and Jack and I went to explore some caves where the Germans stored lots of stuff. We walked for miles underground with a flashlight looking at stuff. It was terribly interesting. Mary flew up to Nancy yesterday in an L-5 and hasn't come back yet, but I guess she'll turn up tonight.

Ten past twelve and there are four G.I.'s from the orchestra listening to records, and I can't make them leave. Tonight I played Ping-Pong until 9:00 steadily. I even won two games and then found out the boy I had been playing with was playing with his left hand! At nine the 1st Sgt. from another squadron came for me, and we loaded coffee and doughnuts into the truck and took them up to his squadron. For your information a bomb group has four squadrons, plus Headquarters (which we are attached to) plus service group, etc. Here they are more dispersed and the men can't get down to the club which is why we go to three squadrons, each one, two nights a week and miscellaneous people, such as engineers and searchlight and ack-ack the seventh night. We are right next the 554th Squadron and Headquarters so we don't have to worry about them. We eat our meals at the squadron near us. The squadrons now all have Officer's clubs and Enlisted Men's clubs where they serve wine and beer, etc. and it is amazing to see them and the ingenuity that goes into building them out of nothing, because there really wasn't anything here when we started. The one we went to tonight is in a rough wooden building, which the boys built themselves. It has lovely naked women all over the walls and the most ingenious stoves made of oil barrels and burning waste oil.

The squadrons send transportation for us, and you'd never think they would be the least bit interested in coffee and doughnuts, but they come in droves and bring us cigarettes (which we are very short of now) and candy and cake from their packages from home. We go back laden with presents. The officers send someone over to bring us back to their club for a drink, and we have to write our names on the walls because we are the only women to ever be in the clubs. Beat up as we are, they sure are good to us.

We have mice by the millions, and the other night they had a little game they played which consisted of squeaking from one corner to another and then changing corners. The route lay across the foot of Mary's bed, so she got up early and found a huge cat, which one of the boys named Mrs. Patrick Fuller-Crap. We had her for one day and she disappeared out the window. That day, our little French boy, Jack, built her a lovely box of sand and when he brought it in our room he said in perfect English, "who is going to teach her to pull the chain." We suspect some of the boys were coaching him. He is very handsome, and Mary is going to bring him back to the states and get him a movie contract. Now we have mousetraps, and they eat the flour in the traps, but we don't catch any mice.

We have a lovely new stove in our room too. Now maybe we'll get some wood so we can have a fire. Must go to bed so I can get up in the morning.

I guess you'll get this letter just about Christmas time so Merry Christmas to you all. I just hope that by next Christmas we'll all be home again.

Much Love,
Fitje

Sunday

Cold and rainy. Mary got back this morning after quite an eventful trip. At one point a bridge was shelled shortly after she had crossed it.

In the courtyard with us there is a place in a shed where they have a movie of enemy planes and the gunners practice shooting at them. This afternoon they didn't have many customers so Sgt. Coppersmith who runs it got a movie, *The Hairy Ape*, from Special Service, and about nine of us went to see it; three gunners, Lt. Paterson, Harry who works for us, Mary, and three transportation boys. There was a lot about stokers on boats in it, and the boy sitting beside me had been a stoker for five years on a tanker. He spent the Christmas of 1936 in jail in Hamburg, Germany.

I lit the stoves tonight because Jack wasn't here and finally got two of them going. Our stove arrangement is terrible, especially in the snack bar. There is no place for stove pipes so we finally stuck them out through the shutters. They smoke like mad. I guess the stovepipe isn't long enough. It is getting cold and I know our outside water tank is going to freeze any day now. Two and a half months until the worst of the winter will be over, and I don't look forward to it. The way we live is like the occasional nights we used to spend in the Buflum's camp in the South County.

Will you see if you can buy a book called *Life's Ebb and Flow* by Frances Countess of Warwick, published by Macmillan, and save it for me when I get home. It is about the estate we lived on when I was with this group in England.[*]

Love,
Fitje

December 20, 1944

Dear Mother & Dad,

I hope my mail is reaching you more quickly now. I get mail from you regularly but it takes quite a while to come the last letter was dated November 20th.

I have gotten two lovely packages from you and thanks so much. The perfume is wonderful of course. It is getting scarcer over here now because the American bought it all to send home for Christmas. Mary and I, not foreseeing the shortage, sold most of ours to the boys who couldn't get into town to get it. It is more fun to get those packages and open them. The Carr's menu, which Rose used as a card, with the lovely slip it, in your box, is worn out so many people have looked at it and decided which meal they would order. We finally put it up on the wall at the snack bar. Lu's slippers have arrived in our lovely nice and warm. By the way, I have spent Lu and Jane some Straw's shoes with rabbit for lining, which the French people around here wear all the time. Mary and I have some

---

[*] Easton Lodge at Great Dunmow

and wear them a lot. Everyone calls them our 'Wabbit and Wacks'. I am trying to find a pair big enough for Anne and a pair small enough for Warren. I am also sending something captured from the German warehouse for you mother, which made me homesick because it reminded me of the 4711[*], which Dad gives you. There is so much more to buy here than England. There are lovely toys now. We should know we have bought 350 for our children's party on Christmas. If only Warren[†] were a girl I would get him a lovely doll.

Christmas tree, 1944

I have lots of pictures of myself but must get them censored before I send them home. They are candid shots and will show you how we live and what we look like most of the time.

We have been working hard getting ready for Christmas. Children from the three small towns around are coming to our party, which is to be in a hall in the town where there is more room. We have been calling on all the town mayors today to get the last details set. We also got a Christmas tree, which we chopped out of the garden of a lady who left with the Germans. All the neighbors gathered and said, "Bosh, cut them all down." The club is all decorated with green things and looks lovely.

My French is improving and I even succeeded in firing someone today. Our staff is wonderful and the club runs in the usual state of chaos that all my clubs have run in. A thousand people in the kitchen all day stealing doughnuts and by the time night comes about half of the ones we've made all day are left. We have enough though and everyone is happy. I wish you could see Bernadette, the prettiest one. Soldiers come from miles around to see her. Marielle the widow who used to like Harry, our old soldier who takes care of the kitchen, now likes the motor pool dispatcher, which makes us unhappy because Harry is unhappy. We get lots of transportation though and that is nice for us. Harry keeps bringing her presents but no use. She says he's too old.

Well Mary is ready for bed so will have to close. I will write a decent letter after Christmas.

I remember wondering last Christmas where I would be this Christmas and here I am; I am wondering the same thing again. I sure hope we'll all be home.

Much love,
Fitje

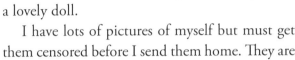

* German Eau de Cologne created and manufactured in Cologne, Germany since 1799, which was favored by Fitje and her mother.
† Fitje's nephew, born to Herman and Ann Pitts on May 25, 1944

December 26, 1944[*]

Dear Family,

Well another Christmas and I thought of you many, many times all day. We did have fun in spite of being busy fighting the war. I could never describe it but roughly here's what we did. Sunday afternoon Mary and I had a party for all the staff, plus Sgt. Garrett, and Lieut. Patterson, who have helped us so much, plus Capt. Zeltner who was always around and who the staff love. They call him Monsieur Jack or the French word for Screech Owl—Hibou—because he makes fun of them when they all get talking at once in the kitchen. We closed the club for an hour and hid out in the lounge. Mary and I filled stockings for the ten on the staff and had two bottles of champagne, and Jack brought two more, and Dick two more. We have more fun filling the sox, which we borrowed from Sgt. Garrett. After we had filled them the mice ate holes in them to get the candy and we had to mend them all. The staff was so excited. They said this is the first Christmas they celebrated for four years and I know they celebrated. The next morning all but one came to work an hour late with hangovers. I thought that none of them were coming and we would have to struggle through the day somehow. Of course we both had to have a kiss on both cheeks from each of them and it was a great success. The morning staff gave us a huge green plant with an American flag and a French flag and two handkerchiefs stuck in the middle of it. The evening staff gave us each a bottle of perfume.

The evening was very hectic. Everyone got drunk somewhere else and then came to see us. We had wonderful food: French-fried potatoes, and they are wonderful here. We collected ingredients from the mess halls and had a baker in town make cake and I wish you could have seen things he made; chocolate éclairs, cream puffs, cookies, and everything. They were delicious. I have never seen anything so good anywhere. He made a dozen extra special sponge things and we gave them to special people for presents, like Jack, Boo-Boo, Col. Corbin, and Wilson, the mess sergeant who collected the ingredients for us.

Christmas morning bright and early, Pat, Lt. Patterson, Jack, and Capt. Charters woke us up bringing smoked lobster French bread and champagne for breakfast and we sat up in bed and opened the stockings we have filled for each other and we all ate.

That afternoon we had a party for French children, all between four and eight from the two nearest towns. The mayors gave us an estimate of 300 but in the end 500 arrived complete with parents, babies in arms, etc. Some fifteen truck loads plus lots who walked. At the most no more than 200 small children will fit in our snack bar at once. You have never seen such pushing and shoving and screaming as when Santa Claus, in the form of Major Howard, complete with beard arrived. I was honestly

[*] Hitler launched his last offensive on December 16, 1944. Fitje never mentions it, the Battle of the Bulge, in her letters although she once told me how nervous the citizens of Beaumont sur Oise were thinking that the Germans might return. For the first seven days bad weather grounded all of the bomb groups, but on the 23rd the weather broke and the 386th flew two missions. The group flew a total of thirteen missions before January 25, 1945 when the German offensive officially ended.

terrified that someone was going to be crushed to death. Luckily we had plenty of everything. I have a boyfriend now, George, age nine, the son of the baker who made our cakes, who wouldn't let go of my hand once. He is awfully cute. He brought me a bag of apples today.

Christmas night everyone in the courtyard had a party, and it was fun. We toured around them, and tried to keep our eyes on the club to. The ordinance company had a dance and asked us, but only one could go. Mary went and came home exhausted because she was the only girl. Later in the evening all the drunks came in. Jack gets furious that I have so much patience with them. He stood and watched for a while and almost got in a fight with one of them. They are such kids, the gunners especially. Roy Brink has a smear of lipstick on his cheek where I kissed him under the mistletoe. It has been there for three days, and he swears he won't wash it off until he finishes his missions. (One more to go.) He thinks it's good luck.

We finally got to bed exhausted about 1:00, and meant to sleep late in the morning. Harry brings us coffee now as soon as the fires are lit so we don't get up until 9:00 or so. This morning, however, the water tanks froze, as it has done for the last three mornings, and I had to get up to find someone with a blowtorch to thaw them out. I suppose we will go through the same process every morning until spring. Tomorrow we will wrap straw and canvas around the pipes, but I'm sure they will still freeze. We fooled around all day and tried to get our room cleaned up, (The size of Lou's room with us, and our staff, and all the Christmas stuff in it.) and finally got a jeep and went over to the hospital for a bath, my first in three weeks I think.

And so ends another Christmas.

Thanks so much for your packages and for the slippers, Lu.

Much love,
Fitje

December 27, 1944

Dear Tim,

Thanks so much for the Christmas box, which arrived, amazingly enough, the day before Christmas. It was full of things, and I had more fun opening it. Roughly: powder, stockings, two pink slips, baby pins, toothbrush, tooth powder, pins, cigarette case, some wonderful herb farm toilet water, which I love, etc. Honestly I don't see how they get so much in one box.

I hope you got home for Christmas. It was amazing here and very drunken. We had a party Christmas Eve and another Christmas day, for 500 French children. What a brawl! I have never seen so many pushing, shoving kids. I was scared to death of some of them were going to be smothered. Christmas night we went around to several different parties and there were a lot. I was glad when it was all over, as I am getting too old to take it.

It has suddenly turned very cold over here. Our outside water tank has frozen three days in a row and finally this morning the pipes burst so we have been carrying water from the nearby squadron all day. I suppose eventually something will be done about it. Anyway maybe the clear cold weather will help us win the war more quickly.

Aside from Christmas nothing particular is happened around here that I can write about. Mary had a friend of hers visiting us for two nights, Capt. Ralph from another group. We had a hysterical time and when he went back he wrote that life was very dull where he was after he had seen how idiotic it could be. What a time we had. It was sort of like the two nights you spent in New York with me.

I wish you what would be sent over here. We would have wonderful fun.

Hoping to hear from you soon.

Much love,
Binnie

1945

January 4, 1945

Dear Family,

Just a short letter to let you know I haven't frozen to death yet.

Today two things happened; we got some coal, wonderful, a whole ton, and it is snowing, dammit. Mary is going to make some snow ice cream after it gets a little deeper. We have a fire in our room and it is wonderful to be warm. Yesterday Capt. Zeltner gave me some lovely heavy GIs shoes with iron heels and cleats so I ought to be able to keep my feet dry.

New Year's was worse than Christmas but lots of fun. We had French fried potatoes and apple fritters, and a variety show in the club, and it was a madhouse. Most everyone was drunk and the next day we had to close the place to clean it up.

The water tank is still frozen and so are the pipes but we are managing to struggle along. Just to show you how valuable fuel is here where everyone has to forage for their own, the other day we had a landing crack up, and a plane was absolutely smashed to bits. By a miracle no one was badly hurt, but in the crash a telephone pole was knocked down. When the ambulance arrived to rush the crew off to the hospital the copilot calmly loaded the telephone pole on the ambulance and took it back to his tent for firewood.

Well, Sgt. Carl Williams has just come in and is talking so much I can't concentrate any longer.

I am enclosing a picture of me and Mary and Santa Claus. Everyone looks happy but the kids. If you could have seen the howling bunch of kids around us you would've understood the worried expression on my face.

Much love,
Fitje

January 9, 1945

Dear Mother & Dad,

Lots of snow in the last couple of days and every time I go out of the building I get a snowball down my neck.

What do you think? I am going to have a weeks' vacation to Cannes on the Riviera. Isn't that wonderful? It seems that there are some extra Red Cross girls here right now so we got a substitute and Mary went first. When she gets back I will go. The week doesn't count travel time so all it will be straight into about two weeks. The new girl, Betty Hardman, is terribly nice. She arrived from England on Christmas day and is finding it a little rough here, but she will soon get used to the cold and the plumbing. I am really glad for this vacation. Without it I would be so beat up at the end of the winter I would never looked like anything again. (Someone just threw a snowball through the windows, which accounts for the smears.)

Haven't heard from you for a long time now and I'm wondering what you all are doing. Is it cold in Providence? I imagine it is.

Poor Jack was in an automobile accident and is in the hospital. Personally I think he's goldbricking but he says he has a sore back and is in bed with a board under his mattress. Major Reffe, Boo-Boo, Cpt. Charters, Gil, Betty, and I went over yesterday and took a bath and washed our hair (Betty and I) and had dinner with him. He is having a lovely time and lots of company. I wish he would get well because I want to work on him for a door from the lounge to the snack bar so everyone doesn't have to go outside and in again, and also for a coal bin so we can lock up our coal. Everyone steals it. At last we did get the water tanks moved into the kitchen so that will help a lot. Oh well in a couple of months the winter will be over anyway.

Did you ever get the box of clothes I sent home? I am going to send some more soon. All my civilian clothes are worn out and I never wear them anymore. I am enclosing pictures taken in England of me and the kittens, and me and Jack, and Boo-Boo, and Mary.

Must go to chow.

Much love,
Fitje

January 18, 1945

Dear Family,

Have just washed my hair and we have a lovely fire in our stove. Betty is not rugged like Mary and I are so we have a fire every day now. This afternoon I have washed three heads of hair. Dick Moncure, field director, fell against a hot stove and burned his hand badly about a week ago. He asked me to wash his so I did, and when Harry (G.I. in the kitchen) heard, nothing would do but to have his washed too. The process is very complicated, as all water has to be carried from the kitchen. We are very fortunate in having a basin in our room, which the engineers who were fixing the runways installed for themselves before we got here.

When I get home it will be terrible. I will probably carry all the water from the tap in the garden to my room; throw dirty water out the window, and empty my coffee cup on the floor in the dining room when I have finished all I want. I hope my language will be all right. I am very careful in front of the GIs, but Mary and I have some choice expressions we used in our room.

I am sending you a cartoon from *Stars & Stripes*, which probably won't be funny to you because you're not here but we think it's a screen. It appears every week—also picture of Betty and I, which Jack took the other day. It shows the snow and the lovely flying boots we wear.

Tomorrow I am off for the south and I'm looking forward to it. I have four books to read, from Mrs. Aldrich, and I am very grateful for them, and some socks to knit. I am planning to sleep most of the time. This vacation couldn't have come at a better time I am really beat up.

I am so sorry to hear about Alan and will write Katrina[*] while I am away. I hope Lu is all right. Your last letter was dated December 5th but the one before that was dated December 26th so I'm a little confused as to news. How is Jones? You haven't mentioned him in ages.

Thanks so much for the lovely green stockings, Mother. They are wonderful, exactly what I need. Did you get my box? I am going to send another shortly with some shoes for Jane and Lou.

We are beginning to hear about a rotation plan for us, thirty days at home after we have been here for two years. I have five more months when I am eligible. Let's hope it is all over with anyway, and then I can see the Pacific maybe.

I am as bad as you, Mother. I keep worrying about what will happen when I'm away and I almost don't want to go. I have a horrible fear that the war will end, and I won't be here to celebrate with everyone, but I remember being afraid of the same thing when I went to Scotland way back last summer. I can't imagine ever being home again. You can't possibly realize how different it is here. Especially how things that you never thought of before become very valuable, like wood. I will never walk past a piece of wood again without wanting to bring it home for a fire and bath. I'll take six a day the first year I'm

* Allan and Katrina Maybock were Fitje's close friends in Providence. Allan was killed during the Battle of the Bulge

home, and food, when I think of drugstores and ice cream and hot dogs I almost die. Not that we're not well fed because we are, but there hasn't been much variety in my diet for almost two years—Spam, C-Rations, pork and beef, cabbage and potatoes. Cole slaw is wonderful over here.

A guard just looked in the window and saw me with my head covered with bobby pins and said I wasn't worth guarding.

I must comb my hair and go eat before it's too late.

Much love to everyone.

Fitje

January 25, 1945

Dear Family,

Can you imagine me in Cannes on the Mediterranean? Well here I am. I wish you could see my room at the Savoy Hotel. A huge double bed, and does it look wonderful, and a bathroom with the bathtub and hot water. Unbelievable and it's mine for six days.

What a trip down here. I almost turned around and went back three times because it didn't seem worth the effort. Finally got a message from Mary saying she was back in Paris, via a truck driver, as telephoning is impossible. I went in on Saturday and got caught in a blizzard, and she drove the car back, and I stayed in Paris. (A new English Hillman is our latest acquisition.) I was so weary I didn't even start trying to get down here until Monday but stayed in a small hotel for Red Cross people and took five baths in two and a half days. Hot water is very unusual even in Paris and I guess this hotel is one of the few to have it. Paris is amazing when it snows. Everyone throws snowballs, and an American girl is at the mercy of hundreds of GIs. Even old Frenchman throw snowballs at each other.

Monday I finally pulled myself together and went to the RTO (Rail Transportation Office) for a ticket. All army people have to have travel orders to travel by rail and that includes us. I finally got a ticket by rail to Lyon and met up with three much older and even more beat up Red Cross girls who were also going. One had just gotten out of the hospital having had all her insides removed. We struggled on the train Tuesday night, and to make a long story short, having missed every possible connection, finally arrived at Marseille late Wednesday night. The best fun was the train from Lyon to Marseille. GIs, whom I quickly got to know, ran it and I spent the last half sitting up in front with the engineer. When we got to Marseille we were completely lost. We went to the army billeting office and got billets in an old hotel that smelled strongly of disinfectant, (bugs) no sheets, or pillowslips, and old worn-out mattresses. I was too tired to care. At 7:00 two of us rose to start struggling for a ride to Cannes. No trains, no buses, no nothing. Finally went to the Red Cross, having exhausted all our Army and Navy possibilities, and after four hours of arguing they gave up and gave us a car and driver.

It was a warm, lovely ride along the Mediterranean. We only had one flat tire on the way. Palm trees and everything. The coast really looks beat up from shelling and landings, etc. But the sea is beautiful and I can hear the surf from my window. It is now at 8:00, and I am going to take a bath and go to bed.

January 28, 1945

Well, tomorrow early I start back. I guess it was silly to come all this long way for three days, but I can't make myself stay away any longer. I just hope Mary has gotten the snack bar whitewashed. With luck it will only take two days to get back to Paris and another day to communicate with the base and get someone to come for me. I should be back Wednesday night.

The weather was perfect today, sunny and quite warm. We walked way up to a church on the hill in got a wonderful view of the city, and the blue Mediterranean, and it really was blue. The other days have been cold and cloudy but still much warmer than Paris and vicinity.

I forgot to say that this hotel has been taken over by the Red Cross for beat up Red Cross girls. It is very small and comfortable. There are only about ten girls here. We have breakfast in bed whenever we want it and eat the other two meals in an army mess in a nearby hotel. I have been in bed most of the time. Go to bed right after dinner and stay in bed until noon. I don't feel like doing a darn thing so I haven't. When I get home I'm going to stay in bed for a month at least. In spite of this lovely bed with sheets, I am so used to my dirty bedroll that I can hardly wait to get back to it.

I have read the two books Mrs. Alter sent me and like them both a lot: *Bermuda Calling* and *Anna and the King of Siam* also *The Razors Edge*, *Strange Fruit*, and *The Thunderhead*, which three of the GIs gave me before I left. Have also knit two pairs of socks for myself, and Mary.

Will mail this when I get back to Paris. Hope there is some mail from you awaiting me at the base.

Did I thank you for the green stockings mother? They are wonderful.

Much love.

Fitje

February 5, 1945

Dear Mother & Dad,

Well, back again and I must say I was glad to get here. The trip back took three whole days. We left Cannes at 6:30 in the morning on Monday and arrived in Paris at 7:00 Wednesday night. Tuesday night we took a train from Dijon, which was supposed to leave at 9:30, but we sat in the RTO office at the station until 4:30 in the morning before it finally came and it didn't leave until 6:00 A.M. As a matter of fact it was the most fun of all. There were about thirty-five people waiting; five French civilians, two British officers, an American civilian and several American enlisted men and officers, besides the two of us. By the end of the night and the next day in the train we knew each other very well. The funniest thing was watching an English wing commander teaching two French civilians how to shoot crap. In the end the two civilians and an American Sgt. took all his money. My best friends were six G.I.'s on their way to some infantry school who found a blow torch, and with it heated C-Rations for me and made me coffee.

When I got back here I found out that in my absence all the repairs that I had been agitating for since we got here had been made. They were furious that I got back before it was quite completed. It is so much better. We have new tent stoves that keep it much warmer; the snack bar has been white-washed and a stone door put in and a the windows were air light, and a door cut through from the snack bar to the kitchen. It is much nicer. The drainage system is almost finished and we have been painting all the trimmings red. The snack bar is now open in the morning and afternoon as well as the evening so we are very busy.

The mud is terrible and comes almost to the top of my rubber boots. Col. Corbin said to let him know when it went over the top and he'd do something about it. It is warming though and all the snow has melted.

Just got your letter dated Jan. 22nd, Dad. Am so glad the Christmas box arrived even though late. I am also so happy to hear I'm going to be another Aunt, Lu. Won't that be something with three new people in the family when I get home? Just hope I get there before they grow up. I sent a pair of shoes home to Jane today and will send Lu's when I get some more paper to wrap them in and if I can find a big enough pair.

When I got home there were two Christmas packages from you all, and they were wonderful. Thank you so much. We had a cocktail party to celebrate my return and I opened them in the middle of it. I love the slippers and the slip and the Pate de Foie, which we ate with French bread. The candy I shared with all the staff because they never see things like that now. The pictures of Warren were so cute. I wish I could see him. He must be awfully cute now.

I am enclosing a picture of us cutting wood, also one of me, which everyone says I shouldn't send home I look so beat up. We really sawed that wood too, and chopped it up. In the background is the barn that is our mess hall.

Fitje and Mary cutting wood at Beaumont sur Oise, January 1945

Don't worry about me Mother. Nothing upsets me anymore and in a lot of ways we are better off here than we were in England. I don't mind the physical discomforts, although Mary is so fed up and I am very glad the winter is half over. Col. C. is urging us to move to the small nearby town for the next two months but transportation is too difficult so I'm going to stay right here. We are probably warmer here anyway as there is no heat in town, and I don't know where we'd live anyway.

I am getting optimistic and even have a bottle of scotch and I am saving it for the day the war ends. We are all beginning to talk about that day.

Don't let Jones get too fat. He must be almost seven years old now. There are lots of new puppies around here and they are awfully cute.

Much Love,
Fitje

February 6, 1945

Dear Jane,

Thanks an awful lot for your letter about Christmas. It sounded about the same except the babies and the absences.

I am trying to write this letter in the snack bar because I haven't had another chance. One boy sitting beside me just said, "Who can read that scribble, I can't hardly figure out what you're writing." What a madhouse. You should see it.

February 7, 1945

Mary and I are having drinking hour. We just polished off a bottle of champagne with Lt. Paterson, one of the pilots. This afternoon we took time off to go into town to Col. Corbin's house (he and two other Cols. have just moved to a tiny house in the very small nearby town). It's wonderful for us because we can take a bath there. We sat in front of the fire and Sgt. Wilson, who runs the joint for me brought up sandwiches and coffee while he heated the water for our baths. The novelty of living in a barn wore off a month ago and it is very bad for us to go near a warm clean place. We are working for Col. C's trailer now that he has moved out of it, but he says he's saving it for a summerhouse.

We have been very busy painting lately and the place looks very fancy. I wish I could send you pictures of the outside though. Mud knee deep—what a mess. We gave up trying to keep the inside clean long ago. We are all looking forward to peace day and Mary and I are hoping we will stay sober long enough to remember it. Mary is quite a character. I know you would like her. She reminds me an awful lot of you as a matter of fact.

I would love to write you a letter about life as it really is over here, but I guess it will have to wait until I get home. When I think back over the last two years and realize how it has been and what I have done and how I have changed I die at the thought of coming home. I mean it scares me. In spite of it all, I am sure I am better for the experience. I hope I am right.

I am so excited about Lu. It is hard for me to believe. Why don't you buy her anything you think she would like? I am enclosing a money order for $100 for my share. With what is left will you take out anything I owe you for the other stuff you sent and then if there is anything left will you <u>buy and send a bath robe</u>—a nice pretty one—don't care how much it costs. Pink or blue quilted or something like that. Am tired of everything old and dirty and not pretty. My old one is worn out. Don't worry too much about warmth, as it will be spring when it gets here. Don't try to be practical! I want something pretty and feminine and you would too if you lived the way we do. If there is any money left send a silk <u>nightgown</u> with sleeves along with it—size 36 and bathrobe size 16. Thanks a lot.

Fitje and Mary, 1945

Mary's sister, Madeleine, is having a baby just about the same time Lu is so it will be exciting in July and we will be waiting for news. Wish you would send some up-to-date pictures of Warren. He must be awfully cute.

What do you hear from Johnny? Do you know where he is now? How is Pat? Is she divorced yet?

Am sending this home to be forwarded as Dad wrote that you had gone to Washington for two months and I don't know your address.

Much Love,
Fitje

February 8, 1945

Dear Mother & Dad,

It seems like ages since I wrote but I guess it hasn't really been so long.

We have been concentrating on our new quarters, and a police dog puppy, which we are taking care of for someone else, and I hope to be able to keep permanently, so the time has flown by lately. Also, I hitch hiked a ride to Belgium for one night and got back last night. We had a lovely time seeing new territory, and spent a night in Charleroi with the nicest Belgian family, and a huge soft bed, and eggs for breakfast. I am so pleased with all the French I have learned and can actually carry on lengthy conversations on elementary subjects. The staff teases me and say, "Mlle. couldn't speak French with her hands in her pockets," because I gesticulate so much with them.

Our dog is terribly cute. We call him Hidi-o-Hush, which means something awful in Russian. (Mary says)

Mary on far right with French staff at Beaumont sur Oise

Our new quarters are lovely. They are completed except a place to hang our clothes, and that is being done this afternoon. Tomorrow we will get it cleaned up and move in.

I am enclosing a picture of some of our staff and Mary. The husbands of the two on either end are prisoners. The one on the left of Harry is Bernadette, the pretty one, and the one on the right is Marcel whose husband was shot by the Germans. Have had a hectic week. Harry got drunk and stole the car and we had to get the MPs to pick him up. He was so remorseful that we forgave him, of course. We caught one of our French boys stealing so fired him on the spot, but luckily got Pierre, a much better one to take his place. It seems like all the crises come at once.

Haven't heard from Tim for a long time and wondering if he will turn up over here.[*]

Did Lou get the lace collar I sent? Have the shoes arrived yet?

Much love.
Fitje

February 9, 1945

Dear Mother & Dad,

We are having a party with the box of food, which arrived today. The fact of the matter is it arrived at 8:00 this morning while Mary and I were still in bed. Jack came down and we opened it and he sat on Barry's footlocker putting anchovies on crackers and feeding them to us for breakfast. We ate the box of crackers and two cans of anchovies. Now we are eating a can of sardines and the Triscuits and

---

* Tim was not yet in Europe. He graduated from OCS in October 1944 and was posted at Ft. Blanding in the Infantry Replacement Training Center (IRTC). He sailed to Europe in late February 1945. His first letter from France was dated March 1, 1945.

Lt. Patterson is here helping us. It is wonderful to have food of my own because I am always eating everyone else's.

I also forgot to mention how I love the little balsam pillow in my Christmas box. It's sleeps with me every night and makes me homesick for Maine.*

We have worked hard today. This morning we went to town and got some whitewash. We get it from huge bins behind the factory where it is some sort of a byproduct. This afternoon with the help, and hindrance, of about twenty people we whitewashed the kitchen and painted the doors a lovely gray, or rather Mary managed that detail. I just got in on the end of it because I had to do the accounting all over again for the two weeks I was away. It was so messed up. Just goes to show how invaluable I am.

Harry, our GI, has reverted to drink again, and has been drunk for three days, and I've had to send him away. We are so organized that I guess we will be able to do without him and I hate to keep him when he gets to be a nuisance.

Did I write you that Mary's sister is having a baby just about the same time Lou is? We will be very anxious for news, come August. I hope we are still here, unless of course we are home and that seems very doubtful.

Got a long letter from Priscilla. She is getting a divorce and I am sorry. I like them both so much. Also one from Trelsie who now lives near Ellie Wilson Jordan who has twins, and they are very good friends. I think my friends are very good to write considering I never find time to write anyone but you.

Today while we were in town I saw the nicest police dog puppy and now I'm angling for someone to get it for me. I asked the people to sell it but they said no so I will have to find someone who can bargain with them.

I am enclosing a money order for $100, which I have made out to you, Dad, and after it was made out I decided to send it to Jane to pay for a wedding present for Lou and some money I owe her and some things I want her to send here. So will you keep it yourself and send her a check for $100? Thanks. When I have $2400 in the bank will you start buying me a $75 dollar bond every month out of my checking, or investing it in some stock or something whatever you think is best? I will try to send $50 home every month now because when I finally get home I want to have lots of money to spend.

Just ate another can of anchovies. Anytime you want to send me some more I'd love to have them—also canned lobster. It's wonderful with French bread, toasted, and champagne.

How is Bridget? Give her my love and tell her there are several very nice Irish girls working for the Red Cross over here. I am sorry Jones is getting fat. You will have to put him on a diet? I wish I could see Warren. When do the babies learn to walk? Answer this!! Every day some boy comes in to talk about his baby. Most of this group's babies are about 11 months old and they all ask, "When do babies learn to walk."

---

* Fitje's family had a small cabin on Saddleback Lake in Rangeley, Maine.

I am reduced to wearing G.I., O.D.* panties and G.I. O.D. slips only because everything else is dirty after my long vacation.

Well must go to the snack bar.

Much love to you all.
Fitje

February 16, 1945

Dear Mother & Dad,

I have received much mail from home lately, and lots of clippings, etc. The latest letter from you, Mother, was dated February, although I couldn't read the date. I am so glad my Christmas package and my clothes arrived safely. I have also sent the shoes for Lou and Jane and am shortly going to send more old clothes. Speaking of clothes, would you send me four or five summer dresses size fourteen? I forget what I sent home, but if anything good, send it back. I left most of my things in England so have no way of knowing. Did I send home the green and yellow plaid silk dress like Jane's? If so, why not send it back? Not the others, as they are too impractical in the mud. I could use three or four warn dresses, like the plaid, though—something Town and Country has to offer. I will send some winter clothes home on the assumption that I will be home next winter. However you may have to send them back to me. If you see a wonderful spring silk print dress that I can wear to Paris (with black shoes) I would love that too.

The newspaper article about us made us laugh. It is only slightly true and could be enlarged upon greatly.† Like rain pouring in the windows, and also drunks, Frenchman, and everything else. Which officers we will tackle for what we need—our methods are horrible—I never thought I'd stoop so low. The GIs were not even playing Ping-Pong while the girl played classical music, only because Mary hid the Ping-Pong balls and paddles. The fact of the matter is that two enjoy it, and the rest get furious. "How can we play Ping-Pong with that going on?" The missing door was not to our room, but to our latrine—much more serious. I might add that we still have none. As for Bernadette burning the candle, she did it once for Lt. P., but as far as we know, the only thing she burns now is perhaps the midnight oil in some pilots' tent. As for Mary having untiring energy, no one in this world ever had less, as she only too well knows. Col. C started to tease us about it but his was worse. It refers to him as the "handsome but shy base commander." He is very handsome but we never noticed that he was particularly shy. Judy has written some wonderful articles though and she herself is an amazing character.

The weather has been warm and beautiful for a couple of days. Let's hope it continues so we can

---

* Olive Drab

† The article, *Build G.I. Club At Plane Base: Red Cross Young Women Supply Doughnuts*, was written by Judy Barden, Staff Correspondent for The New York Sun.

fight our share of the war. I think we can start getting sunburned any day now. We spent today painting all the outside doors.

No fires for a week; it's wonderful not to have to worry about coal. Of course it is not exactly spring but we are much warmer.

I have written Mrs. Aldrich to thank her for the books and I have already written you that I receive the packages. They did all come in case you didn't get the letter and I enjoyed them so much.

Much love,
Fitje

February 23, 1945

Dear Lu,

Am sorry I haven't written you before this. I have certainly thought of you often enough. I have never been able to believe you were married so of course I just can't believe you are going to be a mother. The exciting thing is that Mary's little sister is going to have one in July too. Her husband is in the Air Corp too and was on Ascension Island for a year but is now back in the States. I have been away so long now that everything that happens seems very remote. Mother sent me a letter that Johnny had written her and I have read it over about a dozen times. I can't believe he has grown up so much.

Was in Paris yesterday getting food for the club and noticed especially all the cute baby clothes. They are so cute but terribly expensive. $60 for a dress, so I guess I won't buy any. There are lovely things in Paris but the prices are more than anyone can afford to pay, as there is no price level here. If you have cigarettes from home, however, you can get for a few packages of cigarettes what would cost in money three or four thousand francs sometimes. After the cigarette shortage, though, and seeing what it's like for the soldiers to have to go without, I can't bring myself to give any to the French people.

We are very excited lately because we at last have new quarters and it will be much nicer. We have been working on it for weeks. Mary had the detail at first and used the feminine approach, and got nowhere. She spent hours driving around with Col. C. and finally got mad and gave up. Then I got furious because the room we want has been vacant ever since we got here five months ago, so I just went and sat in his office until he said, "You can have the room if you'll just get out of here!" Then we went to work on the engineers and they are going to build partitions so we will each have a bedroom and a living room, all very rough of course, but now that we are more settled here there is no reason for us not to have a little peace and privacy once in a while. I won't live through the war if I can't at least get a few hours sleep once in a while.

Today is a beautiful day. I got up early and ate four oranges, which someone brought to me, for breakfast. This afternoon Lt. Paterson and I are going to walk to town and try to buy some Ping-Pong balls and a paintbrush. Mary is off in Paris for a couple of days with some Captain from another group.

Did I write you how much I liked the slippers you and Bill sent me for Christmas? I have worn them a lot; in fact they are nearly worn out.

How is Ann MacLead and what is she doing these days? How are Ibby and Terry? Give my love to Carol and Ann Grosvenor and everyone else.

Much Love,
Fitje

March 15, 1945

Dear Mother & Dad,

At last we are in our new quarters and it is beaucoup better. We painted busily last week. Mary's room is light blue with red woodwork and mine is cream with red woodwork. The window frames are all red and it really looks nice. The living room is whitewashed. We even made curtains and stuck pictures up on the walls. We have very little furniture but maybe we'll be able to pick up some more.

We have been here for two days and have had two parties the first for the three Colonels and the three engineers officers who got the work done for us, and the second, for an actor friend of Mary's who has been staying with us before he departs for the states. We are almost living in style now—in a hayloft.

Did I write you about my scrawny little police dog puppy? I am taking care of her for someone else but am hoping to be able to keep her. She is just like Danny was, a terribly sissy, has worms and fleas, and no one can bear her but myself. She loves me and I step on her all day long because she follows me around all the time and is right underfoot. She was acquired in Normandy and I guess she was something the Germans left behind.

I am sending you a picture of the guard with our window in the background. The Madonna we salvaged from the bombed church across the street. We always refer to him as "our guard" but really he guards the motor pool, which is in the courtyard. He is only there at night, and we are only a secondary concern as naturally the motor pool is more valuable. He has proved very useful on occasion though. We are never bothered with anyone who would do us harm but often by some boy who is drunk and who just wants to talk to us. People used to come in at all hours of the night but now he keeps everyone out after 11:00. We only had our own when we were just here. I am sure no one has any trouble unless they ask for it and the respect with which we are treated is amazing. It sure amazes me. When the

Unidentified guard outside Fitje's room at Beaumont sur Oise. Note the statue of Madonna in the window

French KPs first started to work in the mess halls they whistled at us just once and got such hell from the Americans that they hardly speak to us now. I sure am spoiled. You should see the presents we get, eggs, food from the home, lots of things.

Mary and I discussed how to describe Jack to you and finally decided it wasn't possible. He is just a character and by far my best friend here. He is from NYC and is strictly a dead-end kid. (He says so himself). He hasn't had much education. His parents are Swiss and speak broken English. His brother, Bob Zeltner, is assistant manager at the Taft Hotel. (Why don't you look him up if you are ever there, Dad?) Jack is S-4 officer and a very good one. He is very bright and strictly self-made. He hasn't even a slight touch of polish. He has lived a plenty rough life and sure has educated me. On the other hand I amaze him because he calls all women B_____S and can't believe one exists with any values. He always goes to bat for us and sees that we have what we need. He was responsible for our new quarters and all the improvements in the club. He has a wife in NY. You will have to meet him after the war. It isn't possible to describe him. Enclosed is a rather poor picture of him. He isn't handsome, but he sure is nice.

Mildred Eberle is going to be married in Paris on April 14th and I am going to be a bridesmaid. That will be fun.*

The picture is <u>not</u> of me. I flew over here with the bomb group, just Mary and me. I guess I couldn't tell you that the other time.

Got a letter from Ginni Graham the other day saying her husband, Phil, was killed over here on January 2nd.

Much Love,
Fitje

March 16, 1945

Dear Tim,

I'm so excited at the prospect of maybe seeing you. If by any chance you should get here go to the ARC headquarters in Paris and see Mark Sanborn. He knows how to telephone me and how to get here. If he isn't there see Anna Aab or Mrs. Gould. I will leave directions with them all next time I am there. Ask for "Fitje!" No one will know who in the hell Binni is.

Wouldn't it be amazing if we meet in Paris? I am anxiously awaiting another letter.

Much love,
Binnie

---

* Mildred Eberle of Providence, Rhode Island was marrying Major Harry Rothrock of Billings Montana. Kathleen Kennedy, the Marchioness of Harrington was the Matron of Honor and Fitje a bridesmaid. A reception was planned at the George V Hotel.

Tuesday, March something or other—20th

Dear Mother & Dad,

So far this is been by far the craziest trip I've been on in France anyway.

Our group has a hotel in Néris les Bains, way south of Paris where about sixty men (officers and enlisted man) go each week for a rest. This week Jack was going and Saturday about 11:00 he came over and said, "Hurry up and pack you're going with us and we're leaving at three." I never had a chance to think it over, which was just what Jack was counting on. At 3:00 I found myself on a plane with Jack, Maj. Reffe (Boo-Boo) and Lt. Joe Lyons, and off we flew as far as a tiny place called Avord, south of Paris. The plane took off again immediately leaving us stranded in the middle of the runway (an old bombed out German field), but French civilians gathered quickly and finally some French gendarmes drove us to the station. Just as we were looking up trains, a French truck came along and we hitchhiked a ride with ten smelly workmen to Bourges. There we unloaded our luggage and sleeping bags in front of the best hotel, but no rooms. Jack and I sat in the café across the street keeping an eye on the stuff and drinking cognac while the others combed the place for rooms. Finally, after two hours of no luck, the lady in the best hotel dug up two rooms and Jack and I moved in. When the others got back they were furious because they had finally rounded up a place and had to go back and cancel it.

We met up with a French civilian who ate dinner with us and got us the black market menu, so we had a delicious dinner and then in the evening we went pubbing and made a great hit because there were no other Americans in the town. Of course, everyone asked us for cigarettes and we must have given out an awful lot.

I stayed in bed and had breakfast there the next morning while the others looked up trains and we struggled to the station and took the train at 4:00 that everyone else from the group was on. They had a whole car, but it was full when we got on, so we sat on our luggage in the entry. It was a five-hour trip to go sixty miles. Jack and Joe Lyons got more and more impatient and spent most of the time barging into the freight car behind us reminiscing about how they used to bum around the country.

Finally they couldn't stand it any longer so when we got to St. Armand they told Reffe to take care of our luggage and said, "Come on Fitje," and we got off the train about fifty kilometers from our destination. We ducked in a café and had some wine while we waited for the train to pullout. Then we started walking. First we walked a mile on the wrong road and had to start over again. Then we walked until 10:00 that night, for four hours, and not one vehicle ever passed us, not even a bicycle, nor did we go through a town. We sang songs of the open road and had a lovely time. It was a beautiful night, moon, and stars, and warm. We had a bottle of cognac but I never had any of it because every time I got the bottle to my mouth Jack would say that's enough and take it away from me. Finally after about fifteen miles we arrived at a town called Urcay, but of course everyone was asleep. We found one light and went in. There was a very nice French family, an old woman with a wooden leg, and a young girl, whose husband had been killed, took us to the two tiny hotels, and we woke

Fitje, Jack Zeltner and Joe Lyons on train to Néris les Bains

up the proprietors, but no room. Just as we were getting ready to sleep in a field, she got the idea of taking us to see the mayor. That was very complicated because we banged on all the windows and couldn't wake him so finally had to wake his grandsons wife, who lives across the street, and she woke them. The mayor had one room with two beds but being French of course thought nothing of putting us all in the same room. We finally got to bed and I'm sure I went to sleep before I had a chance to draw a breath.

The next morning we got up early and had bread (no butter) and horrible French coffee (I'm sure it made of chickaree and acorns) for breakfast, and took a train at nine for Montlucon. From there the hotel was only a four-mile walk so we bought a loaf of French bread and started off. We stopped beside a lovely stream and bathed our aching feet and drank the rest of the cognac and ate the bread and I went to sleep for an hour in the sun. Incidentally, I have a lovely sunburn.

Just as we were starting off again a truck came along and we got a ride. I don't think I could have walked another step. When we arrived everyone was sweating us out because no one knew what had become of us.

They had gotten a room for us at a little pension across the square because they thought it would be better for me than a hotel full of men. I have breakfast in bed and it is lovely. I can be in bed all morning and get sunburned through the window. I eat my other meals at the hotel and the food is wonderful. Army rations, but cooked by French cooks, and they can even make C-Rations taste good. There isn't a thing to do but lie in the sun and eat and sleep. I went to bed at nine last night and it's about nine now and I'm going to bed soon. The best thing is, it's a vacation strictly in the line of duty, as Col. C has wanted us to come down here. Néris les Bains is a bath resort and the baths are reserved for us every afternoon, so everyone spends the afternoon in them. It is really a lovely spot and so nice and warm and sunny.

I will finish this letter before I leave, as I'm sure there will be something to add.

March 22, 1945

We have been having a wonderful time. The weather continues to be perfect and I have a lovely sunburn. The bags under my eyes have completely disappeared.

We have walked miles. Yesterday Jack and I spent all afternoon walking around on dirt roads. The apple trees are all in bloom and we saw lots of women washing clothes in the river and pounding them with wooden paddles. Every sorts of animal, even the cows, are hitched up to plows, and there are goats all over the roads, grazing with dogs and old ladies watching them. In the evening Jack, Joe, Boo-Boo and I, walked four miles to a town called Commentry and drank some red wine and walked back again. I could hardly move my legs when I got back. This afternoon we are going to Montluzon to a French movie and for dinner.

I got up for breakfast this morning and had pineapple juice, apricots, two eggs, two pancakes, bacon, coffee, and French rolls. I am eating like a pig. This little town is so cute. All the water comes from pumps. There is a pump, with hot water from the springs, right outside the hotel and all sorts of characters come and fill pails in pitchers all day long.

March 23, 1945

We are about to eat lunch and then take the train. I hate to leave here.

This morning I got up early, ate two eggs and sausage for breakfast, and went and took one last bath. Yesterday we walked to a little tiny church, St. Joseph's, way up on a hill. The view was lovely and the houses around here have red roofs.

Reading this letter over it sounds as if the war hadn't traveled to this little town at all. I am so used to it now that it will be strange to get home because destruction is getting to seem sort of natural. Most of the shops are closed and boarded appear and only very essential ones are open. There is one gift shop and I bought a few things; a wooden tray, some shoes for Warren and Lucy's baby and some china ashtrays, which I will send home. There is a French military hospital nearby and lots of soldiers on crutches, etc., walking around. I don't believe there is any place in France where you can feel that there isn't a war.

I guess Tim is over here now* as I got a letter from him written on the boat I hope I will be able to see him and I'm sure I will eventually.

Much love to you all.

Fitje

* Tim was in Germany. He was with the 76th Infantry Division, 417th Regiment, E Company, which crossed the Rhine River at Bopard on March 27th.

March 26, 1945

Dear Mother & Dad,

Home again and the place looks dirtier than ever.

It seems that while I was away, one morning early, the priest who used to have the bombed out church across the road came to get the statues that we had in the club, for his new church. He took the three in the lounge while Mary watched and then asked about the little one of St. Bernadette that Mary has. (It is in the picture of our window that I sent you.) Mary loves it and wants to keep it so she said it used to be around but she didn't know what had become of it. The priest smiled and said unmistakably in French, "It is in your room, Mlle." Apparently he has his spies among our staff. Seeing Mary's utter confusion at being caught telling a lie he added, "But you may keep it Mademoiselle if you will pray for me." Since then he has sent us flowers twice, and bread, which he blessed. The staff are much amused that Mary told the priest a lie.

One night at Néris les Bains, at the bar, Jack was getting drinks and he asked the bartender for four doubles. I said I only wanted a single and moved my glass away. When I looked back I had a double too, and the bartender said to me, *En France, c'est le monsieur qui commands.*[*] Jack was very amused.

I am in closing these three French postcards because I know you can't get anything like them in the U.S. Aren't they pretty?

March 31, 1945

Mary and I have spent the whole week goofing off. Things are running much too smoothly with us, and we only had one fire in the kitchen this week for excitement. I guess everyone feels that the war is at last drawing to a close because the atmosphere around here has been wonderful lately. Everyone is in a hilarious mood.

The highlight of the week: we went to the Headquarters Officer's dance at a Château near here, which they took over for the occasion, and had a lovely time. The best part of it was dinner, ham, chicken, and some other kind of meat, about twenty different kinds of pastry, and ice cream, chocolate, and coffee. Mary and I sat on the stairs and stuffed ourselves while people kept bringing us more and more just to see how much we could eat.

Mary noticed a strange smell in her room and finally located to dead mouse in the very bottom of her footlocker.

Mary and I spent all day yesterday in Paris having a lovely time. We explored every junk shop on Rue Montparnasse, but could hardly afford to buy a thing except some junk. We both tried to find a dress for our respective sister's babies, but there wasn't a one for less than $50, and that seemed a little expensive. We tried to find wine tasters in the junk shops—the only one cost $33 so I didn't get it. Everything is

[*] In France, it is the man who orders.

Fitje and Mary Haynesworth in photo taken by Captain Charters

terribly expensive. I finally bought a peculiar teacup for $3 and a few pictures. I think we must both think we will be home someday because we are both beginning to collect things to bring home with us. There are so many lovely things I would like to bring. I think Paris is the most beautiful place. All the store windows are red white and blue. If sweaters are featured, they are red, white and blue. And the hats, I wish you could see the hats, they are out of this world. When the war is over I want to wait in Paris until I go home, unless I can stay with this group. I wish I had learned more French, but the staff understand my sign language so well that I seem to have stopped learning. They are learning all the worst possible American words from the soldiers and sometimes I am nearly embarrassed to go in the kitchen.

I will not send any of my winter things home. Mary and I were saying yesterday that when we sent our summer things home last fall we never thought for a moment we would still be here to send for them again this summer.

Did I write you that Tim is over here? I can hardly wait to see him, and hope to meet him in Paris sometime. Did Leo Arsalanianan ever get in touch with you? He is a sergeant that I knew from bomber command who was going home. He lives in Providence.

Tonight we are having eggnog and French fries potatoes for supper. Our laundress bought us four eggs.

Last night Mary and I had our pictures taken by Captain Charters the photo officer. I am hoping they will be good as we went to lots of effort and so did he.

Easter

It's raining, dammit, and nothing special except the staff brought lots of flowers for the club. A hospital plane landed here because of the weather and the flight nurse stayed with us.

What you said about my friends in your last letter mother led me to a serious discussion between Mary and me as to whether we are "moving in the right circles." We wonder if you and Mrs. Haynesworth would like our friend Joe who "shacked up" in a hotel with a French "babe" and got "rolled." When he came to, everything was gone, even his clothes, and he walked back to the base at six in the morning wrapped in the quilt. Or our friend, "Jitter," who has decided to forgive his wife who just had a baby in spite of the fact that he has been overseas for over two years, or our friend Mike who stole Fr. 25,000 from another French babe and is in beaucoup trouble. Two other friends who we call "Dreamy Eyes" and "Pappy" who have come to us for advice about the girls they have gotten in trouble. These are some of the things that have happened to our friends in the past week. They are all our friends and we are here to be their friends. You could never understand how it is and wish you were here yourself because everyone is at their worst, and also at their best. Our presence here and our relationship to them and theirs to us couldn't be, at home. In order to live at peace with everyone we must be strictly impartial and "friendship," like it is in your own hometown, doesn't even enter into it.

You can imagine how I felt when I caught my friend Jack stealing coffee out of our storeroom to sell in town (for a fabulous price as is no coffee here) to pay a gambling debt. In the end I lend him the money and he is paying it back in monthly installments, which he has not missed so far. He is still my friend. He was drunk when he did it, and was so ashamed. On the other hand I'm sure you would like our three friends Paul, Carl, and Tubby, three gunners with the cutest dog named VD, who gets drunk frequently and comes over to the club and has every once in hysterics. I never saw a drunken dog before and it is the funniest sight. Before the war Paul was an acrobat in the circus, Toby was a fireman (and is always moaning about the lovely three alarm fire's he is missing in St. Louis), and Carl who was born and brought up in Alaska where his father is a jeweler. When boys like that don't get back from the mission you feel like you have lost a very good friend.

Tim is already in Germany so guess I won't see him for a while.

Much love,
Fitje

CHAPTER 11

Even V.D. Has a Hangover

April 13, 1945–May 8, 1945

In order to support ground efforts more effectively, as allied forces pushed their way to the Rhine River, the 386th needed to be closer to the front. The bomb group moved to St. Trond Belgium, six hundred miles northeast of Beaumont sur Oise, arriving on April 9, 1945. In the week leading up to the move, Mary Haynesworth left to work in a club mobile. Fitje's new assistant was Louisa "Babs" Garfield, from Carlisle, Massachusetts, whose great grandfather was President James A. Garfield.

The living conditions at St. Trond were a significant improvement from the Spartan conditions the 386th endured at Beaumont sur Oise. Officers were housed in modern buildings with heat, reliable electricity, running water and hot showers. To the delight of everyone, real bathrooms replaced slit trenches. Enlisted men were billeted in the old Belgian War College building, which, while not as luxurious as the officer's quarters, was still a big improvement over what they had.

St. Trond was larger than Beaumont sur Oise, making it easier to hire local citizens to work in a variety of positions on the base. Fitje could speak passable French but no Flemish. As her translator, she hired a multilingual Austrian secretary who escaped from a concentration camp and hid in a convent for over a year, until the Americans came.

Built for the Belgian Air Force, during the German occupation the airbase at St. Trond was the base for one of the most effective Luftwaffe night fighter squadrons. It had bedeviled British bomber crews as they flew to Germany. The 386th, which occupied base for the last thirty days of the war, flew their last seventeen combat missions from St. Trond.

On May 7th Fitje wrote saying she had just received news that the war was over, although it would not be official for another day. It was a bittersweet moment. The news left her "strangely cold." It was a moment to reflect on, "all the men I know and we all know who have died in a war that we knew we were going to win anyway."

The celebrations that night were boisterous, for the citizens of St. Trond who had suffered German occupation for almost five years, as well as the 386th. Fitje wrote on May 8th: "What a night! It is so quiet around here today. Haven't seen a soul so far and it's after 10:00. Even VD has a terrible hangover and was sick several times last night. Everyone danced and yelled on the square until well after 2:00. There was an effigy of Hitler hanging from the town hall, with a dead herring in his mouth, and toward the end of the evening it was burned."

April 13, 1945

Dear Mother & Dad,

Just a quick note to let you know I am still alive but I know you will understand that I have been busy.

Everything is lovely! We have a wonderful new set up, bathtub and all, and I am enjoying it. Mary has left me, but my luck continues. I have a very nice assistant named Louisa Garfield, from Cambridge. The last week was rather hectic as Mary left in the midst of everything and I had it all to do alone. She was tired of the rough life and had always wanted to be in a club mobile so she got a chance and transferred. All that was without knowing that living conditions were about to improve. Anyway it is for the best because Louisa works hard and Mary never lifted a finger.

I was alone for week during which I got all the work done and had a wonderful time. Went to Paris one day with Jack, Boo-Boo, and Major Haire. Jack bought me a French doll, which I will send to my first niece. We went to the Folly's in the evening and rode back to the parking place in a buggy. One night I went to dinner at the Colonels and spent another afternoon racing up and down the river in a speedboat. Louisa joined me at the last moment and here we are.

Am enclosing a picture of Mary and myself, which I know you'll like.

Forgot to say that I have a dog at last. I have written you about V.D. (I have changed her name to Virginia in polite society). Well Carl and Tubby couldn't keep her so they gave her to me. The only trouble is she is used to sleeping on an air mattress and an air Corps sleeping bag. We fight over mine every night but she is gradually learning to sleep on the floor.

I will write more details in another letter.

Much love.

Fitje

Fitje and Babs Garfield,
probably in Belgium, 1945

✐

April 13, 1945

Dear Tim,

Am afraid my last letter got mislaid in the rush, as I wrote it but don't remember mailing it. Anyway I didn't say much except that you can locate me through the Red Cross headquarters in Paris and maybe I could meet you in Brussels or Paris when you get some leave.

As you can see there has been a change in my life but it is lovely and much for the better. A green tile bath tub and all modern conveniences and you may be sure I am making the most of it.

Other changes of note besides locations: I have lost my old assistant, Mary, and have a new one—terribly nice—Louisa. I have a dog, named V.D. She used to belong to one of the gunners but he couldn't keep her so gave her to me. She is wonderful but causes me no end of trouble because she is an alcoholic and I can't drink a thing without having her climbing into my lap and doing her best to reach the glass. Also, being a true Air Corps dog, she likes to sleep on air mattress bedding rolls and I spent most of the night pushing her out of bed until we got a night watchman, to take care of her.

We are in town in a dismal building, but lovely compared to our former barn. We hope to have the club open by Saturday and have been busy getting things ready. Our quarters are wonderful, two rooms and a living room. I guess you're not having it so good compared to us, but you sure are doing well judging from the news, which incidentally, I am at this moment with no success trying to get on the radio. I am so proud that you are taking part in it, and in my own way I am praying that you are safe.

I know I am going to see you over here and that it is only a question of "sweating out" when. You must meet my crazy friend Capt. Jack Zeltner, a dead-end kid from New York and my staunch supporter ever since I joined this group.

Hope to hear from you very soon.

Much love,
Binni

✐

April 14, 1945

Dear Mother & Dad,

Wish you could see our set up. We are in town for a change, in an old building that was used as a German club of some sort. It has a kitchen and snack bar downstairs and lounge, writing room, Ping-Pong room, office, and our quarters upstairs. Our quarters has two bedrooms and a living room. Best of all there is a courtyard in the middle, which we can use for something.

We got here late Thursday and opened the club today, Saturday, which is record time, and I feel very proud. It was so simple, with modern conveniences, after the last place. The only hitch as we still have to use the field ranges, but only to make donuts as we have a huge German boiler for coffee.

The staff we have gotten together seems very good, the only hitch being that most of them speak only Flemish. However we got an English-speaking Austrian secretary who translates for us and it certainly simplifies matters. The Nazis killed her husband and parents. She hid for year and a half in a convent in Belgium before the Americans came, after having escaped from a concentration camp.

Today was a market day and we went to the square at 8:00 to buy flowers. We bought ten lovely plants. Right in front of the club is the arrival street and I wish you could've heard the pigs squeal and the sheep baa and seeing them all in baskets waiting for a buyer who usually picks them up by a leg or an ear and carries them away.

It is about a fifteen-minute walk for us to go to the mess hall—just right—and we can hitchhike if we so desire. There are lots of lovely orchards along the road and the trees are all in bloom. The Belgian people here are terribly friendly and all rush out to say "hello" and "okay," which are the two American expressions they all seem to know.

There was a lot of furniture here, even beds with mattresses, so I can give my sleeping bag a rest as soon as I procure some sheets and blankets. We have a night watchman as it is impossible to lock the joint and he even lets the dog out during the night.

I am dying to get to Holland and Germany and will make an effort to grab a ride as soon as possible.

I am enclosing two pictures of me, both the same as you can see. Pretty good I think.

Too bad about Roosevelt. Too bad he couldn't see the end of the war. One of the Belgian women was crying about it yesterday.

Much love.
Fitje

April 17, 1945

Dear Mother & Dad,

Just a note to enclose a letter from Mrs. Witherington that she sent me because she lost your address, also a picture of Jack and I on our trip to the rest home standing outside a hotel in Bourges. In the background you will see my bedding roll.

Your letters say that the weather is lovely and warm at home. It is the same here. I don't remember such nice weather since I've been overseas. Today the two men, Gaston and Antoine, who work for us, started fixing the garden. It is going to be nice—roses and pansies, etc. We are going to plant vegetables too.

We have a jeep and trailer and are having a lovely time taking donuts and coffee around the field each afternoon. It seems so amazing to have running water and modern conveniences. I never knew how nice they were before. Last night sixteen soldiers going through here spent the night on the floor of the lounge. They were so happy when they saw the bathtub I almost cried. They left at six this morning after coffee, which our night watchman made for them.

Last night when we were walking through the Square on our way to dinner at the base, truckload after a truckload of German prisoners went through town, packed, standing in trucks with no tops. I wish you could've seen the Belgian people rush from everywhere and stand and cheer and laugh at them. It was wonderful. They sure didn't look like superman. There are pictures of Roosevelt all over this town and people will stop you on the street and tried to tell you how sorry they are.

Did I tell you that they have ice cream here? The first practically since I left the states, although we have had it on the base on very special occasions—anyway the first in real ice cream parlors.

Did the other shoes ever arrive? I have lots of things to send home but am afraid they won't get there. Have something for Johnny for his desk at medical school, which I know will shock you, but they are in all the store windows here.

VD is standing in my lap licking my face so I must close.

Much love.
Fitje

∽

April 23, 1945

Dear Mother & Dad,

I am certainly getting continental. Last Sunday I went across some of Holland and into Germany with Jack and some other people to pick up supplies. We saw three windmills and lots of tulips in Holland. We went into Germany right through a lovely pine forest that smells exactly like Maine. It is so sad to see the destruction in Holland, little towns knocked to pieces with hardly a soul living in them and wreckage still filling the streets, much abandoned German equipment and white tape marking mines. The sign "Mines Cleared To Hedges" is as familiar here and in France as "Speed Limit Strictly Enforced" is in Rhode Island. Jack's mother was born Hamburg and we all tease him about what a wonderful storm trooper he would've been had circumstances been different.

Last week Babs and I went to Brussels for the day to look around—saw the little statue of the boy—fountain that is so famous.* I am dying to get to Luxembourg and Cologne. There is so much to see.

Mother, I don't know what my plans are. I am sweating it out now. I wish you could see the pictures I saw yesterday that an army photo officer showed me, which he took himself while he was at the front. They were horrible and made me more than ever want to stay until the war is over. I don't have to do anything but I probably will if I get the chance. It's just as easy to get home from one place as from another. Let's just hope the whole thing will end soon so everyone can go home.

I got three packages from you all at once the other day. I love the dresses. Louisa, our maid, shortened them for me. Now of course the weather has gotten cooler so I haven't worn them yet. We have been living on anchovies and last night ate the lobster with Belgian bread and champagne. We have an electric plate in our living room where we can toast bread and baked cocoa. Thanks so much for it all.

---

* Manneken Pis: meaning "Lil' Piddler" in is a small bronze sculpture in Brussels depicting a naked little boy urinating into a fountain's basin. It was designed by Hieronymus Duquesnoy the Elder and placed in 1618.

I wish I could send you some of the loot we got out of Germany. Our club is all furnished with stuff including lovely rugs that you would love to have. I forgot to write you that one of the officers gave me a German car. It is now at the motor pool having a spring fixed but aside from that it isn't perfect condition. I am going to get it tomorrow. Imagine having a car given to you. Someone is trying to get me a fur coat.

Chaplain Hemens here knows Chaplain Comfort at the 397th and one of these days he's going to take me up to see him. I know what happened to make him feel as he does about the American Red Cross, but I also know that, like most people of his calling, he didn't bother to find out the facts, which actually were nothing at all, but only listened to the rumors. My faith in his profession has not been restored over here.

I guess I wrote you that I did not get to Mildred's wedding on account of moving. I have heard however that it was lovely and that her husband is a very fine person. They're honeymooning in Cannes now.

Have you been getting the pictures I have been sending?

Much love.
Fitje

May 1, 1945

Dear Mother & Dad,

Well, I guess the war is about over, isn't it, although you hardly know what to expect from those damn Germans. Rumors are flying around here but no one seems to know much of anything.

We have had a very interesting week. Last night a little Irish soldier in the English Army straggled in and we put him up for the night. He had been taken prisoner in Crete in 1941 and had been near Berlin all this time. Last Friday he and the other prisoners were released to make their way back as best they could. The Germans told them that Germany, the U.S., and England had declared war against the Russians and to save himself from the Russians, We gave him eggs and toast and sat in our living room until three talking. Jack was there or he probably wouldn't have said much, as he was very shy. I couldn't begin to tell you all he told us and he seemed so sincere that I'm sure it must have been true. All about the raids on Berlin and the terrified women and children and atrocities he had seen with his own eyes. This morning he took a bath and Jack gave him clean clothes and had him driven to the nearest British headquarters. The propaganda that he had been told by the Germans was amazing. He said they wouldn't have been able to live without the Red Cross packages and used to trade chocolate from them for bread. I wish I could tell you some of the things he told us.

I went to Bomber Command over the weekend to visit my friend Col. Styles. They have a beautiful setup now. Thirty-five of the Colonels, and Majors live in one huge beautiful chateau where I stayed. They had a very nice dance Saturday night and it was wonderful fun. I saw all my friends again.

You will laugh at my two new friends here, two English nuns. One has been in the convent for forty-five years and the other for eighteen years, Sister Valentine and Sister Helene. They came to ask us for our old newspapers and invited us for tea. We went and they were so nice. They showed us all over the convent, which has a boarding school attached to it. The most interesting thing was the lace room where about twenty women make lovely lace all day, for a living. There are children as young as six, learning the trade, and I ordered a handkerchief made by the cutest little child, which I will send you. They told us a lot about the German occupation and the days when the Germans were retreating. One of them threw tacks and broken glass on the road hoping to hold up the retreat. You can imagine how much good that would have done. When the Mother Superior reproached her for taking such a chance she said, "Well, you know, nothing ventured, nothing gained."

Wish you could see my dog. She is lovely.

Later

The dumb dog just scared us to death. She bit an electric wire and was lying on the floor in convulsions. It took us a moment to see what was wrong and pull out the plug and she still kept on acting like she was having a fit. We were scared to death. She is OK now and all tired out.

Much love.
Fitje

May 5, 1945

Dear Tim,

Was very glad to get your letter and know that you are all right. I certainly am tired of worrying about all of my friends and I sure am glad the war's practically over. But isn't it wonderful!

This is a poor excuse for a letter I know, but wanted to write it immediately. I have written two or three times. Haven't you gotten any of them? Anyway I am in Belgium now, so come to Liege if you get a chance and start looking. I have probably been fairly near you as we get very far on excursions and I am starting another one tomorrow.

Tim, I don't like what you say about the rear echelon. Around here we have lots of it and many have been through a lot and anyway they have sweated out months in this godforsaken part of the world and that's worth a lot. Anyway most of them fought all the way across France and are only now being relieved by newcomers like you. I will tell you about a few Jewish heroes I have known when I see you.

If you get here look up the S-4 officer, Capt. Zeltner, my very good friend (function headquarters building) and he will locate me for you. Go AWOL or something, as I am dying to see you.

Love,
Fitje

May 5, 1945

Dear Mother & Dad,

I can imagine everybody at home is very excited at the prospects of the war being over, on this side of the world at least. It has been very exciting here, what with truckloads of liberated Belgians coming back and rumors flying around like mad. If someone in town comes home the houses are all decorated with flowers and the whole neighborhood turns out. Last night there was much celebrating in the streets because of Denmark and Holland and Northern Germany giving up. It makes me feel wonderful to think that poor London doesn't have to worry about Buzz Bombs and such anymore.

Last night we gave a huge dance for the Bomb Group, which was a lot of fun. We have a Jewish boy, Private Rudner, who is assigned to us to drive our jeep. He used to work for us in England and he more or less engineered the deal here. He just came down here with the jeep everyday until Captain Post, the transportation officer, got so used to the idea that he assigned him permanently. Rudner is wonderful. He can do practically anything. He gets here at 8:00 and makes our coffee for us. Then he wakes us up and says, "Well girls, what's for today?"

Fitje with Urban Rudner
and her dog, VD

I really think that he is running the club. Last night he ran the whole food department for the dance and still found time to look us up every few minutes to be sure we weren't involved with any drunks. Usually I would be having a lovely time being entertained by a drunk and Rudner would cut in and say, "Were you having trouble," pick out a sober person and say, "Here, dance with her." Exactly like a brother. His jeep is amazing. It has every accessory; strange lights, horns, ashtrays, even sides so it is warm. He is always busy putting something in it. He was a taxi driver in New York before the war. What a character!

Monday, May 7th

At exactly 2:30 this afternoon Major Reffe called to tell me that the war was over by secret Teletype, although it won't be official until Wednesday. Everyone is celebrating though. We gave the staff each a drink and told them to go home and not to come back until they wanted to tomorrow. That will keep Babs and I sober to make coffee, etc. The town is covered with flags and it is wonderful to think that it really is over for the Belgians.

The funny thing is, it leaves me strangely cold. It seems to me that I have looked forward to it for so long and have always wished I remembered the day the last war ended. It seems like years ago that we got up early down in the country to hear the King declare war against Germany, and years ago when

I was with the Matteson's and we heard over the radio about Pearl Harbor. I can only think of all the men I know and we all know who have died in a war that we knew we were going to win anyway. Now Jack, Madeline, Babs and I are sitting here talking. Madeline has lost her husband and parents, and Jack has just been telling us about his aunt with three sons; one killed, one lost a hand, and the third an arm.

In the afternoon we got a letter from the nuns saying, "Is it really true? We can't believe it until we hear it in English." Jack and I went to see them immediately and they were so excited. This town is famous for it's lovely chimes and in the past three days we have been hearing them practically all the time. They are lovely, but they keep us awake at night.

At this very moment the sirens are blowing. VD is standing on the window howling and Madeline is lying on my bed crying. I predict an amazing evening. The clock is striking and everyone is saying, "Let's go out on the square and see the excitement."

April 8th

What a night! It is so quiet around here today. Haven't seen a soul so far and it's after 10:00. Even VD has a terrible hangover and was sick several times last night. Everyone danced and yelled on the square until well after 2:00. There was an effigy of Hitler hanging from the town hall, with a dead herring in his mouth, and toward the end of the evening it was burned.

The Belgian King was supposed to have come back to Brussels yesterday. I would have loved to be there.

I am wondering what you all are doing.

Much love.
Fitje

CHAPTER 12

Behind the Hedgerows

May 16, 1945–July 19, 1945

After D-Day as the Allies drove further into France and other occupied territory before reaching Germany they erected signs along the sides of the roads saying, "Mines Cleared To Hedges." After the 386th moved to St. Trond, Fitje took several long road trips through Belgium to Holland and Luxembourg. There were no rest stops, gas stations with convenience shops or public restrooms. When nature called, cars and trucks stopped and men relieved themselves along the side of the road. As Fitje was often the only woman in the group, it was not so simple for her. To have privacy she had to go to the other side of the hedges. The men would laugh: "Be careful Fitje, don't step on a mine!"

On May 11, 1945, three days after Germany surrendered, Jack Zeltner requisitioned a command car and two, two-ton trucks for a trip to Czechoslovakia. Fitje was the lone woman with three officers and six enlisted men. They drove south from St. Trond, crossed the Rhine River on a pontoon bridge at Remagen where the Ludendorff Bridge once stood and stopped in Karlovy Vary (Carlsbad) on the northeast side of the Ohre River. Soviet forces occupied the other side of the river.

Fitje's letter of May 16th, which is a marvelous account of the trip, signals a winding down of her official responsibilities and the beginning of a new chapter in her adventure. She seems to relish the attention she was receiving in Europe: "Every time we stopped Americans would come up and want to shake hands with me, and the drivers in the trucks behind us said they thought we must have Hitler in the Command Car, we were attracting so much attention! We drove with the top down, and I have a lovely sunburn. How I can ever come back to the US after being such a novelty here, I don't know."

Although still responsible for the clubs, she is freer to travel, and uses her last seven months in Europe to see as much as she can. Before the 386th left Europe she traveled to Antwerp with her assistant Babs Garfield, stopping on the way to see the concentration camp at Breendonk, now used by the allies as a prison for collaborators. Her letter of June 7th is a funny account of her twenty-eighth birthday, which she spent swimming and aquaplaning on the Meuse River, before being feted at a surprise party. She traveled back to England with Jack Zeltner, drove to the American Military Cemetery in Luxembourg, and went to Paris.

The 386th stayed in St. Trond until mid-July when, mission accomplished, it returned to the states. It was a bittersweet time for Fitje. After being gone for so long she debated what to do next. Her letters mention the possibility of staying in Europe, and she even mentions transferring to the Pacific. She writes that she will probably be home by Christmas. After the 386th left she wrote, "I feel like my last friend left Europe with the bomb group."

⚭

May 16, 1945

Dear Mother and Dad,

I am sure you will think that I don't do any work anymore when I tell you that I have just returned from a five-day trip to Czechoslovakia. I am sure I got farther than any other American girls, right up to the river that runs through Carlsbad. We couldn't go any further because the Russians were on the other side of the bridge.

We started on Friday, Jack, Lt. Leone, and Lt. Smith in a command car with the driver, a Mexican boy and Sgt. Patsy Fontana, who works for Jack. Also with us were two, two-ton trucks, each with two drivers, all characters and all horrified at the idea of taking a woman on such a trip, (although in the end they all told me that I was a definite asset.) In all there were six enlisted men, three officers and myself.

We started at 6:30 and drove all day. At about 7:00 or so we reached Frankfurt where we spent the night with an infantry outfit, the one that took Saarbrucken to be exact. Of course, we had to hear the whole story from the CO of the outfit, a very nice Captain. They love to see a stranger, and literally force you to sit and listen to the story of the action they had seen. I used to think parts of England were beat up, but I wish you could see Germany. Towns like Duren and Frankfurt are completely destroyed, hardly even walls, just piles of stone and rubble. The people are bomb happy and go around laughing as if nothing had happened. The little kids already wave and ask for chocolate. It is very hard to ignore them. They are the cutest kids. The older people would sort of smile. It was the ones in between that really gave you a stony stare. Of course, the young girls were very conscious of the soldiers, and I guess there will be plenty of Americans married to them before they get home.

The next day we went through the most beautiful country, ending up in Huls on the Czech border. It seems strange that people with such a lovely place to live in could be so nasty. At noon we had a picnic, of C-Rations of course, beside the road. A skinny little German girl came and stood and watched us eat, which took all our appetites away. The boys wanted to give her some chocolate, but Jack wouldn't let them and finally yelled at her in German to get away. I will never forget her expression. She started to cry and ran off.

Traveling is slow because the roads are beat up and practically all the bridges are down. We got lost on detours innumerable times. We crossed the Rhine on the Remagen Bridge, which was exciting.

In Huls we spent the night in a hotel, which had just been taken over by Americans for billets. We were the only people there except for three British soldiers who had been prisoners since Dunkirk and were going to fly back to England the next day. We shared our C-Rations with them, and we all cooked them in the kitchen of the Hotel. They were fascinating and pathetic to listen to. They were very thin. They had a radio, which they had hidden in the prison camp so they knew how the war was progressing. They said the last five weeks seemed longer than the four years they had been prisoners, and then one morning they woke up and the Russians were right across the road. They gave me a sheepskin fur coat and a rabbit fur jacket. Incidentally, I came back with more stuff. Everyone we met gave me something. As we drove by Americans they would yell things like "That looks like a white girl." Every time we stopped Americans would come up and want to shake hands with me, and the drivers in the trucks behind us said they thought we must have Hitler in the command car, we were attracting so much attention! We drove with the top down, and I have a lovely sunburn. How I can ever come back to the US after being such a novelty here, I don't know.

The next day we divided into groups to get the stuff we wanted, which was parachutes from a German warehouse, and cognac from another German warehouse. I was on the cognac detail. In the end we all ended up in the same place, as some Belgian officers controlled both warehouses. After much persuasion (I had to have my picture taken about twenty times with each Belgian officer's arms around me) we got the stuff and loaded up the trucks quickly before they could change their minds—seventy gallons of cognac in two kegs, and other stuff the boys just picked up, also lots of parachutes. I got a white nylon one, and a camouflaged one. We had lunch with the Belgians, and they gave me more stuff, slippers, a tablecloth, a knife with a swastika, etc., also a German Motherhood Pin, and from that time on all the boys called me Mother Pitts. The Belgian officers all got drunk, and we drank toasts to everything under the sun.

After lunch we started for Carlsbad. That was the most interesting trip of all. Refugee Germans, trying to get away from the Russians, slave laborers, free at last, trying to get home, and German soldiers trying to get to a PW camp, crowded the roads. No one even stopped the German soldiers. There is a huge PW camp, which we passed and most of them were going there, I guess, very thankful to be away from the Russians. The liberated slave laborers were pathetic, whole families in some cases, but mostly younger men and women struggling along with a homemade cart for their belongings and a homemade flag of their nationality on the cart or on them somewhere. If you stopped you were besieged by them wanting rides.

We did pick up an English soldier, a prisoner for five years, and took him to Carlsbad. He said he was hunting SS men and had a murderous look in his eye. We thought he was crazy. We had seen refugees all across Germany, and also German soldiers, walking and riding, but never in such quantity as there.

Carlsbad was a mess with bombing and refugees and all, and Jack wouldn't stop because he was afraid we'd get into trouble with me along, so we turned around and went back near Huls where we spent the night with another infantry company, this time the one that took the Remagen bridge, and was also at Bastogne. They were nifty to us, fried us chicken for dinner at 9:00, and put me, and the three officers, up in a house, and our enlisted men with theirs. While we were listening to their officers tell the story of all the action of the company our enlisted men had to listen to their enlisted men. Not to be outdone, however, our enlisted men said they were gunners with about 100 missions, and Pvt. Mauran, who was a stoker on an oil tanker for five years, told such a good story that one of the Infantrymen gave him a Lugar for his autographed hat. In fact, our enlisted men shared ten bottles of some horrible stuff they had gotten from Huls with them and literally drank them all under the table. All of which was unfortunate because sometime during the night some of the infantrymen stole one of the thirty-five gallon barrels of cognac, emptied it into seven and a half gallon water cans, and strapped it onto trucks so it looked like gas cans. We found it after much trouble the next morning, and after the CO said he would court-martial everyone. We felt very badly about the whole thing, as they had been so nice to us, and then we got them all in trouble.

I forgot to say that on the way to Carlsbad we passed fields of German equipment; helmets, bayonets, etc., that they had just dumped there when they surrendered en masse. I got a helmet and a bayonet but we couldn't stop long on account of the refugees and we were too scared of booby traps to look around too much. I didn't get a gun.

The last night we spent somewhere or other not far from the Rhine. This time we arrived about ten and went to the town mayor who gave us a whole house that they had just moved a German family out of. There were still clothes in the closet. I had the detail of cooking breakfast and washing dishes while everyone else reloaded the trucks. By that time I was ready to sleep all day, but Jack got us up at 6:00 every morning.

Babs left during my absence to be a Director of another club, so I am alone and Madeleine has moved in to live with me until someone else comes.

Do you know I am in Belgium now? You haven't mentioned it, so I am wondering if you got that letter. Just found out I can tell you where I am, St. Trond, Belgium, near Liege.

Much Love,
Fitje

May 17, 1945

Dear Tim,

Just got your letter with map enclosed and was terribly interested to see where you have been. Maybe you could get up this way soon. I know I could get someone from here to fly me down to your vicinity, but am afraid chances of seeing you would be too slim when I got there if you are moving around and I probably wouldn't be able to let you know. Anyway, this place will fold up soon, and then I plan to be in Paris for a few days and then take two or three weeks vacation in Cannes before I do something new. That will probably all come about just after August 1st so maybe you can have some leave around that time. After that chances are that I will be in Germany too.

Also, got a wonderful birthday box from your mother—stockings, soap and bath powder. It was so nice of her to bother. My birthday was amazing, and roughly consisted of spending the day with the Colonel in his boat on the Meuse River, (He stole the boat while we were in France) and a huge white sheep, which I found in my bed when I got back, (A present from three drunken G.I.s and later called for by a very excited Belgian woman, three gendarmes, and two M.P.s) and a very successful surprise party in the evening. I was completely surprised and everyone got very drunk.

Last week I goofed off to England with Capt. Zeltner and stayed with some friends of his. It was wonderful fun. The only thing was the pilot who came over to get us went to the wrong field and we waited all day at the one place while he waited at another. It was an RAF field and they were wonderful to us. Called us "Redskins" and gave us transportation and a place to spend the night. The next day they finally showed up but the weather closed in and it was Friday before we finally got home. Capt. Z is a swell guy, strictly a dead-end kid and very much a character. Don't know what I'd do without him.

V.D. is going to be a mother, I think. I carefully kept all the male dogs away from her until I went to England. When I got back and started chasing them out the staff all said, "Oh it's too late Mlle., she's had it." (Or words to that effect in French.)

Well, much love to you—see you soon, I hope.

Love,
Fitje

May 21, 1945

Dear Mother & Dad,

Just a note to send a couple of pictures—also my income tax thing for 1943 and 1944.

Dad, could you get someone to figure this out and pay it for me? I hate to let it go and have maybe three years of tax to pay when I get home. I paid a tax for 1942. Isn't there a refund on that or something? I don't know why there are two slips for 1943, one from February 1st and one from May 1st, unless it is because I was overseas or something. The one marked 2/16–12/31 shows my whole income anyway. The one marked 5/16–12/31 doesn't make sense to me as it just repeats.

I know you are going to ask me when I am going to take steps to get home so I will tell you in advance. I do not become eligible for rotation until next November, theoretically July, but it works out twenty-nine months instead of twenty-four months. Between now and November any number of things may happen. Actually they need more of us over here now than while the war was going on because there are so many more leave centers, etc. If I do go from here to the CBI it is just as easy to get home from there as it is from here. Tell Johnnie not to worry about feeding starving Europeans. Nothing would induce me!

The nuns are making me some lovely underwear out of the parachute silk I got in Germany. I took Jack over there for tea the other day and they thought he was wonderful. They are making him a pair of pajamas.

Tell Jane we now have a darkroom in the club and I am learning to develop my own pictures. I took eight truckloads of GIs and Belgian girls on a picnic yesterday and swam all day in the Meuse River. I am still exhausted.

Much love.
Fitje

May 23, 1945

Dear Tim,

The war being over I can now tell you that I am in St. Trond, Belgium, near Liege. Also that I must have been right near you the week the war ended, as I went way up to Czech (Carlsbad). Had a lovely time for five days and got lots of loot. I'm now having some nuns make me negligees, etc., out of parachute silk. I went with three officers and six G.I. truck drivers, two trucks and a command car, strictly as bait. I always enjoy going on trips with Capt. Zeltner (S-4 officer) because he gets more loot with me along. We brought back seventy gallons of cognac too.

I asked around trying to find your outfit but I didn't have much luck. I'm sure you must be near there though.

Best you get leave and come up here immediately.

V.D. just chewed up twelve Ping-Pong balls at Fr.18 each.

Much love,
Binni

May 24, 1945

Dear Mother & Dad,

Enclosed are two pictures, one of me with V.D., and the other of me and Madeleine our secretary, about whom I have told you.

Mother, could you possibly send me a few yards of linen for the nuns as they can't buy it here and they need it for handkerchiefs. I am enclosing one for you. The cutest six-year old child made the lace. My negligee is finished and it is lovely. It is made of camouflaged German parachute silk and trimmed with the white cord with a huge full skirt. I think all the nuns helped make it. They were more excited than I was.

At last I am putting things in boxes to send home. One package contains children's books I got in England and France. The best ones I have not sent because I'm afraid something will happen to them. One has a tiny present for each of you and the others have just junk the people have given me. Will you save the cups and glasses until I get home? There are two pairs of small straw shoes (Watch out for the glasses I packed inside them) and a doll for some nieces I hope to have.

How do you like V.D.? Isn't she cute? In the last two days she has eaten a dozen Ping-Pong balls at Fr.18 each. She has also learned how to climb up on the table in the kitchen and grab a doughnut when no one is looking. She never eats them but loves to play with them. She is now busy bringing all the staff's shoes (they change into wooden shoes when they get here) one by one from the kitchen to the office.

Must stop and develop some pictures.

Much love.
Fitje

June 1, 1945

Dear Family,

Here are some German stamps I thought would interest you.

Just to add to the confusion, the nuns gave us a tiny kitten last week. V.D. just adores it. She thinks she's its mother. She stays with it every moment and almost kills it with attention. Now both of them are sick and we're afraid they have distemper.

Last week Babs and I went to Antwerp and on the way stopped to see Breendock* the concentration camp where the Germans had most of their prisoners. Now it is full of collaborators. It is quite a sight to see. We have met several Belgians who were there. Antwerp sure is a lovely city. I wish we could have stayed longer.

Yesterday was the official day that the group got the presidential citation. The ceremony was out on the runway with each squadron standing at attention and all the dogs fighting in the middle. General Sanders† gave the award and also lots of others to the men. Col. Corbin got the Croix de Guerre from the French. Just at the right moment sixteen of our planes buzzed the Field, four abreast right over us at low level and it really was a lovely sight.

The fame of my negligee and Jack's pajamas that nun's made has spread even up to Bomb Division. It is perfectly beautiful. Jack asked them to the celebration and they finally got permission after much discussion as to how many civilians would see them, etc. We took them all over the base even into the bar and into Jack's room. They drank a Coca Cola and I was scared to death Jack had had rum put in it. Col. Corbin made a special point of coming up and speaking to them and they had a wonderful time. Afterwards they came back for tea, and we had huge big strawberries.

Much Love,
Fitje

* Originally a Belgian fort, Breendonk was used by the Germans as a prison camp for political dissidents, captured resistance members and Jews. Most inmates were quickly transferred to larger camps in the East.

† General Richard C. Sanders was the youngest general in the history of the United States Air Force. In June 1944, at twenty-eight years old, he was promoted to Brigadier General and in November became Chief of Staff of IX Bomber Command.

❀

June 7, 1945

Dear Mother & Dad,

It's a bit late to wish you many more wedding anniversaries. Anyway I thought of you and wondered how you were spending the day.

I had a wonderful birthday! I decided to stay in bed all morning and did in spite of people walking in and out in a continual stream. The day staff gave me a lovely glass vase and the evening staff a plant. The nuns sent me flowers, strawberries and two delicious cherry pies. In the afternoon the Colonel took me and Jack, Major Burris, Capt. Capp and Lt. Doliker out in his boat, which he keeps at Liege on the Meuse River. It is the same boat he had in France. We had a lovely time swimming and aquaplaning in filthy water and had a very late picnic lunch. The weather was perfect.

We got home about 8:00 and when I got in the living room I heard a strange noise coming from my bedroom. I opened the door and there right in the middle of my bed was a fat, white, half-grown sheep. The room looked like a barnyard. Apparently it has been there for quite a while, as it was on excellent terms with V.D. and Ginni (the kitten). Amid much screams of laughter from the staff Jack carried it downstairs and out into the garden where it immediately ate all the flowers. I was just beginning to get fond of it and decided where we could keep it when in walked a very excited Belgium woman with three gendarmes and two MPs. It seems that three of my drunken soldier friends had stolen her for me. We pacified the woman with donuts and they took the sheep off in a jeep. The boys said, "Never mind, Fitje, next time we'll steal one from further away."

Jack had told me in the morning that Dick Moncure, the Field Director, who had an apartment in town, wanted us to stop in for a minute for a drink in the evening. All the time the sheep episode was going on Babs and Jack keep saying, "Hurry up, hurry up, let's go see Dick." Jack wanted to take the sheep and Babs kept saying she had to get back at 9:15 and to change my clothes. I looked awful. Finally we started out and I met another drunken G.I. friend of mine who insisted that we have a drink on him on my birthday. Jack and Babs didn't want to and I was furious so we had the drink but they kept hurrying me. Finally we got to Dick's and walked in the door and guess what—a surprise party! There were fourteen people there, Babs and I, and three French girls and nine officers; Col. Corbin, Jack, Dick, and the other six I guess you've never heard of. Everything was so nice—a wonderful dinner of fried chicken, ice cream, etc., a birthday cake with "Happy Birthday Fitje," a table full of presents and beaucoup champagne. We had a lovely time. Dick told the true story of his black eye. Apparently a Russian girl hit him with a bottle during a political argument.

I never suspected a thing and couldn't find out who did the work—someone must have done a lot—or when they did it. I thought I knew everything that went on. A lot of the enlisted men helped get the staff together and they were all down early this morning to see if I had a good time. It was wonderful.

We have met a terribly nice Count and Countess of Salisbury who live in a lovely place just out of town. We have had lunch with them a couple of times, and today we went out there for tea. They have the most beautiful roses and gave me a huge bunch for my birthday. Their orchard is full of cherries, which are huge and delicious.

I don't believe I thanked you for the wallet—anyway I love it—it is too nice to use until something special comes along. It is big enough for Belgium money too.

I may go to England for the weekend. Babs flew over last weekend and had a lovely time.

Well, the usual soldiers are beginning to come in looking for a place to sleep. We put up ten or fifteen every night here on couches and army cots.

Much Love,
Fitje

June 15, 1945

Dear Jane,

Just got your letter dated June 2nd. I did write and thank you for the nightgown and housecoat and hope you got the letter. They are lovely, exactly what I needed. Why don't you hang onto the money and buy Lucy something with some of it when the baby comes? Also I will need stuff I know. For instance I am desperate for girdles, the last one you sent is nifty. If you could get me a couple more sort of like that one I would appreciate it; pantie girdles of course. If you have any luck have them sent C/O American Red Cross, Continental Headquarters, APO 887, C/O PM, NYC, because packages take so long and Lord knows where I'll be when it arrives but probably not still with the 386th Bomb Group.

I am sorry to hear about your kidney stone. It must be from too much drinking. It must be a screen to see Rose, Lucy, and Ibby pregnant—especially Rose. I can't quite imagine her with the baby.

I have seen a lot about the 6th Marine division on Okinawa, and have followed all of that very closely knowing Johnny was in it. Didn't know until your letter what regiment he was in. I sure hope he gets home this summer. It would be lovely to think that he and Bill were through with fighting. Myself, I am dying to get to the Pacific and will try every possible way. There is no use in me coming home until the war is over because I would be very unhappy, so I'm not going to even consider it. Don't say this to the family though.

My friend Capt. Zeltner will be in to see you when he gets home, and he can tell you more of my plans. That probably won't be for quite a while though. You will like him a lot; he is a character and has been wonderful to me. He used to be mixed up in unions and stuff and even knows some gunmen, strictly a dead end kid. Just got back from a trip to England with him yesterday. We flew over last Saturday and meant to come back Wednesday but got weathered-in until Friday. We stayed with some friends of Jack's near Dunmow where we used to be stationed in England. Whatever you say about the English they sure can be nice. We waited a day and a half at an RAF base for our plane to pick us up and it was such fun. I never wanted to leave. Those English flyers are wild men. I would never have stayed sober if Jack hadn't kept saying emphatically, "No Fitje doesn't want another drink." In France and Belgium everyone steals everything they can get their hands on, but in England we never had any trouble, and the English are so much cleaner too, and so nice when they know you well. I wish you could meet one family Jack knows. We had dinner there one night. They live in a modernistic house in the country that is the most beautiful thing I have ever seen. Mr. Critfall has some sort of factories and is very progressive about his employees. He has unions, etc. He is always being criticized over here. I guess that's why he and Jack are such good friends.

I hope to see Helen Shoemaker soon. I will probably take all of my vacation when this deal folds up, and will have a chance to look her up then.

Love,
Fitje

June 18, 1945

Dear Mother & Dad,

The lounge completely empty and I am listening to records. I have to know all the latest songs or all the soldiers think I'm a creep.

I was interrupted then by a sergeant in the tank division, now stationed in Germany, who is here on leave. He used to be stationed here during the break through and was just telling me that his driver was killed here on New Year's Day by a Jerry plane strafing.

I meant to write you, now that the war is over, the places I have been stationed, although I guess you know most of them already. Anyway in the first place I came over on the Queen Mary and landed in Grennock in Scotland. Then I was near Ipswich between the tiny villages of Eye and Stradbroke when I was with the 95th, at Marks Hall, near Coggeshall, in Essex with Bomber Command, near Royston, which is near Cambridge, when I was with the 91st, and at Dunmow, or rather between Dunmow and Great Eastern, about fifteen miles from Bishop Stratford when I was with the 386th in England. When we moved to France we flew and were first in Beaumont sur Oise, thirty-five miles north of Paris, and then here.

I flew over to England with Jack last week and we stayed with some friends of his at Thaxted, near Dunmow. They were awfully nice and have a lovely place in the country. We walked over to see Mrs. Widdrington one morning and to see our old field now that the RAF is there. It is quite different. Canon Widdrington is sick in the hospital with pneumonia. He has been sick for a month and apparently not doing too well. They are wondering why they haven't heard from the Washburn's lately. The next night we had cocktails there with Zita and her husband, who was an American officer and then had dinner with the Critfall's, who live nearby, and a lovely modernistic house. They are friends of Jack's and awfully nice. We brought over champagne and Benedictine for them all, a thing, which we regretted because we had to hitchhike from near Oxford, where we landed, all the way to Dunmow. It seems so funny to be in England. I kept embarrassing Jack by making comments in a loud voice about people, nearly forgetting that they can understand. London seems very peaceful although any loud noise made me jump, as the last time I was there was V2 and Doodlebug time.

Getting back was the bad part. We went to Oxfordshire and waited all day at an RAF field for a plane, which never came. We found out later it was waiting at the wrong field. At dinnertime we struggled up to the officer's mess where we got a wonderful reception and I never would have left there on my feet if Jack hadn't kept saying, "No Fitje does not want another drink." The group CO gave us a car and found us billets. The next day bright and early we came out to the field again. About 3:00 a plane finally showed up and picked us up and went up to Colchester to pick up someone else from the group. There the weather closed in and we couldn't leave. The crew was delighted and took off for London and we struggled into Colchester to try and find a place to stay—not a thing. We finally went to the Rose and Crown, which is a club and Jack talked them into letting us join the club so we could stay there. So I now have a membership card to the Rose and Crown, in Colchester. It's a fascinating old building and we were the only guests. We spent a lovely evening in the bar talking to Mr. and Mrs. Turnbull who run it. In the end we found out it had just that day been reopened having had its license suspended for keeping the bar open after hours, and letting non-members in. The next day we gathered early and sat in the bomb bay of our A-26* until noon, when the weather cleared up enough to take off. On the way home we flew over the flooded parts of Holland. It was a terrible site to see.

Here comes VD with a shoe in her mouth. Now she has climbed up in my lap and smeared the ink. We think she is going to have puppies. I tried not to have it happen but it was impossible. I'm afraid it will be hard to find her a good home in her condition but maybe I can keep her.

Saturday night we went to a party that the Count and Countess had. It was wonderful fun—a few American officers and lots of Belgians, all of whom spoke English. We had milk punch and a buffet supper with wonderful wild strawberries, which they grow on their place. Every Sunday Babs and I have a picnic for about 200 soldiers and Belgian girls. We go to a lovely place on the Meuse called Tilff in eight trucks. There are lots of beautiful woods there and they are full of wild strawberries now. They are delicious.

You asked me in your last letter if I had been to Brussels. Yes but not since I got Carol's letter. Next time I go I will look up her friends. I have also been to Antwerp and hope to get to Bruges, Ghent, and Luxembourg within the next two weeks. It is easy to get a truck if you fill it full of soldiers because you can call it a tour, and now that the war is over they are giving us plenty of transportation for things like that.

You asked if what we do is about the same. It is a little different because before we have always been right on the base. Here the club is in town about a mile from the base. Of course we eat there and everything, just as always. Col. C said that after a winter in a barn we should have something good so he picked the spot mostly for our comfort, and for us it is ideal. We don't see as many soldiers from the base because they have to wear Class "A" uniforms to come to town, but we do have lots of transient soldiers, and of course the dances and picnics we have are for our group. Actually it is a great deal easier for us because we have just what we can handle and not hundreds milling around the way it used to be. I would estimate about 300 soldiers come here daily. Also we have a better staff because it is in a town.

---

* The Douglas A-26 Invader arrived in Europe in late September 1944 and assigned to the 9th Air Force.

My job is always the same. I run the club and the other girl runs the programs. Babs is responsible for the picnics, tours, dances, etc.

Actually we really do both together now that Babs is here. Mary was very nice and quite a character, but she never did a damn thing. In fact, she would hardly get out of bed all winter in Beaumont. Thank God Babs, although not such a character, does an awful lot.

Well, have been writing this off and on all evening and must go to bed.

Much love.
Fitje

༄

June 23, 1945

Dear Mother & Dad,

Yesterday I went on a lovely trip with the chaplain down to the city of Luxembourg. I went because Ginny Graham wanted me to look up her husband's grave and take a picture of it for her. He is buried in the American Military Cemetery near Luxembourg City. We started very early in the morning in an old Mercedes which the chaplain had "obtained" in Germany, taking Sgt. Johnson, the chaplains driver, and Sgt. Fail, whose brother is also buried there.

We had a lovely time. It was a beautiful day and we had lunch of C-Rations, by the road at about 10:30, we got so hungry. We went down through Bastogne where there was so much fighting during the breakthrough. There is very little left there, but piles of ruins.

The cemetery was really lovely although spoiled considerably by the smell of bodies, which they work burying and long trenches all the time we were there. They had rows stacked up, wrapped in white mattress covers, Italian POWs digging the graves, and American soldiers putting the bodies in them—no chaplain or anything, although one comes three times a week. A lot the bodies have been brought from temporary graves in Germany and, of course, they're still being dug out of the ruins etc. In the ruined villages here, and in Germany, you can smell that same smell.

We looked around Luxembourg City for a while. It is lovely. Have you been there? Then we came back right through the center of Luxembourg. It was perfectly beautiful, rolling hills and lovely pine-woods. The roads were terrible though. In one place it took us three hours to go fourteen miles. In fact we walked most of the way so there wouldn't be so much weight in the car. The roads are all beat up from shells and heavy tanks. Part of it is a corduroy road put in by combat engineers "between rounds" when the fighting was so heavy there. The woods of course are full of abandoned equipment, tanks and trucks, both ours, and German, all along the road. In some places the trees are all broken off from shellfire. There are very few villages, but St. Vith at the other end of Luxembourg, was completely demolished. Yet there are lots of people living in the ruins in cellars and wandering around the streets. It seems especially sad there, because those people thought the war was over for them until the breakthrough when the Germans came back. We went through Malmedy where all the Americans were murdered in the field and then to Spa, Liege, and home. In that section there are lots of German soldier's graves all along the roads with lots of flowers, which must've been put there by civilians.

Have you gotten any of the packages I sent? Is Bill home yet? Does Jane still think Johnny is coming home? When are you going to send me some more pictures of Warren? Can he walk yet? When is Amy's baby coming? And Rose's?

I think you had better write me to this address at the end of the letter until I let you know differently. Don't be alarmed. I'm not going anywhere very far from here, but I can't stay here alone. When this club folds up in about two weeks, I am going to take all the vacation I can before going to some new place. I would love to go to Switzerland, Italy, or Norway now but am afraid I haven't got much chance. I do not want to go to Germany but that is probably where I will end up. There is a chance that I can get home around Christmas for thirty days but it is pretty slight I think.

Enclosed is a picture of me, which Mary had enlarged, which isn't bad is it? I am getting more photogenic I have had so many taken.

I am so happy Bill is coming home. I am hoping his baby will be a boy.

Much love.

Fitje

July 3, 1945

Dear Mother & Dad,

I feel like I haven't written home in ages or heard from home. I guess it's because the time is dragging a little because of all the changes that we know are coming. Babs and I are anxious to get the club closed up as we are looking forward to a two weeks vacation, with a German car to drive ourselves to Cannes probably. I have been with these people for so long I hate it to come to an end, but then there's nothing to do about it.

I haven't really done much of anything lately. Tomorrow we are planning a big dance for the 4th so we have been busy planning that. V.D. is definitely having puppies, but not until after we leave much to our disappointment. We are giving her to Gaston, one of the men who work for us. He loves dogs so I will I know he will be kind to her. I would love to send her home by plane but am afraid she would never get from where the plane lands to Rhode Island. You would love her though; she is the most affectionate dog.

This is a short letter but I really can't think of anything to say. My two friends, Jack Moran, the boy that used to be a stoker, and Sgt. Whitesides who was wounded on D-Day plus two in Normandy, and was transferred into the group in January when he got out of the hospital, have been here all evening. I certainly wish you could meet them. They work for Jack (he always takes over all the misfits to work for him if he can get them). They are the procurers for S-4 and go on trips all over the place to pick up stuff. They can procure anything and are very proud of it. They just worship Jack, I guess because he is about the only guy who ever put any faith in them. They are never sober, or rarely, and they have just gotten back from a trip. They are trying to get nerve up to call him and report, but they know he'll think they're not sober, and that he'll be mad. They always come here to sober up when they get back. They say they know they're home when they hear me say, "Hello you two drunken bums." They always bring me flowers when they get back and I have to hear the stories of how they got this and that, and what they did.

Here comes V.D. with an old dead fish head. There is a fish shop next-door and she hangs around there most of the time in spite of the fact that she's better fed than most Belgians.

Much love.
Binni

Paris
July 19, 1945

Dear Mother & Dad,

Our mail is all mixed up now and Lord knows when I'll ever hear from you again. I am dying to hear about Lu.

The last week has been very eventful. We closed the club a week ago Monday, packed up all the furniture etc., and sent it to a warehouse in Liege; let all the staff go except the night watchmen, and Thérèse and Gaston, who take care of us in the daytime, and then sat and waited for the Bomb Group to leave for two reasons. I didn't want to go until they did, and we had to wait for the German car they promised us. We had a lovely time all week, lying in the sun all day and having parties all night. We went to the RTO in St. Trond to find out how to get to Bruges by train and talked the RTO officer, Capt. Daniel Boone, into taking us into his Packard, another captured German car. We went early Saturday, Capt. Boone, Lt. Nelson (from the Engineers,) Babs and myself. Went to Bruges and looked around a little and then went to a beach and went swimming. Got back to Brussels about 9:30 and there the car just stopped going—nothing to be done but call for a jeep which we did and then sat, literally on a curb stone just outside of Brussels, from about 11:00 until 3:00 waiting. Capt. Boone, being a fat southerner didn't mind at all. He just stretched out on the sidewalk and went fast asleep. Me, I don't mind anything anymore, but Babs and Lt. Nelson almost died of impatience. The reason it took so long was because Capt. B. had told the driver to pick us up on N3 while all the time we were waiting on N2. Luckily the driver had brains enough to search every route until he found us. Got to bed somewhat after 4:00 and was awakened again just before 6:00 by Jack, to go to the RR yards to watch the trains load up, and say goodbye to everyone. What a happy group they were! The trains finally pulled out at 9:00.

We finally got our car and got a Belgium mechanic to work on the brakes, which were lousy on Monday. Jack, who had to stay until the very end, left Monday after lunch with the last few enlisted men, and at 2:00 Gaston came and took V.D. home with him, so it was a very sad day for me.

We got up at 6:00 Tuesday and Lt. Nelson came and loaded the car for us; it took an engineer to get everything in. Everyone had been very doubtful about us starting off alone in that car and even Babs and I got a little leery. It is a lot different here, of course. You have to carry your own gas and food with you, and if there don't happen to be any Americans around, you've about had it if anything happens. At last we took off about 8:30 and everything went fine until we got to the Camberley. There the brakes broke completely—none left at all. We discovered it when Babs, who was driving, banged into a jeep. The jeep driver told us how to drive with no brakes and directed us to an ordinance outfit nearby. We never found it but we did see a truck and a tank trailer, complete with tank by the road, so we looked in the nearest pub for the drivers. They were very nice and looked the thing over. The truck driver went back to town for a G.I. mechanic and we went in the pub where the French family invited us into their apartment with the tank drivers for coffee and cognac. The mechanic finally came and we took the car back to his Ord. outfit for them to work on. We broke down in just the right place because the flying personnel from our group were staging there to go home, so we ate with them in the officer's mess, picked up the car about 7:30, and started off again. This time we arrived in Paris about 11:30 without mishap. Spent yesterday and today settling the club accounts, buying new uniforms and seeing the Rodin Museum. The RC Hdqrs. is full of confusion due to the fact that many people are clamoring to go home. We were urged to take a long vacation, so Saturday we are starting off for Cannes in our car. We hoped to go by way of Grenoble where Babs lived for a year. We will only stay there a week, as it is an army leave center and you aren't allowed to stay longer. We have planned to take three weeks so may go to England from there. There is really no place to go here except to a leave center because civilian places are too expensive and anyway army personnel are not allowed to stay in them.

The picture has changed a lot in the Red Cross since the war has ended. About the only thing now are clubs in towns and a few on bases, but I think I've had enough of that now that the war is over and there is no more excitement. There is no chance to get to the Pacific from here. I have no great desire to be in Germany with a lot of disgruntled occupation troops and I really think the people who are new over here could do a better job anyway. I am dying to go to Austria though, but all in all I expect I'll be home for Christmas and maybe before. I am beginning to feel so beat up that I think I owe it to the Red Cross to take a 30-day leave at home and also I would love to see you all now that this war is over. I feel like my last friend left Europe with the bomb group.

Will write from Cannes.

Much love.
Fitje

CHAPTER 13

Hanging Around Paris

July 27, 1945–November 11, 1945

Fitje closed the club at St. Trond on July 9th and remained with the 386th Bomb Group until July 16th when the few remaining units left Europe. Taking some vacation time she and Babs Garfield, her assistant at St. Trond, spent a week in Paris before driving to Juan Les Pins, on the Riviera. They returned to Paris on August 6th. On the 11th she joined the 27th Air Transport Group in Villacoublay France.

The 27th, which was attached to the 302nd Transport Wing, was organized as a logistical support organization at Hendon, England in 1943. Commanded by Colonel James H. Douglas, it was an integral part of the war effort. The 27th consisted of eight squadrons, which ferried tactical aircraft and

Fitje in Paris nightclub with Captain Jack Zeltner

delivered medicine and other materials, including gasoline, to the front. They also evacuated wounded to England and transported high priority passengers. The 27th flew C-47 Sky Birds, commonly called Gooney Birds.

The move to Villacoublay marked the beginning of the end of her remarkable adventure. On one hand, she claimed to be busy writing that, "We have three places to run here—a regular aero club for the permanent party on the base, a canteen for transients waiting for planes, and a field grade officer's lounge. The transient canteen serves about 2000 per day so you can see there is a lot to do." On the other hand, her last thirteen letters from Europe read like a travel log filled with trips to Paris, Cannes, Ireland and Switzerland. Not mentioned in the letters is a flight to Berlin with Captain Thomas Mostyn. Captain Mostyn, who she called Matey, was, as she wrote her parents, "my special friend."

Fitje's last day of work must have been in late October, just before she traveled to Montreux, where she stayed in the Swiss Hotel, ". . . looking out over Lake Geneva." After returning to France she spent her last two weeks in Paris before boarding the USS George Washington in Le Havre and sailing home.

July 27, 1945

Dear Mother & Dad,

I certainly wish you could see this lovely place. It is a lot different from when I was here in January because the weather is so beautiful—very warm but life is so attuned to the heat, that you don't even notice it.

As you probably know, the Riviera from Cannes to Nice has been made into a rest center for American troops. The army runs it, although there are naturally lots of French citizens around. All the big hotels have been taken over for billets, and army rations are served in the dining rooms, so disguised by French cooks that you would never know they were army rations. The regular French staff continues to run the hotel so it is not like staying in an army billet it at all. Cannes is for officers and Nice for enlisted men. We are staying at the Belles Rives Hotel at Juan Les Pins, just outside Cannes.

There is every sort of thing to do here. Our hotel is right on the Mediterranean with the terrace right on the water. There are sailboats, bicycles, pedalo, (little boats which you pedal) movies and bars, dancing every night on outside terraces at every hotel. Army trucks go everywhere so there is no need to exert the slightest energy, and lots of people to do everything with. Everyone relaxes completely and does exactly as he pleases. There is a huge sign on each side of Cannes that says "saluting is not required in this area." All 2nd Lieutenants change rank daily and appear one day as a Major or Colonel. Last night I went out with a 1st Lieutenant who chose to be a Brigadier General for the evening and where we went there was a Lieutenant General masquerading as a 2nd Lieutenant. Yesterday we saw an officer walking down the street in pajamas pulling a wooden duck after him. It is amazing. You wear a bathing suit practically all the time and the water is wonderful. The sun burns very quickly, and naturally I have a terrific sunburn. There is a wonderful place to swim called Stone Roc and we ride bicycles out there most every day. There are lots of lovely vacant houses around, lots of them owned by

English and Americans. The mines haven't all been cleared away so it is not wise to do any exploring off the beaten track.

We had a lovely trip down here. It took two long days, spending a night in Lyon, and arriving here about 12:00 Sunday night. We just barely managed to nurse our old car down here, and I don't know whether we will be able to get it home or not. We progressed very slowly due to the fact that we met all sorts of interesting Americans along the way. The first day for instance we went through Fontainebleau and stopped there and had lunch with some officers who were billeted in a little inn right across the street from the castle, where people used to stay while waiting for an audience with the king. Once we ran out of gas but luckily had a can with us, and another time the car almost burned up. We were told it had a broken gasket but we filled it with water and it runs all right so I guess maybe it will get us back to Paris.

Have met two Navy people down here who know the McLaughry's (both went to Dartmouth) but can't remember their names. Spent today with Col. Crawford from Little Rock who knows Phyllis and Charlie Campbell. He works for IBM too.

I'm hoping that when I get back to Paris I will find a letter telling me about Lu—am very anxious to hear. You never did tell me when Ibby and Rose's babies were expected.

Much love to all.

Fitje

July 30, 1945

Dear Jane,

Here I am basking in the sun of the Riviera. It is certainly a wonderful place. The hotel we're staying at is the Juan Les Pins between Cannes and Nice and right on the water. We get up around 10:00, lounge around in bathing suits on the deck chairs drinking Tom Collins all morning, eat lunch about three, and then do something strenuous in the afternoon, like bicycling to Stone Roc, about half a mile away to do more of the same thing, lounge, and drink Tom Collins, or go sailing, or sleep, which I have done half of the time. In the evenings you go to Cannes or stay here with someone and dance on terraces over the water and drink more Tom Collins. It is delightful. After a week of it all my energy has returned and I feel like I'm good for another year over here.

We had wonderful fun getting here. We drove down from Belgium in a German car, which the bomb group gave us when they left, stopping off in Paris for a couple of days on the way. It was a three-day trip and all sorts of fascinating things happened because we had so much trouble with the car. The brakes broke, a gasket broke, we ran out of gas, had all sorts of trouble with MPs who thought we had stolen it, and Frenchman who wanted to steal our gas and the rations. We are sure we will never make it back to Paris!

On account of moving around a lot lately I haven't heard from the family for ages and I'm wondering about Lucy; sure hope she had a boy. Do you expect Johnny home this summer? Is Bill home yet? Have you any recent pictures of Warren?

Anyway the real point of this letter is to tell you that the 386th is on its way home or even home by this time I guess. I have given your address to a few of my friends that live around New York and I hope they will look you up. I hope Capt. Zeltner does as he was a very good friend of mine and I know you'll like him. Although I guess after two years overseas you don't spend your time running around looking up sisters of Red Cross girls.

What's happened to Pat? I haven't heard about her for a long time.

Much love.

Fitje

✍

August 6, 1945

Dear Lu,

Just got back to Paris and found lots of mail awaiting me, including a letter from Mother saying that you and Bill had a daughter born almost on Mother's birthday. I am so glad. I can hardly wait to get back here because I was sure there would be a letter waiting for me. Does it have red hair or can't you tell yet? I don't see how she can escape having curly hair anyway. Isn't it nice that Bill got home just in time? Congratulate him for me.

Finally got back from Cannes late last night and just barely. The car stopped the moment we got it inside the garage and I'm doubtful as to whether it will ever start again.

Now I am fussing around here trying to find out what I want to do now and taking the opportunity to get my teeth fixed up and get some new uniforms. Tonight I am going to have dinner with Pat McParland. Ann sent me some awfully cute pictures of Warren and also told me that she had ordered a baby sister for him. There will be so many strangers in the family when I get home!

Am wondering if you know yet where Bill is going to be stationed. Do you expect to be with him or are you going to stay in Providence? What is Roger doing now? Mother said something about him traveling back and forth from Casablanca.

I will be waiting now to hear what the baby's name is and to see pictures of it. Give Bill my love.

Much love.

Binni

✍

August 6, 1945

Dear Tim,

Your latest letter has been going around in circles because I forgot to give you my new address. Since the 386th Bomb Group has gone home I am now in Paris trying to decide what to do next.

The last few days in Belgium were amazing. Naturally we had lots of parties and got quite accustomed to going to bed at 4:00 and getting up at 6:00 to see a train or a convoy off. The last day was very sad, I thought, because I hated to see everyone go. Of course they weren't the least bit sad to be going home. About 3:00 that night when I finally got around to feeding V.D., while Jack and I drank a last bottle of champagne, I suddenly remembered that it was our last bottle of champagne and the last time I would feed V.D. so I burst into tears. Jack's reaction to that was, "Let me fed the dog if your going to cry about it," so I didn't get much sympathy. The Belgian I gave her to promised to let me know the result of her confinement and I am expecting to hear any day now.

Speaking of that sort of thing, Lucy had a baby girl on July 23rd. I am so glad her husband is home now. In fact the baby was born in the morning and he got home that evening. Jane's husband was at Okinawa and was slightly wounded. Jane expects him to be home in September. Johnny goes to Harvard Medical School in the fall and Hermie and Ann expect another baby in January. Hermie expects to go overseas and may have gone by this time. And that is all the latest news on my family. Has Alice two or three kids now? I can't seem to remember.

I forgot to tell you that after I left Belgium, Babs and I drove down to Cannes for two weeks in a German car that the group gave us for a present before they left. We had a wonderful time there and I recommend it highly if you ever get a chance. We just got back Sunday night and just barely made it. The car stopped the moment we got in the garage and although we didn't try it, I know it will never start again.

I don't know what I am going to do now. May go to Germany, may go home and may go to the Pacific or the CBI from here. I will try to get a ride to your part of Germany. Be on the lookout for a Red Cross girl named Mary Haynesworth. She was the girl who was with me in France and I think she is in your vicinity now.

I will let you know when I decide what to do.

Much love,
Binni

Paris
August 10, 1945

Dear Mother & Dad,

We are just hearing this afternoon the first rumors that the war is over. In fact I was sitting in the dentist chair when the first news came. All sorts of rumors are flying around and everyone on the street is stopping everyone else. I guess it will be very exciting for the next few nights. Isn't it wonderful, because even if it isn't true it must be nearly true and to think, three months ago we thought it would be two more years?

I will get this in the mail quickly as I must start celebrating myself, but just wanted to let you know that I am safely back from con and having been taking a few days here going to the dentist.

Tomorrow I am going to an airfield just outside Paris (Villacoublay) for a short time, probably until

September or October, when I will be on my way home. It is a nifty assignment and I am looking forward to it.

Had dinner with Pat McParland and hope to see him frequently between now and then. He is fine and seems to love his job.

I am delighted about my niece, and have already written Lou.

Hope you're celebrating at home in the proper manner.

Much love.
Fitje

Saturday, August 18, 1945

Dear Mother & Dad,

It is pouring rain and the airplanes are few and far between, so maybe I can finish uninterrupted. No—I have to stop already and drive one of the staff to Versailles.

Sunday, August 19, 1945

This is a terribly busy place and lots of fun because there is so much going on. Planes go from here to England, Germany, Poland, and Norway, all over the place transporting Army personnel on pass and on business. We have three places to run here, a regular aero club for the permanent party on the base, a canteen for transients waiting for planes, and a field grade officer's lounge. The transient canteen serves about two thousand per day so you can see there is a lot to do. We have a central kitchen that makes stuff for all three. Right now they are building us a new and larger transient canteen, which is going to be awfully nice. The director before me has just left to go home to Boston after six years over here. She is married to an Englishman. The other girl with me is very nice, Blanche Curley from Grand Rapids Michigan.

I have my car here and it is wonderful. Although we also have a weapons carrier and driver, the distances are large between places, and it is very convenient to have it. We live off the base in a whole house about two miles away—three bedrooms, two living rooms, and the kitchen. It is a little beat up and no hot water of course, but we have just have locks put on the doors (after a chair and all her rations were stolen) and some of it boarded up so it really is very nice.

The nicest member the staff is Noël, a volunteer from Paris. She reminds me so much of Franny because she has the same hair, and coloring, and wears the same kind of clothes. She is going to live with us too so I hope to learn a little more French.

I don't know where Roger got the idea that I was at the POE[*] with the 386th. I did almost go home

* Point of Embarkation: A U.S. Army command responsible for the movement of troops and supplies.

with them but they left the staging area to quickly, before I could get the accounts and things settled in Paris. I think I will stay until around Christmas. By January there will no longer be need of me anyway. The longer I stay the more money I will have and by then there will be nylon stockings on the market again.

Isn't it wonderful that it is all over with? What will happen to Hermie now, will he go to the Pacific? When is Johnny coming home? I hear there is no more gas rationing in the States. It would be nice if the rest of the world would recuperate as quickly as we will. It is fascinating to watch developments in France. The black market is terrific. You can sell anything and everything even our old and worn out shoes for Fr.2000. Two-piece bathing suits in Paris with no linings cost Fr.3000 to Fr.4000. ($60-$80) The French can't live without buying from the black market. The legitimate ration would hardly feed them a week and they can't even buy what they are allowed because it isn't available except on the black market.

I am waiting for pictures of Lu's baby, and I am so glad Ann is going to be another mother.

Did you get my letter about income tax dad and were you able to pay it?

Much love.
Fitje

⌘

August 22, 1945

Dear Mother & Dad,

At last the weather has cleared up after a week of cold and rain. Both our clubs are in the process of being moved, one to the main gate and the other just across the road, so we have nothing to do but stand around and watch operations. The idea is to decentralize things a little on the base so there won't be so many things in one area. I am glad because the new Nissen huts will be clean for a while anyway and they are terrible now.

Just took my car to ordinance to put water in the battery and in the end they gave me a new battery and redid most of the wiring. I never had it so good. Just think, I would have to pay for in civilian life (that is, if I were ever lucky enough to have a car.) I will have to take a picture of it to send to you.

Yesterday, when I was in Paris, I met Babs Garfield, the girl who was with me the last four months at the 386th and went to Cannes with me. She was leaving for home the next day on an emergency leave as her father is very ill. She is from Boston and will call you when she gets home. She is very nice.

I wish you could see our house. We now have some furniture in the living room and it looks so nice. Why we bother I don't know as we are never in it except to sleep. The people that own the house are fixing the grounds and they are beginning to look nice. I guess the people are mad that we are living in it. It seems sad about the housing situation because most often the houses of the French people who were not collaborators were taken by the Germans then the Americans took them from the Germans

238

and they have no place to live whereas the collaborators who were allowed to keep their houses still have them. Oh, well, there isn't much justice about it anyway I guess.

Has Jane heard when Johnny is coming home? I hope everyone will be home by the time I get there. I am wondering if Hermie is going to the Pacific now.

Much Love,
Fitje

August 30, 1945

Dear Mother & Dad,

Tonight is Thursday and our dance is going on, but as everything runs smoothly I have come down to the other club to close up and write a couple of letters before I go back.

Everything is lovely and I am fine. This is quite a place and quite different from a bomb group. There are two squadrons in this 27th Air Transport Group, which is what I am with. We eat all our meals at the 311th squadron officer's club right near the Red Cross. It is in a lovely château owned by some Swedes now living in the U.S. The officers are the craziest bunch, all mostly young flying officers and terribly nice. Everyone has a special name like "The Nose" or "The Voice" and you are introduced to people that way so you never know their real name because no one will tell you. I am simply "The Fitcha." My special friend here is Captain Tommy Mostyn, a pilot, who is terribly nice. He has two special friends named "The Kraut" and "The Lee." The Lee is Jewish and very nice and very funny. He sings Jewish songs with a wonderful accent. The Kraut was a professor at the University of California but is now a pilot. We have a lot of fun.

This afternoon Tommy and I drove over to see Helen Shoemaker. She is only twenty minutes away. She has a wonderful set up and seems very well and happy and she loves what she is doing.

Our staff here is very good. The cutest is a little fifteen-year-old boy named Jack who works in the kitchen. He speaks very funny English like, "Miss Fitje, I got fifteen years how many you got?" Also Annie who was very pretty and is married to an American soldier from Texas.

We have just finished moving one of the clubs to another building. Next week we are moving the other. It is nice to move into a new place. At least it will be clean for a while. Our house gets better and better. The living room is all furnished and the man

Fitje with Captain Thomas "Matey" Mostyn

that owns it has been fixing up the grounds so they look quite nice. Next door to us there is a tiny black puppy and it is the constant companion of a large duck. It is the funniest thing to watch them playing together.

You will be happy to hear that I sold one of my new uniforms. I have my name on the October list now so we'll probably be home early in November. Send me Jane's new address if she moves so I could get in touch with her the first thing.

Got a letter from my friend Mere Valentine in Saint Trond saying that she has TB, poor thing. Also one from Mme., our manageress in St. Trond, saying V.D. is fine and happy in her new home but that she never had any puppies so I guess we were wrong.

I can really carry on quite a conversation in French now. In some ways I hate to leave just when I am really beginning to learn. Noel helps me a lot, as does the whole staff.

I'm waiting for pictures of "our baby" although seeing the real thing will be much better. Can Warren talk yet?

Much love.
Fitje

September 2, 1945

Dear Jane,

Just a note to wish you a happy birthday although I know you won't get until much later.

I am so glad you saw Jack. He really is awfully nice and I thought you would like him. Today is Sunday and quiet around here. I am up at the aero club and one of the French staff is playing Ping-Pong with one of the boys. She just used a horrible expression one of the soldiers had taught her without having the slightest idea what she was saying. You hear them say some of the choicest things.

The other day Matey,[*] one of the pilots, and I went over to see Helen. She isn't at all far from here, about twenty minutes. She really has a wonderful set up and seems to love it. She is having the same troubles I am, staying away from the bar etc., and deciding whether to go home or not as I guess her outfit is going. Today she called me twice but I wasn't around. I will call her later when the lines aren't so busy. It is very difficult to put a telephone call through over here. I am going to get her over for the night next week. She has to live with 150 nurses, which must be ghastly.

I met a friend of Polly Evans who told me that she had gone to Rheims where there is a huge staging area. I will get in touch with her. I don't envy anyone just arriving here for a job in the Red Cross. The good part's over now. You get here so eager and so innocent that boy, how two years changes one. When I arrived the soldiers were new, and eager, and innocent, but now we've all been here for months and how we've all changed! It's all right for me because I've learned along with them but for someone

---

* Captain Thomas E. Marsden.

new at the racket it must be terrific. I have been very aware of the changes recently because we have a third girl here temporarily who came over with Polly. I spend all my time trying to lessen the shocks I can see she is receiving.

Surely you're not thinking of going overseas just when Johnny and all of us are coming home. I hope not. Send me your new address if you move so I can get in touch with you the minute I hit New York. It will probably be in late October for early November. I want to leave before the cold weather starts because I can't see much hope of staying warm without Jack to keep us supplied with coke.

This is a pretty rough detail. Up about 7:30, work till 11:00 at night and 11:05 seems to find me at the bar regularly. There is a wonderful group of flying offices here and we have much too good a time. They are now beginning to call me Buchenwald Rose because of the bags under my eyes. I am hoping I can hold out until October. If Providence was dull before, I hate to think what will be like now.

My car is still wonderful although they tell me at ordinance that the front wheels are about to fall off and the brakes still don't work at all. The mechanics can't get the German parts to fix it. The two fifteen-year old boys who work for us wash it practically every day. In fact this morning little Jacques my favorite was crying in the dishwater when I went in because Mme. Delapierre, who is the manageress, made him wash the cups when he wanted to clean out the car.

Well I'll probably see you all soon.

Much love,
Fitje

September 10, 1945

Dear Mother & Dad,

Just a note to tell you I am okay but very busy. The weather is wonderful and there are airplanes all over the place.

Helen Shoemaker is coming to spend tomorrow night here and we will no doubt have the usual party. Her hospital is going home but she doesn't know what she is going to do. We are going to try to get a leave to Switzerland together.

Every Sunday evening we get a French artist out from Paris to draw the GIs. They love it, as much as the fortuneteller who comes every Saturday evening. Enclosed is an example of the artist's work. Last night the transportation got all mixed up and at 11:00 there was no one to take him to Paris. In the end we got Capt. Mostyn (Matey) and Lieut. Kitsos (Jack) out of bed and they drove us all to Paris in my car. We had a lovely time driving around Montmartre where he lived and finally came back to our house and made turkey sandwiches out of some canned turkey someone gave us. Today Matey and Jack are out rounding up a load of wood for us. The flying officers have lots of spare time and they love to come down to our house and fool around. We have a key at the club and they come down in the afternoon and put locks on the doors electric plugs on walls and fix windows. They call it the lower house and even keep it stocked with food and whiskey.

Drawing of Fitje sketched by artist at Villacoublay, September 9, 1945

Every morning we go out on the taxi strip to watch the planes load up and take off, usually around 8:30 or 9:00. It's wonderful fun because they are going all over Europe and back on that day. The pilots are always asking us to go but we don't feel we should is they are the ones that get in trouble if we're caught on the plane without orders. I am going to try and get to Berlin though.

I forgot to tell you that Bill Curtis is stationed here. Isn't he that friend of Marjorie's? I had dinner with him a couple of nights ago and he is very nice. I am right now hiding out because I know he wants me to go into Paris tonight and I can't because Helen is coming tomorrow night and I've got to work sometime. I get so tired of saying no. He is going home soon I think. Don't be expecting me home until you hear from me because I will let you know when I plan to leave. As long as my car last and the fun lasts and the warm weather lasts I'll be here.

Mother will you call Mrs. Ford and find out about Carol. I never did know her married name and address and the only letter I ever wrote her was returned marked address unknown. I should writer.

Did my income tax ever get paid?

Much love.
Fitje

September 12, 1945

Dear Tim,

Am wondering where in the world you are since it has been beaucoup time since I last heard from you.

I am now stationed at Villacoublay, the airport outside of Paris, near Versailles, where all the planes from Germany, the Riviera and England land. It is fascinating. I see people all the time that I haven't seen in ages. It's sort of like Grand Central Station. I keep expecting to see you on your way to Paris or London, on leave. Couldn't you come? We could have a lovely time. There is a crazy bunch of pilots here. We have a house off the base and two cases of whiskey. It is a good setup and I really hate to leave, but think I'd better before I get too degenerate, so I'll probably go home around the middle of October or the beginning of November.

You <u>absolutely</u> must come up here. I could fly down there but I wouldn't know where to find you and you can always find me here.

How is everything at home? How long do you expect to stay?

Write soon.

Love,
Binni

September 17, 1945

Dear Mother & Dad,

We are having a lovely time. It is a warm beautiful day and we are at home taking the afternoon off.

Blanche is lying in the sun, I am writing letters, and Jack, Kraut and Matey, three of our flying officers are fussing around fixing windows and putting the electricity in. They are now talking about a doorbell (there is nothing we need less) and are about to take glass from the bombed back room, and put it in the broken front windows. They just love to work around here and of course we love to have them. All I have to do is get the materials and that's easy. Matey and Kraut do most of the work and Jack is rushing around mixing drinks and keeping their glasses filled. I wish it would get cold so we could light a fire. The other afternoon they chopped the wood and we laid a lovely fire with pine boughs for decoration. We even have a radio from a B-26.

Yesterday was a terribly busy day. We had a picnic for about forty G.I.s and French girls at Villences, which is a lovely spot about twenty miles away. Didn't turn out too good though, as the weather was bad and everyone stayed at the bar, and trying to get forty half-drunk people onto trucks was no easy job. In the evening we had a fortune-teller, a caricaturist, and a pianist in the club, all from Paris, so the place was packed. After we closed, I went down to the château and took a bath and washed my hair in Matey's bathroom. I guess that's why I feel so good today. I'm clean for change. We also raided the kitchen and ate piles of fried chicken, leftover from dinner, which we missed because of the picnic.

Did I tell you we have a third girl here temporarily, thank goodness, because two people can't be in three places at once? She came here fresh from the states with practically the identical thoughts I had two and a half years ago. She makes me feel awfully cold-blooded most of the time. I'm afraid I've gotten ready horrible but you can judge for yourselves soon. I can't tell you how I'm looking forward to getting home. I am only staying now because until we get this new club finished I know I am useful and because I want to be able to be home for November and December. Almost everyone I know has gone. Francey Baker just left, and Martha Brush is leaving soon. If it weren't for being lucky enough to have this particular job I would've come home when the 386th left.

I am being heckled as everyone has stopped work, and is sitting around talking about their blisters.

Much love.

Fitje

Sept. 26, 1945

Dear Mother & Dad,

I guess you have either just have or are just going to have the usually stormy September weather, as we are having it here now. It makes it very hectic here because the planes don't take off on schedule and the place is packed all day with soldiers waiting to go somewhere. This afternoon the sun shone long enough for Matey to take off for England with some passengers and to bring back the gang that left for home a few days ago but are still waiting in England, to the officers dance tonight.

This promises to be an exciting evening because of that, and also because we have planted traps tonight to catch the members of our staff who are stealing food for the black market. I can hardly wait, it makes me so damn mad. There are three of them, one boy and two women, and they give the stuff to one of the French bus drivers, who drive the busses that transport soldiers from Paris. Up until recently it has been very minor, only stuff from the kitchen but now they have gotten a duplicate key and we hear through the grapevine (they tell on each other like mad) that a big deal is coming off tonight. We have stooges planted all over the place and if we can trust the stooges it ought to be exciting. We are trying to replace all our French men with Russians, as they are very, very honest and wonderful workers.

Bill Curtis started on his way home yesterday. He was transferred to a group in England that is going soon. I went out with him the night before he left, to the movies in Paris and then to a Russian place in the Montmartre. He is very nice. He is going to call you when he gets home.

Had lunch with Helen Shoemaker in Paris yesterday. Her hospital is on its way and she is going to Cannes on leave. I think she is going to spend Thursday night and Matey is going to fly her down on Friday. She and I wanted to go to Switzerland together but the tours are all filled up until January, so I guess we'll go on a tour to the U.S. instead. We think we'll probably come home together, early in November now.

If only I could bring my car home with me. I guess it wouldn't look so beautiful in the states. Babs wrote that it was days before she could get used to seeing all the shiny cars and well-dressed people. I can't wait to start buying clothes. Are nylon stockings on the market yet?

I am dying to eat fresh vegetables, oysters, mushrooms and steak, roast pork, ice cream, and milk. I hope Lu is still there with the baby when I get there. Is Jane at home now? What does she hear from Johnny? I hope he is on his way by now. I would have loved to have gotten to the Pacific but guess there will be no need of me now. I'm afraid the U.S. will never be big enough for me again. If I had the wanderlust before I have something awful now.

Sept. 27, 1945

We are now at home cleaning ourselves up for the G.I. dance, which we give every Thursday night. We have just lit our little Coleman gasoline stove and are waiting for water to heat, so I will finish this letter. We are browbeating Betty who hasn't taken a bath in the four weeks she has been here. She is only just beginning to approve of our informal way of doing things.

The dance last night was wonderful. We went to bed at 5:00 and got up as usual at 8:00. You would love my friend Jeanine I am sure Mother. She is from Brooklyn but has lived in France for nine years. She has a daughter fifteen and is very much in love with a flying officer at least twelve years younger than she is. She has dyed brilliant red hair, speaks perfect French (so I understand) and English with a terrific Brooklyn accent. She lives mostly on the base in a room with her officer and two others. Last night she sat at the bar crying all evening because she is catching on that her officer doesn't really love her but likes the beaucoup money she has given him from her profits on the *Marche Noir*.* For some reason she considers me her good friend and is continually doing things for me. I feel so sorry for the poor thing!

Uncovering the robbers in our staff didn't turn out so good as they got wind of the fact that we were suspicious. I'm afraid I handled the whole thing poorly anyway. The French people seem to resent it if you won't let them steal from you.

I love the pictures of Lucy Ann that Jane sent me.†

Must go wash.

Much Love,
Fitje

Sept. 30, 1945

Still haven't mailed this so might as well add to it. Helen spent Friday night here and Saturday morning early Matey flew her to Nice. I took her to lunch and saw her on her way to Juan les Pins where she is staying for a week. He also arranged through a friend of his to have her flown back next Saturday. It sure is wonderful to be in the Air Corps. Five hours in the air is much better than 48 hours by these trains. I was dying to go with them but couldn't, as Blanche and Betty both sick with grippe, or something.

October 13, 1945

Dear Mother & Dad,

It seems like a lot has gone on this week, but since it always seems that way I guess it was nothing out of the ordinary.

Last Saturday Matey took the trip to Nice so I went down while he picked up Helen. It is great fun to go on an illegitimate trip as you go to the dispersal area and get on the plane where no one can see you and taxi up to traffic, where the passengers get on. You sit up in the pilot's compartment where it is nice and warm while most of the passengers freeze in the back. It was a lovely trip to Nice, right over the French Alps, and a beautiful day. Matey has flown all over Europe, so much so that he knows every rock and can point everything out. In fact he kept going off course to show me things and I felt sorry for the passengers especially when he buzzed over our house so I could see it on the way home.

---

* Black Market

† Fitje's niece, born on July 23, 1945 to Bill and Lucy Grosvenor

For some reason it reminded me of Dad taking Helen's appendix out and cutting her open a little extra so I could see her liver or something.

We had lunch in Nice and Helen was at the airport when we got back. She stayed with me until Monday morning and then went back to Paris and has now been assigned in Germany. She left for Wiesbaden yesterday.

Wednesday afternoon I took off again, this time for Ireland, with Matey and three other officers for a wedding. One of the officers in the squadron married an Irish girl. It was another lovely trip right along the south coast of England and over the Isle of Man. The engineer on the plane was married to an Irish girl in Bangor so we buzzed Bangor to let her know he was on his way and then landed at Lutt's Corner, just outside of Belfast. The bridegroom left a couple of days before and when we arrived in Belfast we suddenly realized that no one knew the name of his girl or had the slightest idea where she lived. After much difficulty, we finally found billets of sorts, although Matey and I had to stay way outside of town, in a dirty little inn. We had chicken for dinner at the local hotel and then went to a local dance place where Lt. Richards, the groom, used to hang out when he was stationed in Ireland. Lo and behold, just as we expected, he came about 10:00 with the bride and her parents. The bride was very pretty. Matey fed the brides father lots of whiskey and he was very funny. The bride's mother had never been in a nightclub before and didn't look very happy about it.

The wedding was a very solemn affair in a lovely little church. Matey was best man and had all sorts of tricks planned. I could see him change his mind when he saw the minister, a huge white-haired, solemn, Irishman, with a wonderful brogue. The bridegroom looked terrible. He shaved fifteen minutes before the wedding because Matey made him. He had on a dirty shirt and his shoes weren't shined. We were in the pew right behind them and I had an impulse to reach out and button his hip pockets, which were unbuttoned. After the wedding we went to a small wedding dinner and ate chicken again, and then saw the bride and groom on the train to Dublin. We spent the evening seeing Belfast nightspots. The three officers and I and had a lovely time. We ate dinner—more chicken—at the Allied officers club, which is practically closed, as there are very few officers left, and practically no Americans. We only saw about four beside ourselves.

The next morning early we took off. Matey was going to fly down to Dublin so I could see it but it was too cloudy and we couldn't stay below the overcast. The trip back above the clouds was beautiful, although I slept most of the way on a stretcher. It takes about three hours.

That's about all the news I can think of. We finally set a trap and caught the French boy that had stolen all the stuff. Everyone has been very good since then and there has been a very noticeable drop in the amount of stuff we use each week.

Be sure and tell Bridget about my trip to Ireland. I bought her a pretty calendar, which I will bring home to her.

Don't know when I'll be back as everything is held up because of the strikes and losing the Queen Mary and Aquitania. Anyway the weather is lovely right now and I'm afraid only the cold weather will drive me home.

I forgot to tell you that at the wedding we were giving cake in little paperbacks to dream on for three nights. The first night I had a terrible dream that Johnny Mclaughry was trying to murder me by running over me in a jeep. I decided after that that I would rather not know what was in store for me so I threw it away.

Much love
Fitje

October 14, 1945

Dear Tim,

Have gotten two letters from you lately. I had begun to think your were dead I hadn't heard from you for so long. I see by *Stars & Stripes* that Military Government is beginning to fold up by degrees and wonder what that will do to your status. I should think it would be most interesting. I would love to have been in Germany a little more just to have a better understanding of the German people because I guess the next ten years will see lots of upheaval over here.

I am having a lovely time and trying, not too successfully, to get myself in the mood to go home. As things stand now I am pretty definitely to be on my way by the end of the month, or at least in Paris waiting to go. I think my successor will be here around the 21st. The Red Cross is beginning to demobilize and wants everyone with twenty-two months over here to leave. Since I have been here twenty-eight months and only about fifteen others have been here that long, I guess I better go before I'm thrown out. At times I am very eager to leave and see my family, but I hate to think of staying in one place and I'm quite sure the US will never be big enough for me again.

I have a very good pilot friend here so I fly all over the place. Last Saturday I went to Nice with him to bring another Red Cross girl, a friend of mine, back. Wednesday he and I and three other officers flew to Ireland to the wedding of one of the officers in the group. We had a crazy time and almost never got to the wedding as no one could remember the name of the bride, or where she lived. I got back Friday morning exhausted and have been trying to catch up on sleep ever since. It is practically impossible for me to fly to Germany without orders as the security is so strict and I would only get the pilot into trouble if I went. We have a scheduled flight to Munich every day though. If only you could catch a plane and come here, you could eas-

Lt. Tim Pitts, Germany, June 1945

ily get back though, of course you always have to take a chance on the weather. I guess we are fated not to meet here. If only you could get a leave to Paris or Cannes. I could get either place with no trouble at all.

I will certainly write or telephone your family the first thing and probably see them soon, but I expect to rush right home to Providence first and take about a million baths and buy some clothes.

I have no idea what I will do next but as I have beaucoup irons in the fire I am sure something will turn up.

Will write again when I have more definite plans and let you know.

Much love,
Binni

❦

October 21, 1945

Dear Mother & Dad,

Just a quick note to tell you that I think I'm on my way at last, although I'm not positive.

Monday I am leaving here to go to Switzerland on leave for ten days. Isn't that wonderful? You know how I have always wanted to go there. When I get back around the 1st, I will probably wait in Paris until there is space on a boat for me. If it looks like a long wait I will probably come back here but it probably won't be too long. I expect I'll be home between the middle and end of November. I am very excited. I don't mind leaving here so much, as Matey and all the people I know best are going at the same time. In fact we're hoping to be on the same boat.

The weather is beautiful here right now, much warmer inside than out as the insides of all look stone buildings are so damp. Blanche is sick with bladder trouble again and may have to go to the hospital. If so it may change my plans but I'm hoping sulfur pills will keep her on her feet until after I leave.

This afternoon I am going to clean all of my clothes in gasoline so I can be reasonably clean to go home.

I love the enlarged pictures of the babies. The one of Warren is so cute.

Much love.
Fitje

❦

October 29, 1945
Montreux, Switzerland

Dear Mother & Dad,

I am sitting in the window of my room at the Swiss Hotel in Montreux looking out over Lake Geneva and snowcapped mountains beyond. It is beautiful and the whole trip has been like being in a fairy land after all the dirt and ruin in France.

I started out alone from Paris Monday night, Matey and Blanche having put me a train to Mulhouse, on the Swiss border. On the train I met up with Lt. Carlisle Brown and his girl, Elaine St. Maur, a Red Cross girl, and three Sergeants from his company, Billy, Nick, and Frank, all very nice, so have been with them ever since. As you may know, leaves to Switzerland are more or less in the form of a tour. You have a choice of five routes to take and can have only $46 in Swiss Francs (Fr. 200) to spend. We left Mulhouse Thursday morning, spent that night in Lucerne, Friday night in Meiringen, Saturday here, and we will be here until Wednesday. Friday morning we will be back in Paris. You know how I have always wanted to go to Switzerland. I have never seen anything so lovely. The weather has been perfect and we have walked for miles. We can't get over the things we see in stores that we haven't seen since we left the states; good food, clean, snow-white sheets and napkins at the table. There are no signs of war except for a few pillboxes in the mountains and a few Swiss soldiers in uniforms looking so much like German it seems strange at first. The Swiss people are so friendly and the kids so healthy looking after the skinny pale ones in France. They buy you drinks in bars, and stop you in the street and ask you for tea. They do not ask you for cigarettes and gum or come suddenly up to you and ask if you have anything to sell like the French do. I suppose home is more or less like this.

I have a room on the third floor with a balcony, and Billy, Nick, and Frank are directly below me, so they can go out on their balcony and whistle up to me. This afternoon we are going to ride bicycles to Lausanne and they have just called that they are ready. Yesterday we walked down to see Chillon Castle and tomorrow we are going to Geneva for the day. The trains are wonderful here and everything is so clean. We have milk for each meal and wonderful dark Swiss beer. The Fr. 200, incidentally, is spending money so you pay $35 for your expenses before you leave Mulhouse.

Next Day

We never did get as far as Lausanne on bicycles because we kept stopping to look at things. We had tea and pastry at a cute little place. The pastry is simply marvelous. You get four pieces for one coupon and we are given two-dozen coupons at the beginning of the trip. Most things are rationed, of course. For example a glass of milk is one half of coupon, a meal eaten outside the hotel we stayed in, is two-coupons, etc. We have coupons enough for eight tiny bits of chocolate and it is wonderful after our old stale PX rations. Of course everyone is buying watches like mad, but luckily I all ready have two that the pilots bought me from Sweden and Switzerland, so I don't have to spend money on that. So far I have bought a music box and an alarm clock. It seems very strange to be able to buy things. I will probably spend all my money in two days when I get home. I can't get over how well-behaved all the American soldiers are and I'm sure it's because they're treated so nicely for a change. They're so quiet you could hardly believe they are Americans. On the tour I am on, there are three girls, 155 G.I.s, and fifteen officers, but the Swiss run them so well that you were never conscious of being in a crowd.

Is big John home yet? Is Bill a civilian?

Much love.
Fitje

November 6, 1945

Dear Mother & Dad,

Arrived back from Switzerland (in Paris) at 5:30 Friday morning. It certainly was a lovely trip, if a little hectic. Took a bath and ate breakfast, and then went back to Villacoublay. Found many changes there. The new club is almost finished, Blanche is now club director, and there is a new girl there. I didn't do a thing but move the stuff out of our little house, as they are moving to one of the officer's chateaus for the winter, and hang around the bar in the evenings. Johnny Stock, the bartender, said he had closed the bar at 10:00 while I was away because no one was there. In fact, he said all my friends were very well behaved while I was gone, and that I was definitely the evil influence. In fact, everyone said that, as we had a huge impromptu party that Friday night.

Monday morning Matey drove me into Paris in my car, which, incidentally, the ordinance department fixed all up for me while I was away. It runs so beautifully and I hate to leave it, as I know no one else will take the loving care of it that I have taken. I am staying at the hotel Noailles at night and commuting to Villacoublay until the new club is opened. Then I will come home. Marjorie's friend, Bill Curtis, sent me that book, *A Narrow Street* by Elliot Paul, about a section of Paris, and Matey and I read it and then went and roamed all around it. The book is an excerpt from *The Last time I Saw Paris*. The district is old beat up now but some of it is left and it is very interesting.

November 11, 1945

Still hanging around Paris and having a lovely time. It certainly is wonderful to be here. We opened the club Thursday night—a big success. It really is a lovely club. We had stoves and everything and lots of flowers that Blanche and I bought at a flower market just outside of Paris. We have two German prisoners working for us now they are a big help.

Now I am slowly getting ready to leave, although there is nothing much to do except settle the accounts, have shots, and sit around and wait. The Red Cross figures I owe them Fr. 12,963 from last December's receipts, which apparently never got to them. Thank God I have money order receipts for it, so I guess they will straighten it out all right. Also I got another raise so I don't think I can afford to get out of the Red Cross.

Saturday night Matey and I went to a nice black market place and ate squab and oysters while the waitress entertained us with stories of how they ate cats during the occupation. Later someone told us that the oysters come right out of the Seine. I never seem to be able to eat oysters without hearing something awful about them.

Yesterday (Sunday) I had lunch with Noël Thierry, the French girl who works for us who reminds me of Franny, at her home. Her family is very nice, with lots of interesting stories about the occupation. Matey came in for me later (we both hate to leave our vehicles. He has a Jeep, which some colonel gave him for being flown somewhere) and I went out to Villacoublay to a party to celebrate the departure of quite a few pilots today. People certainly are leaving fast. This is the ideal time to be going home.

I suppose it is freezing cold in Providence. I think I will go to Florida for January and February.

Much love.

Fitje

✎

November 11, 1945

Dear Tim,

Well, I guess I'm on my way at last, but without much enthusiasm I'm afraid.

I have been living in Paris for about a week now and having a wonderful time doing practically nothing but enjoying myself. The process of clearing to go home is very simple and only takes a couple of mornings, so I have nothing but free time. Mostly I spend the afternoons and evenings at Villacoublay at the bar. It is such fun and those pilots are such crazy kids. God, I can't bear the thought of dull old Providence. A big group of them left for home today so we had lots of celebrating last night.

I have also gone to a couple of very nice black market restaurants and had squab and oysters and things like that. I have the nicest fella here (successor to Jack), a pilot, Capt. Mostyn who is about to go home too, and he and I have found some nifty spots. He has a jeep that some Colonel gave him in return for being flown somewhere, or something, so we are pretty lucky with transportation and everything.

As things stand now I think I am leaving here on Friday and will probably be sailing very shortly, as they say we go in very small groups and are hardly held up at all. I wouldn't be the least bit surprised if I were back here in Jan. or Feb. though, so we may have that meeting yet.

Quite a few people who have been home are getting back, so I think I will be able to. I would like to have a job in the embassy or something civilian.

Will write when I get home.

Much love,

Binni

Noël Thierry on the cover of
Point du Vue Magazine, March 1946

251

Fitje's November 11, 1945 letter to Tim Pitts is the last letter she is known to have written from Europe. She spent her last two weeks in Paris arranging transportation back to the United States. Fitje booked passage on the George Washington, which sailed from Le Havre on November 17th. After eight hundred seventy days in Europe, she was going home.

What's Past Is Prologue

Fitje hoped to sail into New York, retracing the route she'd sailed on the Queen Mary twenty-nine months earlier. She wanted to be greeted by Lady Liberty, see the towering skyline of New York and bask in the emotion and excitement that so many thousands of G.I.s experienced when they returned. It was not to be; the USS George Washington sailed into Boston Harbor and she disembarked on November 25, 1945. No one met her in Boston; she felt more alone than she'd felt at anytime that she was away.

There were no hero's returns for the Red Cross "girls." No medals, parades or public adoration. They did their jobs and came home. Nothing could have been more emblematic of that reality than Fitje's homecoming. She took a train to Providence, but no one met her at the station. She took a cab to her parents' house expecting to celebrate Thanksgiving dinner, which she thought was being delayed until she arrived. It was a moment she looked forward to. When she walked in the front door to discover that the family had already finished dinner, she burst into tears.

Her tears might have been a mixture of disappointment and relief. The family hadn't bothered to wait for her, as they promised they would, but the war was over and she was home. It was also true she knew she'd been a part of something she could never duplicate. She had memories to share but most Americans, tired of the war, wanted to relegate it to history and move on into the future. Her memories were her own.

Soon after she returned, Fitje resigned from the Red Cross. Her retirement lasted two months. She wrote her cousin Tim that she visited Martha Brush in Zanesville, Ohio in January 1946 where they considered several options, including working for the Red Cross in Washington, D.C. According to her service records, the Red Cross rehired Fitje in February, as the assistant to the director of civilian blood donor services. She stayed until June of that year before once again resigning. Fitje returned to Providence where she took a job with the museum at the Rhode Island School of Design.

Fitje was twenty-eight and single when she got home. Most of her friends were married and starting families. When attached to the 27th Air Transport Group in Villacoublay, Fitje fell in love with

253

Captain "Matey" Mostyn. Matey, who was from the Midwest, remained in the military after the war. Apparently Fitje wanted to marry Matey and thought the feeling was mutual. In early 1946 he visited Fitje at her parents' house in Providence. At the end of his visit he told her that as "you will never fit in my world and I will never fit in yours" it was best they ended their relationship. She was disappointed and must have mentioned the breakup in a letter to her cousin Tim. Tim responded on May 30, 1946:

> *I will merely say that I am terribly, terribly sorry to hear that your mid-westerner is something that you will always regret. Please don't think me nosy. I will not ask anything now nor later. However if I get home and you want to talk, you know that it can be done with no fear of going farther. I feel certain that I have told you stuff that no one else has ever heard and I rather imagine the reverse is true too. I can think of no one who helped me more when I needed it most and often wondered if what little I did helped you a fraction as much. I only wish I could have been there for this deal, whatever it was, so that I could have at least offered my help. It is a darn shame, Binni, that one so utterly wonderful, so completely unselfish, so devoted to the welfare of others and so darn pretty to boot, should go through life as far as you have with so damn little reward and so little of the rich happiness that you need, want and surely should have. I wish I could supply it because I would positively deliver if I could. That is not poppycock and I am sober as a judge. I mean it.*

We don't know with certainty when Tim and Fitje first met, but it might have been at his sister Alice's wedding on September 14, 1940. Alice was a boarding student at the Mary C. Wheeler School in Providence where she and Fitje were close friends. When Alice married Norman Gardiner at Bryn Awel, the family's estate in Glen Arm, Maryland, Fitje was one of her bridesmaids. Whenever they met, Fitje liked to say she fell in love with Tim the moment she saw him.

Fitje had been in Europe for nineteen months when Tim sailed in February 1945. He was a 1st Lieutenant in the 76th Division, 417th Regiment in Patton's 3rd Army. His unit crossed the Rhine River at Bopard on March 27, 1945. During forty-five days in combat he was wounded twice and awarded two Bronze Star Medals for valor. His unit was on the western outskirts of Chemnitz, which the Soviet Army was occupied by when Germany surrendered.

When World War II ended, the military used a point system to determine who went home first. As he had been in Europe a relatively short time and didn't have the requisite number of points to leave, Tim stayed as part of the U.S. occupation force. After several postings in Germany, in December 1945 the army sent him to Vienna, Austria with the 796th M.P. Battalion. The following month he met a Viennese woman named Gerti Strasser*. Gerti was beautiful. She was in her mid-twenties, had long dark hair and brown eyes and two young children.

Tim's letters to his parents reveal much about his relationship with Gerti. They were skeptical—concerned that the relationship was improper and worried that she was using him to find a way for her and her children to escape war-torn Europe. He tried to reassure them, pointing out that her family

---

* The name is a pseudonym at the request of the family.

254

Tim Pitts with Gerti Strasser, Vienna, 1946

was wealthy, more so than his own. They must have softened a bit. At his request they sent each of Gerti's children a stuffed rabbit for Easter.

Apparently Tim spent much of his free time with Gerti, visiting art galleries and museums. They attended the opera at the famed Viennese Opera House, which was damaged by allied bombing and required extensive repairs, the night it reopened. His letters to his parents often mention his desire to remain in Vienna.

Tim's father died in July 1946. After much deliberation, and a phone call from his brother Clinton, he reluctantly returned to Maryland.

My wife Ellen and I visited Gerti in Vienna in 2003. She told us about her relationship with Tim, how he enjoyed playing with her children and how much he loved Vienna. Near the end of our visit she showed us a packet of letters. "This is every letter he ever sent me," she said. "They are too personal to give you now, but I will instruct my sons to send them to you after I die." When Gerti died two years later, her son Christian sent me the letters.

After leaving Vienna, Tim corresponded with Gerti for a year. At first the letters were affectionate, but over time became more about his day-to-day activities. His desire to return to Vienna seemed to take a back seat to rebuilding his life in Baltimore. He wrote on June 28, 1947:

> *For my vacation this summer, I am going to go with some friends on their yacht out into the ocean, up the Hudson River, through various canals and into Lake Ontario, play around the Thousand Islands and then back through more canals, and into the St. Lawrence River and back. We should have a fine time, don't you think?*

According to Gerti, she never heard from him again. The letter never mentioned that his cousin Fitje was going on the cruise with him.

Fitje with her cousin Tim Pitts
at Trade Vic's in New York, August 1947

A photograph of Tim and Fitje taken at Trader Vic's restaurant in the Plaza Hotel in New York in August 1947 hangs in my den. They sit alone at a table, absorbed in each other's company. Fitje, thirty years old, wears a print dress, her hair, parted in the middle, cascades over her shoulders in the style of the era.

Tim, a few days from his thirty-fourth birthday, wears a white suit jacket; a tie bar at his shirt collar gives him a jaunty look. Tall drinks sit on the table in front of them but they don't seem to notice. They only see each other.

According to Fitje, they arrived at The Plaza together. The desk clerk, visibly embarrassed, noted they were unmarried and informed them the hotel had erred in giving them adjoining rooms. Looking at Fitje, he assured her he would make more suitable arrangements.

Tim suggested that the clerk look at their last names: "We're cousins for god's sakes. There is nothing inappropriate about that." Little did the desk clerk suspect as he left the reservations unchanged.

Not long before she lost her memories to Alzheimer's, I asked Fitje about the photograph. The question seemed to transport her back to that night sixty years earlier. "I believe it was the first night we did it."

According to my mother, her own mother once said, "Binni, you will never marry until you get your cousin Tim out of your head." She was right. Second cousins Tim and Fitje Pitts married on March 20, 1948 in her parents' house in Providence. After a brief honeymoon in Bermuda, they set about building their lives together in Baltimore, Maryland.

Tim mustered out of the army soon after he returned from Europe and entered the insurance business, ultimately joining three partners to form their own agency. Missing the military, he joined the Maryland National Guard in 1948. He stayed in the guard for twenty years, eventually promoted to Colonel and Regimental Commander of the 5th Regiment, 29th Division. Our father was sixty-one when he died of cancer on April 11, 1974.

Every marriage has its frustrations and my parents weren't immune. My mother longed to return to Europe, but my father had no desire to go back. She could never convince him to do so. Not long before he died he told her, "After I die, there will be enough money so that if you save, you might finally get that trip to Europe you've always wanted." She did. Three years after he died, Fitje returned to England for the first time since July 1945. Over the next twenty-four years she took thirty-one more trips out of the country, including trips to Russia, Australia, Africa, Polynesia, and Europe.

My mother and I had similar personalities, each of us stubborn and independent. As a result we clashed often. While we resolved our conflicts, it was not by conscious decision. We simply reached that point in our lives when whatever stood between us didn't seem to matter any more. After reading the letters, I feel as if I know her, not only as a mother, but as the woman she was during a remarkable chapter in her life. I thank her from the bottom of my heart for saving the letters.

Fitje Pitts died on Halloween morning, 2008. Nine years after she died, through her own words, she introduced us to the incredible life she led before she was our mother.

Postscript

To the best of my memory my brothers and I only met two of the individuals our mother knew and wrote about during the war: Martha Brush and Mary Haynesworth. One of the many reasons I regret not reading the letters before she died is that so many of the unforgettable individuals she wrote about will forever remain a mystery. That said, I located the children of some and learned something about their lives after the war. There was a common thread: none of the parents talked about their experiences during the war except in the most general way. Through our contact I provided them with information and photographs they had never seen.

Jean Plageman, the director of the Red Feather Club, stayed with the 95th Bomb Group until the end of the war, then returned to her hometown of Portland, Oregon in August 1945. Jean played competitive golf before the war. In 1932 she was the Oregon amateur champion. She continued playing when she returned. Early in the '50s Jean moved to Santa Cruz, California. She stayed active with the Red Cross and several other philanthropic organizations. Jean died on February 2, 1978.

Martha Brush, Fitje's assistant at IX Bomber Command, returned to Zanesville, Ohio. Later she married Bill Eyster and moved to York, Pennsylvania. Fitje saw her several times before Martha died in 1975.

Mary Haynesworth, Fitje's assistant at the 386th Bomb Group returned to the States soon after V E Day. An actress before the war, she joined the cast of the Broadway show *The Big People*, starring George Mathews. The play, which was a flop, resulted in romance; Mary and George married in 1951. They lived in New York until 1974 when George retired, then moved to Greenville, South Carolina where George died in 1981. Fitje stayed in contact with Mary, visiting her several times. Mary died on May 6, 2011.

Babs Garfield was Fitje's assistant in St. Trond after Mary transferred to a Red Cross Club Mobile unit. After the war she returned to Massachusetts. She married Ted Browne in 1946 and had four children. After training at the MGM Language Institute she taught and tutored children with Dyslexia at the Carroll School in Lincoln, Massachusetts. Babs died on November 18, 2012 in Concord, Massachusetts.

Jack Zeltner returned to the States with the 386th Bomb Group. Not long after returning he had lunch with Fitje's sister Jane in New York. He married Marguerite Robb in 1948 and had two children. According to his son John, Jack worked in the garment industry in New York until recalled to military duty during the Korean War. Jack died on August 28, 1965 and buried in Arlington National Cemetery.

On November 2, 1948 while reading the morning edition of the Baltimore Sun, my father read that a military C 47 flying out of Sheppard's Air Force base had crashed near Muldrow, Oklahoma. Witnesses said the plane broke into pieces during a violent thunderstorm; all eleven people on board died. While the article withheld the names of the dead, one witness said he had found a bag with a nametag. It belonged to the pilot, Captain John E. Mostyn.

Roger Freeman completed his required number of missions and returned to Providence where he met his one-year old son Terry for the first time. He and Ibby had three more children, another son and two daughters. Roger went back to school after the war and earned an engineering degree from MIT. Later he earned his MBA at the University of Rhode Island. Roger worked at Manufacturer's Mutual Fire Insurance Company, later Allendale Insurance Company. Roger was seventy-five when he died in April 1997.

Both Warren "Red" Farwell and Jack "Hinkie" Hinkle survived the war. They were lucky, as the life expectancy of rear gunners was nine missions, and they were along on some of the most costly missions the 91st Bomb Group flew.

Red returned to his home in Eagle Rock, Missouri. He attended the University of Missouri where he met his wife, Rachel Barrett. They married in December 1946 and had five children. After they married Red and Rachel moved to Charleston, Missouri where Red taught agriculture to veterans before becoming the principal of Eugene Field Elementary School. In 1966 the family moved to Plattsburg, Missouri where he was the principal of Ellis Elementary School for nineteen years. Warren Farwell died on October 2, 2012.

Hinkie returned to Bell Bottom, Tennessee where he bought a farmer's supply company in the late 1940s. Later he built a real estate development company. He married Sally Hines in March 1952 and the couple had three children. According to his daughter Sally his real love was farming. He bought a hundred acre farm in Franklin, Tennessee where he raised thoroughbred horses.

In October 1988 the Tennessean carried a story about the time Hinkie met the future queen of England. King George VI and his family visited the 91st Bomb Group to christen a B-17 the Rose of York. According to Hinkie, "It is the rule that one doesn't speak to royalty unless spoken to. We were told not to look King George in the eye. He stuttered some. He talked but not to any of us. The daughters talked to me and I learned that Elizabeth and I shared the same birthday, April 21st. She was dignified but affable, a lovely lady." Jack Hinkle died on December 5, 1991.

Acknowledgements

I undertook this project thinking it would be simple. I was wrong. My mother was a prolific writer, and I needed to transcribe her letters. One hundred sixty-three letters survived, approximately one hundred and fourteen thousand words. As the letters show, she was a gifted observer and storyteller. Nonetheless, my mother often ignored accepted rules of grammar, rarely capitalized words and made "m" and "r" interchangeable. Her handwriting was such that on occasion interpreting her scrawl was as vexing as I imagine breaking the Enigma code to have been. Undertaking this project was a team effort.

First and foremost, without the support of my wife Ellen this project would never have become a reality. Not only was she supportive, she helped transcribe and edit the letters and offered always-valuable advice. You are the perfect partner.

No small amount of credit goes to my brothers Toby and Steve who were always available when I needed advice. This project could not have been if not for your help.

Thanks to my cousins, John Pitts, Terry Pitts, Warren Pitts, Sarah Andresen, Mary Winkes and Jenny Hand, all of whom shared stories and provided information about my mother's siblings.

Ibby Taft Freeman, my mother's childhood friend who still lives in Rhode Island, helped identify individuals my mother mentioned in the letters. Ibby's husband Roger was a navigator during the war and for a time stationed at Great Dunmow with my mother when they were with the 386th Bomb Group.

I engaged several of my former students at The Hun School of Princeton to help with the project. Joey Crivelli, a recent graduate of Hobart and William Smith Colleges, helped transcribe the letters, no easy task for an individual unfamiliar with my mother's handwriting. She did a terrific job transcribing fifty letters.

Samantha Troilo and Stephanie Quirk helped "clean up" many of the seventy-year old photographs I used in this book. Sam, a former student and Stephanie are recent graduates of the Savannah College of Art and Design.

Alexa De Paulis, an extremely talented recent graduate of Syracuse University, designed the cover. I think she nailed it.

Anna B. Knighton designed the book; the results of her efforts are terrific. Thank you to my cousin John Pitts for the introduction.

Phil Samponaro, Andy Garner and Ray Howlett made themselves available when I needed help with questions about the 95th Bomb Group. Phil is a history professor at the University of Texas and Andy and Ray live in England close to Horham, which was home to the 95th. All three are active in the 95th Bomb Group Memorial Foundation.

Acknowledgements

Through an Internet search, I connected with Betty Claes, a curator at the Museum Of The Winter of 1944, in Borlo, Belgium. Betty provided me with valuable information about St. Trond before and after liberation.

Loraine Jackson Riemer gave me valuable information about her grandfather, Dr. Sumner Jackson.

Jerry McLaughlin has done extensive archival work for the National Museum of the Mighty Eighth Air Force and was always available when I had questions. Jerry's book, *D-Day + 60 Years: A Small Piece of History* is a terrific read.

Thanks to Tom Turner, Tina Kelly, Robin Gold, Tess Link and Amy Condon, all talented writers and friends who offered advice and encouragement when I needed it most.

Andy and Carolyn Steigmeier were both supportive. Carolyn read and commented on parts of the manuscript. Andy is the president of the Eighth Air Force Historical Society Birth Place Chapter and offered sound advice whenever I needed it.

Janet Vass, Steve Corrsin, Carri Stoltz and Jim Bruton read and commented on parts of the manuscript. Thank you.

I spoke with several children and relatives of my mother's wartime friends including John Zeltner, Sally Hinkle, Ray Farwell and Ed Brush Eyster. Every conversation was helpful and enlightening.

Tim Pitts is a retired teacher. After retiring he and his wife Ellen moved to Savannah, Georgia where they live with their dogs Charlie and Buster. Tim is available for speaking engagements. He can be contacted at timpitts.author@gmail.com.

52045554R00154

Made in the USA
Columbia, SC
28 February 2019